AMERICAN FEDERALISM
AND
PUBLIC POLICY

Random House Series in Political Science

STEPHEN J. WAYNE
George Washington University
General Editor

AMERICAN FEDERALISM
AND
PUBLIC POLICY

HOW THE SYSTEM WORKS

Thomas J. Anton
Brown University

Random House New York

First Edition
98765432
Copyright © 1989 by Random House, Inc.

LIBRARY OF CONGRESS
Library of Congress Cataloging-in-Publication Data

Anton, Thomas Julius.
   American federalism and public policy: how the system works/
Thomas J. Anton.
      p.   cm.
   Bibliography: p.
   Includes index.
   ISBN 0-394-35362-5
   1. Federal government—United States.   2. Intergovernmental fiscal
relations—United States.   I. Title.
JK325.A75 1988
321.02′0973—dc 19   88-17553
                                                                             CIP

Manufactured in the United States of America

12/21/00

PREFACE

This book is an attempt to develop a conceptually coherent analysis of the relationship between federalism and public policy in the United States. Although federalism technically refers to the constitutional relationship between the national government and the states, American policymaking today is strongly influenced by local as well as state and national governments. From a behavioral point of view, therefore, it is important that the interactions among all three levels be included in any serious analysis of modern federal politics. Defined this way, federalism clearly is the preeminent institution of American domestic policymaking, and it is an increasing influence in foreign policy as well. Nevertheless, scholars continue to analyze public policies as though they are initiated and implemented by separate levels of government, acting independently of one another. Thus we have studies of Congress or the President, or we have studies of individual states or groups of states, or we have studies of cities or groups of cities that contain much useful information but little recognition of the interrelationships among levels that are the defining characteristics of American public policies. Today, when federalism has become a major political issue, it is more important than ever to understand how the federal system works. Achieving a better understanding of that system is the major purpose of this book.

With all of the books and articles that have been published recently on this subject, one might think that our knowledge must have improved quite substantially. In fact, however, the literature on American federalism suffers from several serious problems. One is that much of the writing is polemical, designed to advance a particular political or programmatic cause rather than to offer serious analysis. Because federal relationships are impossible to define with precision and are constantly changing in response to new conditions, it is always possible to argue that federalism is either a barrier to or a support for some preferred policy. Arguments of this kind often are politically interesting, but they seldom improve our general understanding. This study attempts to be more analytical, in order to illuminate the conditions under which political arguments of any kind are likely to be influential. We do not yet know nearly enough about such conditions, which is why polemics remain analytically unpersuasive.

Another problem is the reluctance of American scholars to search for patterns. We have been so fascinated for so long by the wonderful diversity of state and local governments that we have paid little attention to their similarities. Yet structural and procedural patterns abound, if we are willing to look for them. One of my most important objectives, accordingly, is to move beyond the old saw that "everything differs from state to state" to the identification of recurrent patterns of federal and intergovernmental relations. I am acutely aware, of course, that this is a rather risky business. The words chosen to identify patterns may be ambiguous, while data to measure recurrent actions are rarely good enough to resolve such ambiguities. I intend to take that risk nonetheless in order to stimulate further thought about the patterns that characterize American federal politics. If the patterns identified here are ultimately replaced by others that are more precisely stated and more adequately measured, this effort will have proved successful.

Finally, and most significantly, the federalism literature suffers from a lack of utilization of analytic concepts capable of organizing the wealth of available information into general statements regarding system structure and change. As we shall see in Chapter 2, some conceptual frameworks offered by scholars are so abstract that they inevitably miss much of the rich detail present in the system. Reacting to such abstractions, other scholars point to the diversity and complexity of federal relations as justification for not using any explicit conceptual apparatus at all. Clearly, one way to resolve this dilemma is to identify some conceptual framework capable of organizing information from a large number of individual cases into statements that, while more general, are not so abstract as to lose sight entirely of particular details.

My review of the literature persuades me that such a framework is in fact widely used by scholars, although their usage is often implicit rather than explicit. In this study I make this "benefits coalition" framework explicit and use it to generate conclusions of the middle range–that is, statements that move beyond individual cases but do not necessarily encompass everything that might be considered relevant. I make no claim of orginality; indeed, this framework has been used for decades by numerous scholars. I do claim, however, that explicit use of the framework can help us to organize available information better and thus improve our understanding of an extraordinarily complex reality. Readers themselves will judge the merits of this claim.

My subtitle, "How the System Works," is meant to alert readers to the major focus of the book: the *actions* taken by public officials as they craft and implement public policies. I consider legal philosophies that have been used to structure debates over intergovernmental issues in Chapter 1, and I assess alternative analytic formulations in Chapter 2. The remainder of the book, however, is concerned with the behavior of officials who operate the federal system, not with legal, constitutional, or ethical philosophies. Such philosophies enter the analysis from time to time, but only as they affect actions taken by federal officials.

Finally, let me add a note about my own perspective on American federalism and intergovernmental relations. Much of the recent literature on this subject has been extremely critical, emphasizing the complexity, confusion, conflict and inefficiency that often characterize relations between our governments. While I agree that these qualities can be found in the system, I do not share the view that they constitute indicators of imminent breakdown. A fair reading of the evidence seems to me to make clear that, although certainly complicated, American federalism is neither out of control nor on the verge of breakdown. It is, instead, a system on the move, confronting some problems while ignoring others, through processes that are sometimes cumbersome and sometimes remarkably effective. These varied processes and outcomes do not lend themselves to sweeping generalizations about system failure, perhaps, but they reflect what I take to be the realities of federal politics and policy. If we are to work effectively as citizens to improve the system, we must first work effectively as analysts to understand it.

Thomas J. Anton
Providence, R.I.

ACKNOWLEDGMENTS

Because this book is a self-conscious attempt to synthesize a large body of literature, I am more indebted than most authors to the hundreds of scholars who have produced the material on which my synthesis is built. I am especially indebted, however, to Trudi C. Miller of the University of Minnesota and Richard P. Nathan of Princeton University, both of whom generously provided opportunities for me to engage my interest in federalism and public policy in the United States. Samuel H. Beer of Harvard University, David B. Walker of the University of Connecticut, and Aaron Wildavsky of the University of California at Berkeley consistently have provided uncomfortable but appropriately stimulating criticisms of my work that I hope are reflected in the following pages. Finally, the insightful commentaries of my colleagues Darrel M. West and Martha Weinberg of Brown University helped enormously to improve the quality of this book.

The A. Alfred Taubman Center for Public Policy and American Institutions at Brown University provided both a congenial environment for scholarship and some marvelously talented people to assist me in preparing the book. Karen Kane was a whiz at locating fugitive documents, teaching me how to spell, and pointing out ambiguities in my arguments. Kathleen Young was as diplomatic as she was incisive in suggesting more effective ways of organizing and presenting the argument. Susan Juhasz made so many contributions as editor, researcher, and manager that it is impossible to say which of her many talents should be most highly prized. I am exceedingly grateful to each of these people for their assistance, and to the Taubman Center for allowing me to make use of their extraordinary talents.

Thomas J. Anton
Providence, R.I.

CONTENTS

AMERICAN FEDERALISM
AND
PUBLIC POLICY

CHAPTER 1

THE FEDERALISM ISSUE

Americans are born, educated, married or divorced, employed, housed, and cared for according to policies shaped by the institutions of American federalism. Anyone who has moved from one state or city to another knows that the policies produced by these institutions—from speed limits to tax limits—are often very different. Yet anyone who has gone to school or applied for a job also knows that many policies, such as antidiscrimination laws, reflect an equally apparent sense of national uniformity. Both the uniformity and the diversity are products of a political system that allocates governmental responsibilities among one national government and fifty different state governments, each with its own local governments. In this book I hope to develop a better understanding of how these many governments work together to produce the policies that shape our lives.

HOW POLICIES SHAPE OUR LIVES

Improving our understanding of the impact of federalism on public policy is vital, for at least three reasons. One is that the policies jointly pursued by the various American governments really do shape our lives. The ability of individuals to succeed in life is strongly influenced by the amount and quality of the education they receive, which in turn is largely determined by federal policies. Whether people live in healthy or polluted environments depends very much on the joint activities of local, state, and national officials. Job opportunities, health care, housing, and assistance for individuals unable to support themselves are all conditioned by federal policies and procedures. Even in retirement, Americans rely on a number of public policies that provide sustenance and shelter through the cooperative actions of many levels of government. Federal policies, in short, have a profound effect on the quality of all our lives.

Federal policies are also increasingly expensive. As governments have assumed greater responsibilities, the costs of meeting those new responsibilities have risen dramatically. New responsibilities have spawned new or expanded agencies employing millions of additional government workers, particularly among state and local governments. New activities also have led to new and more expensive technologies, such as computers to process

1

information, electronic traffic control systems, and sophisticated new weapons systems. Driven by service, employee, and technological expansion, government costs have grown from less than 10 percent of gross national product a few decades ago to a third or more today. Although this is far from the highest proportion in the advanced world, it is sufficiently high to have caused widespread and continuing concern among American taxpayers.

Third, cost increases and program growth together have stimulated proposals for reform that now occupy a prominent position on the national agenda. Ronald Reagan's interest in the federalism issue and his willingness to use the presidential office to advocate reform clearly have been a major source of renewed interest in the issue. But interest in reform has a much broader base than the White House alone. As we shall see, the nation's governors are vitally interested in reform, a prestigious national commission has developed proposals that have attracted broad support, several members of Congress and senators have offered their own proposals, and so have professional organizations and even some academics. Reform of American federalism, in short, has become a hot topic. And if we are to evaluate properly any of the proposals for change, we need a clear understanding of how the system works, and why.

Increasing numbers of scholars have responded to this analytic challenge in recent years, vastly improving our knowledge of federal politics and policy. The results of these efforts, however, remain paradoxical. On the one hand, the thousands of descriptions of "how they did it in Oshkosh" or "what happened in Hoboken" provide marvelously detailed and often valuable information. On the other hand, such information is very difficult to place in a general theoretical framework. Because scholars have studied a great many different things, or used different languages to study similar things, we are left with a mountain of details, but no widely accepted theory or theories that allow us to evaluate the significance of those details. Empirical studies of American federalism, in short, are descriptively strong but theoretically weak. One consequence of this weakness is that scholars are generally unable to provide much help to politicians seeking to reform the system.

What is clearly needed at this point is some effort to synthesize this vast and expanding literature in order to identify patterns and thus illuminate what is true in general as well as interesting in particular. I propose to attempt such a synthesis, building upon a conceptual framework I believe is implicit in many of the detailed empirical studies. The familiarity of this "benefits coalition" framework will be readily apparent when it is explained in Chapter 2. This framework will be an organizing device for the chapters that follow. More important, using the framework to organize a vast amount of material should reveal many aspects of federal policymaking that are now largely hidden from view. This explicitly conceptual approach, in short, should help us to think productively about the interaction between federal institutions and the policies they produce. But first we need to be clear about the meaning of federalism and the reasons why it is an issue that is never finally resolved.

WHAT DOES FEDERALISM MEAN?

Formal and Procedural Distinctions

Defining federalism can be a forbidding task. Indeed, one scholar has identified some 267 different but overlapping conceptions of the term (Stewart, 1984, 1982). For our purposes, however, a simple definition is adequate: *Federalism* is a system of rules for the division of public policy responsibilities among a number of autonomous governmental agencies. These rules define the scope of authority available to the autonomous agencies—which can do what—and they provide a framework to govern relationships between and among agencies. The agencies remain autonomous in that they levy their own taxes and select their own officials, but they are also linked together by rules that govern common actions.

Since all modern states include a large number of government agencies, it is perfectly legitimate to ask what differentiates a federal system from other systems. Even highly centralized systems officially controlled by a single executive or a tiny committee find it necessary to give some authority to other agencies, particularly if their responsibility extends over a large physical territory. Once diffused, the pieces of authority available to these noncentral agencies allow them to act autonomously in many situations, regardless of the formal system (Taubman, 1973). Similarly, states referred to as "unitary" typically operate with rules that assign formal responsibilities to a variety of subnational governments, as well as to the central state agencies (McKay, 1980).

The answer to the question of how federalism is different lies in the degree of autonomy available to the constituent units. In principle, federal systems allocate broad powers to all constituent units, each of which can act in these broad areas without the approval of any other unit. All constituent units, furthermore, are guaranteed existence so long as the system exists because they *are* the system. Neither condition prevails in unitary or centralized states. The authority available to subnational units in such systems typically is carefully and narrowly constrained, and even these narrow responsibilities are subject to change or even elimination by the central government. Central government action can often be quite remarkable. In Sweden, for example, parliamentary action initiated by the governing political party led to elimination of 90 percent of all governments between 1952 and 1975 (Anton, 1974). A change of that magnitude, initiated by national officials, would be unthinkable in the American context.

A more behavioral answer is that federal systems have a broader base of political participation than unitary states, and they guarantee that such participation will take place. Allocating broad responsibilities to constituent units means that a large number of individuals will have some real interest in participation. Allocating responsibilities to units that are autonomous, as well as responsible, guarantees a level of participation within those units that can equal or exceed participation in the multi-unit system. Federal systems, in short, encourage greater political participation than is typically found in unitary systems; federalism contains a built-in bias in favor of participation.

These formal and procedural distinctions between federal and unitary political systems imply that the scope and distribution of public benefits are different in federal systems than in others—or, to put it differently, that federalism matters. Some years ago, the idea that federal institutions affected policy outcomes was viewed as wrong. Scholars who failed to find differences in outcomes that could be clearly attributed to federalism argued that federalism was either unimportant or far less important than factors such as wealth or tastes (LaPalombara, 1975; Riker, 1975). More recent scholarship, however, has demonstrated that citizen and governmental behavior in federal states differs systematically from such behavior in unitary states and produces different patterns of benefit distribution (Krane, 1984; Rose-Ackerman, 1981). Federal systems are not all alike, embedded as they are in different historical traditions, cultures, and economic systems, but it now seems clear that federal institutions have an important independent impact on both public benefits and the processes through which they are distributed.

WHY IS FEDERALISM AN ISSUE?

Multiple Governments

The participatory bias of federalism is clearly evident in the United States, where federalism has helped to produce the most "governed" state in the world: At last count, more than 82,000 separate units of government were in existence (U.S. Census, 1985). Fifty states, whose autonomy and continued existence are guaranteed by the federal Constitution, are active in a broad range of policy areas, and continue to expand their areas of responsibility through innovative actions in highway safety (seatbelt laws), environmental protection (bottle bills), and the economy (economic development programs). Each state has created its own legal and administrative system, giving the nation 40,000 municipal governments, another 26,000 special districts, and more than 15,000 school districts. Except for 12,000 or so special districts, each of these units has taxing power, its own officials, and authority to act on behalf of some defined public. More important, nearly 500,000 elected officials work with more than 13 million appointed officials in performing these state and local responsibilities (U.S. Census, 1985). When the president and vice-president, members of Congress, and the roughly 2 million civilian employees of the national government are added to the list, it becomes clear that federal government in the United States is an important participatory sport.

And here, surely, is one very important reason why federalism is a recurring issue in American politics. The number of separate governments is so large that they are bound to bump into one another in the course of pursuing their normal operations, and many of these collisions are bound to be sources of conflict. A city that chooses to build a garbage incinerator on its own outskirts, but adjacent to an expensive residential development in a neighboring city, will probably hear from its neighbor. A state that prohibits oversized trucks on its highways will almost certainly receive equally clear messages from officials in all the municipalities whose streets become congested—and more expensive to maintain!—with trucks prohibited from using the state highways. A national agency that proposes regulations to improve the quality of prepared foods will receive strong statements from states whose regulations are different, no matter whether they are more or less stringent.

Note that none of these examples presents a clear case of right or wrong, good or bad. On the contrary, all are cases that can fairly be described as good against good: One government, in pursuit of a desirable public policy goal, comes into conflict with another government, also in pursuit of a desirable public policy goal. In a system with so many governments, the reasonable pursuit of reasonable ends by reasonable people is therefore one major source of intergovernmental conflict.

Political Autonomy

In theory at least, one quality of the American federal system should act as a barrier against conflict. The federal Constitution makes no mention of local government, leaving the states entirely free to design and implement their own substate systems. For this reason, American local governments have a status not unlike the status of local agencies in unitary states: They are not legally autonomous; the "pieces" of authority available to them are carefully defined and strictly interpreted; and their existence can be terminated at any time by action of the state legislature. Given the clear legal superiority of states in relation to their local governments, one would expect state legislatures to be in a position, through careful specification of responsibilities and close supervision, to minimize or avoid conflict altogether.

State legislatures do in fact devote a great deal of attention and effort to local government activities in their annual or biennial sessions. However, the continuing prominence of local government affairs on state legislative agendas suggests that interlocal and state-local conflict continue to occur with considerable frequency. It is also true that few states have attempted local government reform comparable to the massive restructuring of local and regional governments enacted recently by several nations in Western Europe (McKay, 1980). Intergovernmental conflict continues to require attention in the American states, but the responses have not reflected the legal superiority clearly enjoyed by the states. Why are state governments so reluctant to make full use of the authority available to them?

Whatever the formal structure, in America local governments enjoy a substantial degree of operational autonomy, based in part on tradition, in part on sentiment, and in part on political clout. Throughout New England and the mid-Atlantic states, local government jurisdictions predate the federal Constitution by a hundred years or more. Towns and boroughs of colonial origin reflect a tradition of local governance that was spread across the country as settlers from the Atlantic seaboard moved west. The strength of that tradition is apparent from the continued growth of local government units: During the 1970s some 2,000 new units were created (U.S. Census, 1985).

It is also important to remember that municipal incorporations are voluntary actions, initiated by groups of individuals in some geographic area who come together to achieve the benefits that flow from legal status, ranging from the right to pass zoning ordinances that might keep away the developers, to local police protection, to bonding authority. In all such cases, the impetus and the initiative derive from local residents who seek designated benefits available only through incorporation. The tradition of local control is thus joined to a characteristically American practicality that understands the value of municipal or special district status. As new local units age, the voluntarism and instrumentalism implicit in their existence may become cloudy, but their value remains clear—local government is best because it represents what people want, and what they are willing to pay for. Few politicians can afford to challenge those sentiments.

Serious challenges are unlikely in any event, because local governments and their associated interests are powerful forces in every state legislature, on guard against efforts to weaken their authority. In states with large urban centers, political leaders from those centers are often far better known within the state, or even the nation, than are most state leaders. Mayor Edward Koch of New York City, for example, was a far more significant figure in Albany and Washington, D.C., than the relatively obscure state senator who defeated the mayor in a race for governor. Koch remains an important figure even though Mario Cuomo, as governor, has achieved national prominence. Mayor Richard Daley of Chicago certainly was far better known—and conceivably far more influential—than any Illinois governor of his time.

Even in states without glamorous big city mayors to do battle for a local cause, that cause is not without its champions. State municipal leagues, township associations, school district associations, municipal employee associations, real estate boards, construction unions, and a host of other organizations whose interests overlap the interests of local governments are a permanent presence in state capitals. There they offer not just opinion, but expertly produced information to buttress opinion. The substantial autonomy enjoyed by local governments, in short, is in good measure a product of their political power. Municipalities remain less constrained than they might be, and almost wholly uncoordinated. Conflict, and the issues it breeds, remains common.

Shared Authority

There is another, equally important, source of the recurrence of federal issues in the American polity—namely, overlapping jurisdictions. Conflicts arising from two or more units each pursuing its vision of "good" policy do not arise only in neighboring jurisdictions; such conflicts often arise within the same jurisdiction because two or more different governments share authority for the same public purpose. A city, a county, and a state may all operate hospitals within the same jurisdiction, forcing constant attention to matters such as what kinds of patients will be admitted to each hospital, how bills for poor city patients will be paid if they are in the state hospital, or how bills will be paid if the poor are state but not county residents, and they are in the county hospital. A city, a county, a state, and a national government agency may all have responsibility for the highways running through an area, forcing constant attention to maintenance, patrol, and emergency responsibilities. Should county or city equipment be used to plow the access road to Interstate 90 after a snowstorm, and who makes that decision? Will the state increase its support if the cost of plowing cannot be met from the current budget? Will the national government provide more to the state to help keep its own interstate highway system clear? In the United States such questions are endless, because authority for any given public service in any given geographic area typically is shared by several governments, rather than monopolized by a single one.

From the point of view of service, shared authority seems wasteful in the extreme. Why should cities, counties, and states all operate their own police departments? schools? or libraries? And from the point of view of citizens, shared authority certainly is confusing. Few of us can identify the services provided by the governments that surround us, much less allocate responsibility for those services to the officials who provide them. Even property owners, whose real estate taxes continue to provide most of the funds for local government service, have difficulty understanding tax bills that may include levies for ten or more separate governments (see Chapter 6). If our system seems so wasteful, and so confusing, why don't we change it?

One answer is that we do change it. American politicians make thousands of changes in government structure or procedures every year (Anton, 1985). A more precise way of putting the question is to ask why we have been reluctant to alter the shared authority built into the structure of the system itself. Asking the question this way allows us to explore the fundamental values served by American federalism, as well as the tension between those values and other equally significant priorities.

Just as federalism as a system is biased toward more rather than less participation, federalism as Americans practice it reflects a widely shared belief that citizen participation in public affairs is a major civic virtue (McClosky and Zaller, 1984). Demonstrating that virtue requires opportunities to define and debate matters of "public" concern—hence the existence of so many governments whose responsibilities overlap, but whose presence guarantees that opportunities for participation will be regular and plentiful. Indeed, from a participation point of view, overlapping jurisdictions is good, because it creates even more issues for public debate and more opportunities to participate in their resolution.

It is also important to remember that the historic American fear of centralized authority remains alive and well, sustained by generations of politicians and civic leaders who have repeatedly preached the virtues of small government, carefully controlled by a participating citizenry. From this point of view too, the existence of many overlapping governments is a guarantee against excessive power exercised by a single agency that is too large and too distant to be controlled by citizens. Americans, in short, believe in the value of participation, but they do not want too much government. The paradoxical result is a system with a great deal of government, cut up into so many small pieces that no one piece can easily achieve any objective other than providing opportunities for citizen participation.

Participation and limited government are enduring values in the American polity, but they are not the only values. Americans also value efficiency in the delivery of public services and accountability for officials who operate public programs. Both of these latter values are often in conflict with the former. Maximum feasible participation is a worthy enough goal, but pursuit of that goal through a large number of governments causes duplication, high costs per unit of service, and excessive employment levels, none of which contribute to efficiency. Shared authority among overlapping jurisdictions, moreover, obscures rather than clarifies accountability. Obviously, if several different governments are all operating hospitals or roads in the same area, there is bound to be confusion over which officials are responsible for which services.

Americans generally have regarded inefficiency and political confusion as acceptable costs for securing a high level of participation in limited governments. From time to time, however, efficiency and accountability become dominant, fueling cycles of reform designed to reduce costs or improve performance. While such reforms often do some good, it is important to remember that redundancy is designed into our system and is not primarily a result of evil or incompetent officials. Unless the design itself is changed, the tension between values will remain (Downs and Larkey, 1986).

Constitutional Ambiguity

The most important reason for the persistence of federalism as a political issue in the United States is that spheres of autonomous action lack precise definition. As suggested earlier, federalism can be defined as a system of rules for allocating public responsibilities among autonomous governmental units. But the most notable characteristic of our system is that the allocation rules are ambiguous. The rules are set forth in the U.S. Constitution—which, at first glance, appears to offer clear guidelines. A national government created by agreement of the autonomous states was to have authority over a series of governmental functions that were "enumerated" in the constitutional document itself. All functions not mentioned in the Constitution were, in the famous Tenth Amendment, "reserved" to the states or to the people. This formula seems simple, but two centuries of dispute and tinkering have made plain that the original division of authority among autonomous units was far from precise.

The enumeration of congressional powers in Article 1, Section 8, is straightforward enough, but the last sentence of the same article authorizes Congress "To make all laws which shall be necessary and proper for carrying into Execution the foregoing Powers, and all other Powers vested by this Constitution in the Government of the United States, or in any Department or Officer thereof." Extending congressional authority beyond enumerated powers to any powers required to carry out the enumerated powers largely destroyed the significance of enumeration.

Together with an essentially unlimited grant of power to levy and collect taxes for the "general welfare of the United States" (Article 1, Section 8), the implied powers written into the Constitution give the national government free rein to undertake whatever policies, in whatever areas, it deems worthy of national attention. The enumeration contained in the Constitution expresses powers thought to be essential by the Framers, but the document itself makes plain that a broad and open-ended grant of additional authority was also envisioned.

From the state point of view, the Tenth Amendment, which reserves all nonenumerated powers to the states, fails to indicate just what those "reserved" powers might be. Although there are a few powers the states are expressly prohibited from exercising—for example, states may not make treaties, coin money, or grant any title of nobility—in general the states are free to define the scope of authority available to them as "reserved" powers. Not surprisingly, the states have made use of this undefined authority to undertake activities in areas already covered by national government policies, just as the national government has invaded many areas already covered by state policies. Instead of a clear demarcation of responsibilities, then, the U.S. Constitution offers little more than hazy assertions, virtually inviting national and state governments to jointly occupy whatever policy space they prefer.

In retrospect, then, the persistence of federalism as a political issue is no surprise. A Constitution that offers ambiguous rules for allocating authority, a population that historically has placed more value on participation than on competing political values, a preference for small governments, a proliferation of governmental units with overlapping and shared responsibilities, all help to structure a system in which interactions among governments are constantly under consideration. These are systemic qualities, not the products of individual acts. That is, ambiguity, redundancy, and inefficiency are built into the system and cannot be eliminated unless the framework is altered. Efforts to alter the framework are common, as we shall see in Chapter 9, but none has yet succeeded. Instead, we continue to tinker with various aspects of the system in an unending effort to improve rather than change the structure.

HOW THE FEDERALISM ISSUE IS FRAMED

The Efficiency Framework

The essential federalist question is which government should undertake what activity, and on whose budget? Answers to that question vary enormously, because philosophies of government vary enormously. Among the varied conceptualizations that have shaped answers to the question, however, are two that often recur. One, reflecting both rationality and public distaste for government excess, is the framework of efficiency. The other, reflecting the flexibility guaranteed by constitutional ambiguity, is the framework of national purpose. These frameworks are occasionally intertwined, but they more often are used independently, to organize debate on different aspects of the American policy process.

The efficiency framework is commonly found at all levels of government, but is probably used more frequently, with greater success, among state and local governments. Its use is often triggered by public reports of official corruption, waste of tax funds, or candidates for office who find it effective as a campaign device and a program for action if the office is achieved. When triggered by reports of corruption or waste of funds, the framework commonly focuses attention on the alleged wrongdoers, insisting that they be brought to justice and that their wrongs be corrected, usually through some kind of internal reform such as new reporting requirements or new qualifications for employment. When used as an electoral or government program, the efficiency framework typically focuses on the waste caused by program duplication or governmental behavior, and leads to proposals for greater coordination among governments or government consolidation, or both. With impressive frequency, such proposals are produced by "blue ribbon" committees of business leaders whose knowledge of business is presumed to justify the recommendations made to public officials (Downs and Larkey, 1986).

Whether based on corruption or perceptions of waste, the efficiency framework carries the same message: Government should do its job at the least possible cost to taxpayers, producing the maximum possible product per tax dollar spent. The popularity of this message is apparent in the dramatic reduction in the number of school districts in the United States, from 108,579 as recently as 1942 to little more than 15,000 today, as well as in the constant tinkering with government structure that occurs in all states, all the time (Anton, 1984). But the message is heard in Washington as well, causing periodic efforts to reduce waste or eliminate overlapping agency responsibilities within the national government. The well-publicized efforts of President Reagan's Private Sector Survey on Cost Control—the so-called Grace Commission—are the most recent example of a national interest that typically follows a well-worn script: A committee of prominent business leaders is appointed; they "contribute" a good deal of time to deliberations over wasteful spending; and a largely undocumented report is issued, claiming the possibility of large savings if waste is eliminated (GAO, 1985). Such reports seldom have substantial impact, but they serve to dramatize the national government's commitment to efficiency. Since so many of the programs discussed in such reports are jointly operated by the national and state governments, the federal sources of waste are also dramatized.

The National Purpose Framework

Just as "efficiency" frames many federal debates over existing government operations, "national purpose" provides a conceptual framework to debate proposals for new activities. Although less effective in resolving issues than the efficiency framework, national purpose typically generates far more attention, primarily because its opposite is "states' rights." Thus, proponents of new national government programs typically must counter arguments that such programs are properly the business of the states, rather than the national government. Among state and local governments, proponents of programs often face opposition from those who argue that the activities proposed should be national, rather than state or local, responsibilities. At issue in all such debates is the fundamental question of national purpose: What government actions should properly be regarded as national responsibilities, and what actions should properly be undertaken by the states and their localities?

Constitutional ambiguity on this question prohibits a "final" resolution. Instead, we debate the desirability of new programs in terms that imply constitutional precision. Reflecting the legal doctrine of *dual federalism*, which asserts a clear distinction between the powers of the national government and the powers of the states, politicians often assert that programs with which they disagree are "unconstitutional" because they are state rather than federal responsibilities, or vice versa. In his efforts to eliminate a number of federal programs, for example, President Reagan has relied extensively on an image of constitutional clarity, recently confounded by promoters of new government programs. In his 1983 Budget Message, the president asserted:

The Constitution provides clear distinctions between the roles of the Federal Government and of the States and localities. . . . During the past 20 years, what had been a classic division of functions between the Federal Government and the States and localities has become a confused mess. Traditional understandings about the roles of each level of government have been violated. (OMB, 1983)

Mr. Reagan's solution to the problem he imagined was a series of proposals to reduce or eliminate a number of federal grant programs by turning back to the states responsibilities for such programs, as well as enough federal revenue to maintain them if the states chose to do so. Most of the programs he proposed to turn back to the states were social assistance programs for which the president had little sympathy (Palmer and Sawhill, 1982). Like many other American politicians, Mr. Reagan used the presumption of constitutional clarity to support his own policy preferences.

The image of constitutional clarity is not without intellectual foundation. Studies of the Constitutional Convention have made clear that many of the Founding Fathers did in fact believe that the Constitution they created contained a perfectly clear division of responsibilities between the states and the new national government (Hofstadter, 1954; Landau, 1961; May, 1976). Steeped in Newtonian physics and Lockean rationalism, many of the Founders believed that natural laws governed politics as well as nature, and that such laws could be both discovered and applied by reasonable men. Indeed, the Constitution was a good example of just such an application, in which a well-defined and carefully balanced governmental machine was created for a new nation. For many of the Founding Fathers, the enumeration and balancing of powers among separate agencies and levels of government was an important attempt to apply the clear principles of natural law to the problem of human governance. Mechanics, rather than politics, was the underlying intellectual metaphor. But the problem, of course, was that the principles of mechanics had to be applied to a real document. To secure support, principles had to be stated ambiguously, or not stated at all, in the search for acceptable language. Whatever the intellectual pretensions of our eighteenth-century forebears, in short, what they produced was and remains a political document, full of compromises expressed in ambiguous language, rather than a clear plan for a well-oiled machine.

No one has better demonstrated the inherently political quality of the Constitution than Rufus Davis, whose examination of constitutional concepts makes clear that distinctions between "national" and "local" are entirely subjective, as are similar distinctions between "common" and "particular," "important" and "unimportant," and so on. Depending on the interests or purposes of politicians, any governmental activity can be designated as national or local in significance, and a designation made at one point in time can be altered at some later point. It follows that a "federal" constitution can be no more and no less than:

> . . . a political bargain, struck by political bargainers—the "Founding Fathers"
> —who assemble from a variety of motives to create some degree of permanent

union between communities where previously there was none, or to create some degree of diversity where previously there was complete union. . . . the process which goes by the name of the "division of functions" is a unique form of division, containing its own procedure, its own technique, and its own fictions. What is divided in this process is the world of known or conceivable political activities and the principle of division is mutual satisfaction. What functions are vested in the general government, and what is left to the regions, what activities are expressed and what implied, what activities are protected, and what activities denied only emerge from an elaborate system of political "horse-trading" in which the variety of interests seeking expression must be compromised. . . . There is neither science nor theory in this process. It is not a mathematical division where high exactitude is possible. There is only the skill of translating a precedent to local circumstances, and the draftsmanship to express the compromised purposes of the key bargainers in language to satisfy them. (Davis, 1967)

It is precisely because "the world of known or conceivable political activities" changes through time that initial constitutional bargains are continually modified by successive generations of politicians. "At best," Davis concludes, "the federal compact can only be a formalized transaction of a moment in the history of a particular community." Circumstances change, and the changes alter community understandings of appropriate divisions of responsibilities. As Austin MacDonald pointed out more than a half century ago: "The concept of a function as national or local varies with time and place. Highway construction may properly have been a local obligation only three decades ago; the advent of the automobile may have transformed it overnight into a matter of national concern. Public health may properly be a national function in the United States and a local function in another country, because of widely varying conditions" (MacDonald, 1928).

In addition to the intellectual tradition of constitutional clarity, reflected in the legal doctrine of "dual" federalism, Americans thus enjoy another tradition that is equally at home in the Constitution: political pragmatism. As social change produces demands for new public programs, some politicians oppose the proposals on the grounds that they are not authorized by the Constitution, or are state rather than national responsibilities. Other politicians, aware of politically caused constitutional ambiguity, support new programs as efforts to solve serious problems. If political support is sufficiently powerful, national government action will occur to attack problems in which there is a demonstrated national interest. Dual federalism continues to frame the issue by focusing on constitutional authority for national action, but for most of our history, political pragmatism has structured the emergence of more and more programs to solve problems of national concern. What are the appropriate boundaries between national, state, and local action? From a political point of view, the best answer is "whatever the current politicians can agree they should be."

None of this should be taken to mean that the Constitution imposes no restraints on governmental action. Constitutional restraints are real enough, but they are not expressed as clear and unchanging "principles." Rather, they emerge from the document itself, which sets up a framework to guide the continuing debate over who should do what. The Constitution, in this sense, does not answer all questions of governance so much as it creates structures through which answers can be found.

The Current Context

Recent decisions of the U.S. Supreme Court help us to understand both the terms of this debate and its present significance. After decades of federal government program growth, supported by a permissive Supreme Court, in 1976 the Court issued a ruling that seemed to place new limits on national power. In *National League of Cities* v. *Usery* (426 U.S. 833), the Court held that the Commerce Clause of the Constitution did not empower Congress to enforce the minimum wage and overtime provisions of the national Fair Labor Standards Act against the states "in areas of traditional governmental functions." The case had been initiated by the National League of Cities and a number of other state and local governments in reaction against 1974 amendments to FLSA that extended provisions of the act to employees of virtually all state and local governments. According to the League of Cities, the 1974 amendments trespassed on the powers reserved to the states by the Tenth Amendment.

The Court agreed, holding that ". . . insofar as the challenged amendments operate to directly displace the States freedom to structure integral operations in areas of traditional governmental functions, they are not within the authority granted Congress by the Commerce Clause." Although Mr. Justice Rehnquist, who wrote the majority opinion, did not attempt to define the phrase "traditional governmental functions," he did list a few activities he believed clearly fell within its orbit: fire protection, police protection, sanitation, public health, and parks and recreation. Depending on what other activities might be defined as "traditional," the Usery decision was a potentially major limitation on federal power.

As Rufus Davis might have predicted, however, finding a definition of "traditional" that could be applied consistently to individual cases was extraordinarily difficult. Litigation of the issue after the Usery decision produced a series of confused and inconsistent results. Regulating ambulance services, licensing automobile drivers, operating a municipal airport, or operating a highway authority were held to be "traditional" functions protected by *Usery*, while regulation of traffic on public roads, regulation of air transportation, operation of a mental health center, or provision of domestic services for the aged and the handicapped were judged to be nontraditional. An opportunity to consider what, if anything, distinguished one group of services from the other was presented when Joe G. Garcia and other employees of the San Antonio Metropolitan Transit Authority filed suit to force the Authority to pay them overtime wages in accordance with FLSA. Was the San Antonio transit authority a "traditional" governmental function and thus exempt from FLSA rules on overtime pay? Or was it a nontraditional activity and thus required to follow national rules? Could Joe Garcia get his overtime pay or not?

In *Garcia* v. *San Antonio Metropolitan Transit Authority,* decided February 19, 1985 (105 S. Ct. 1005, 1011), the Supreme Court not only ruled in favor of Garcia, but took the opportunity to overrule *Usery.* Taking note of the confused efforts to classify some activities as "traditional," Mr. Justice Blackmun wrote: "We find it difficult, if not impossible, to identify an organizing principle that places each of the cases in the first group on one side of a line and each of the cases in the second group on the other side. The constitutional distinction between licensing drivers and regulating traffic, for example, or between operating a highway authority and operating a mental facility, is elusive at best." Nor was historical precedent likely to help identify such a principle since, taken strictly, a historical approach would prevent the Court ". . . from accommodating changes in the historical functions of States, changes that have resulted in a number of once private functions like education being assumed by the States and their subdivisions."

Justice Blackmun's reading of history, in fact, suggested to him that attempting to place functions into traditional or nontraditional categories could easily be a matter of "historical nearsightedness." Today's self-evident "traditional" function is often yesterday's suspect innovation. Driving this point home, Blackmun noted that the National League of Cities listed parks and recreation as an example of a traditional service and observed that:

> A scant 80 years earlier, however, in *Shoemaker* v. *United States,* 147 U.S. 282 (1893), the Court pointed out that city commons originally had been provided not for recreation but for grazing domestic animals "in common," and that "in the memory of men now living, a proposition to take private property [by eminent domain] for a public park . . . would have been regarded as a novel exercise of legislative power." (p. 15)

For Justice Blackmun and his majority colleagues, efforts to develop clear distinctions of the sort attempted in *National League of Cities* were "unlikely to succeed regardless of how the distinctions are phrased" because of a fundamental problem with such efforts:

> The problem is that neither the governmental/proprietary distinction nor any other that purports to separate out important governmental functions can be faithful to the role of federalism in a democratic society. The essence of our federal system is that within the realm of authority left open to them under the Constitution, the States must be equally free to engage in any activity that their citizens choose for the common weal, no matter how unorthodox or unnecessary anyone else—including the judiciary—deems state involvement to be. Any rule of state immunity that looks to the "traditional," "integral," or "neces-

sary" nature of governmental functions inevitably invites an unelected federal judiciary to make decisions about which state policies it favors and which ones it dislikes. . . . We therefore now reject, as unsound in principle and unworkable in practice, a rule of state immunity from federal regulation that turns on a judicial appraisal of whether a particular governmental function is "integral" or "traditional." (pp. 17–18)

The Court in this case made clear that constitutional restraints on national government power over the states was procedural rather than substantive, inhering ". . . principally in the workings of the National Government itself, rather than in discrete limitations on the objects of federal authority" (p. 23). Or, to put it differently, politics determines the boundaries of acceptable action: ". . . the principal and basic limit on the federal commerce power is that inherent in all congressional action—the built-in restraints that our system provides through state participation in federal governmental action. The political process ensures that laws that unduly burden the States will not be promulgated" (p. 27).

The sweep of the Garcia decision, together with the confident language with which it is asserted, indicate that the Court was well aware of the significance of its ruling. Interestingly enough, however, the decision was made by a slim 5 to 4 majority, just as the overruled National League of Cities decision had been made by a similar 5 to 4 majority. Important and thoughtful as the Garcia ruling may be, therefore, we should not imagine that it signifies an end to the debate. Like all of its predecessors, *Garcia* represents no more than the current view of the present Court. Should the membership of the Court change, or should the views of present members change—as Justice Blackmun's views appear to have changed from *National League of Cities* to *Garcia*—the political pragmatism of *Garcia* could easily be replaced by the dual federalism notions of an earlier period.

The debate will continue, in short, because there is no "final" answer. There is only the process bequeathed by an ambiguous Constitution, offering rules for finding answers, but not the answers themselves. If this system seems uncomfortably ambiguous, there is at least this much to be said for it: Each new generation can solve its own political problems without tying the hands of future generations to outmoded solutions.

SUMMARY

Important as federal governance is to our everyday lives, understanding it presents a formidable challenge. Constitutional ambiguity regarding who can or should do what allows separate institutions to share power over similar activities. Power-sharing inevitably breeds intergovernmental tensions, but resolution of those tensions seldom leads to more than a temporary respite in an unending process of change. Even the major political frameworks for debating federal policy issues, referred to earlier as the efficiency and national purpose frameworks, are defined somewhat differently by each new generation of federal politicians. American federal governance, with its endless debates over divisions of authority, constant adjustments to changing circumstances, and ambiguous political rhetoric, can easily seem too chaotic to comprehend.

Fortunately, scholars have developed a number of conceptual tools to simplify and organize these complexities. In the next chapter three important analytical approaches are examined critically, in order to lay a foundation for developing a more useful conceptual approach. This "benefits coalition" approach is then used in succeeding chapters to analyze the distribution of federal benefits, the coalitions that support such benefits, the dynamics of system change, and major problems such as finance, regulation, and reform. It will become clear, I hope, that beneath the apparent chaos of American federal governance there are patterns of behavior that are revealed once an appropriate analytic language is used.

REFERENCES

Anton, 1974. Thomas J. Anton. "The Pursuit of Efficiency: Values and Structure in the Changing Politics of Swedish Municipalities." In *Comparative Community Politics*, ed. Terry N. Clark. New York: Halsted Press.

Anton, 1984. Thomas J. Anton. "Intergovernmental Change in the United States: An Assessment of the Literature." In *Public Sector Performance: A Conceptual Turning Point*, ed. Trudi C. Miller. Baltimore: The Johns Hopkins University Press.

Anton, 1985. Thomas J. Anton. "Decay and Reconstruction in the Study of American Intergovernmental Relations." *Publius* 15: 65–97.

Davis, 1967. Rufus Davis. "The Federal Principle Reconsidered." In *American Federalism in Perspective*, ed. Aaron Wildavsky. Boston: Little, Brown.

Downs and Larkey, 1986. George W. Downs and Patrick D. Larkey. *The Search for Government Efficiency: From Hubris to Helplessness*. New York: Random House.

GAO, 1985. U.S. General Accounting Office. "Report to the Chairman, Senate Committee on Governmental Affairs: Compendium of GAO's Views on the Cost Saving Proposals of the Grace Commission." Washington, D.C.: Government Printing Office.

Garcia v. *San Antonio Metropolitan Transit Authority*. 105 S. Ct. 1005, 1001 (1985).

Hofstadter, 1954. Richard Hofstadter. *The American Political Tradition*. New York: Vintage Books.

Krane, 1984. Dale Krane. "Does the Federal-Unitary Dichotomy Make Any Difference?" Paper prepared for delivery at the 9th Annual Hendricks Symposium. University of Nebraska, Lincoln, November 14–16.

Landau, 1961. Martin Landau. "On the Use of Metaphor in Political Analysis." *Social Research* 28 (3): 331–353.

LaPalombara, 1975. Joseph G. LaPalombara. "Monoliths or Plural Systems: Through Conceptual Lenses Darkly." *Studies in Comparative Communism* 8 (3): 305–332.

MacDonald, 1928. Austin F. MacDonald. *Federal Aid: A Study of the American Subsidy System*. New York: Crowell.

May, 1976. Henry F. May. *The Enlightenment in America*. New York: Oxford University Press.

McCloskey and Zaller, 1984. Herbert McCloskey and John Zaller. *The American Ethos: Public Attitudes Toward Capitalism and Democracy*. Cambridge, Mass.: Harvard University Press.

McKay, 1980. David H. McKay. "The Rise of the Topocratic State: United States Intergovernmental Relations in the 1970's." In *Financing Urban Government in the Welfare State*, ed. Douglas E. Ashford. New York: St. Martin's Press.

National League of Cities v. *Usery*. 426 U.S. 833, 1976.

OMB, 1983. Executive Office of the President. Office of Management and Budget. *Budget of the United States Government, FY 1983*. Washington, D.C.: Government Printing Office.

Palmer and Sawhill, 1982. John L. Palmer and Isabel V. Sawhill, eds. *The Reagan Experiment*. Washington, D.C.: Urban Institute Press.

Riker, 1975. William Riker. "Federalism." In *Handbook on Political Science*, vol. 5. Boston: Addison-Wesley.

Rose-Ackerman, 1981. Susan Rose-Ackerman. "Does Federalism Matter? Political Choice in a Federal Republic." *Journal of Political Economy* 89 (1): 152–165.

Stewart, 1982. William H. Stewart. "Metaphors, Models and the Development of Federal Theory." *Publius* 12: 5–24.

Stewart, 1984. William H. Stewart. *Concepts of Federalism*. Lanham, Md.: Center for the Study of Federalism and University Press of America.

Taubman, 1973. William Taubman. *Governing Soviet Cities: Bureaucratic Politics and Urban Development in the USSR*. New York: Praeger.

U.S. Census, 1985. U.S. Bureau of the Census. *Census of Governments*. Washington, D.C.: Government Printing Office.

CHAPTER 2

ANALYTIC APPROACHES TO FEDERALISM

Because the Constitution is so vague in allocating responsibilities among different levels of government, all efforts to define the distribution of authority among governments have been unsuccessful. Efforts to impose some alternative intellectual order on this large and diverse group of governments have exposed the enormous difficulty of stating generalizations that are not subject to endless qualification—except, of course, for the truism that politics and policy "differ from state to state." Some scholars have reacted to the size and complexity of our system by rejecting the existence of comprehensible patterns of activity that can be defined, described, and understood. For them, federal politics is so varied that patterns seldom emerge, or if they do, they seldom last long enough to explain very much. From this scholarly perspective, American federalism is a "wilderness of single instance" (Davis, 1967), comprehensible only through close examination of individual cases and events.

This book proceeds from a different approach. Although federal politics and policies are difficult to understand, patterns do exist and they can be described. Understanding these patterns requires a dual strategy. First, we should focus our attention on the behavior of public officials. Too many studies go astray by accepting political or legal rhetoric as a basis for analysis. Political formulations are always available, since federalism is a recurring issue, but the exaggerations of political debate seldom bring us very close to reality. Focusing on official behavior offers the possibility of discovering patterns of action, where they exist, as well as the possibility of relating such patterns to the attitudes and opinions that shape actions.

Second, observation of behavior must be guided by analytic concepts appropriate to the task of discovering behavioral patterns within masses of particular details. Concepts identify and define fragments of social life that we consider important and by doing so call attention to specific aspects of action. For example, we might believe political party identification to be important in explaining some policy. By carefully defining the concepts "party identification" and "policy," we might then attempt to match them against observed behavior in an effort to discover the significance of party identification for the policy outcome in question. Note that in this case we focus on a single presumed cause—party identification—and exclude other plausible causes of policy outcomes, such as ideology, education, gender, age, and so on. Other plausible causes could have been considered, singly or in combination, but defining one significant concept has the effect of excluding other possible factors. Stating a concept, in other words, not only tells us what to look for, but in doing so excludes other aspects of behavior from consideration. Developing useful concepts is thus an important first step in any study of social life.

Unfortunately, many studies of federal politics and policy seem either unaware or uninterested in the problem of conceptualization. One result, most evident in the hundreds or perhaps thousands of so-called case studies of individual policies or events, is the use of frameworks that are implicit rather than explicit. These bootleg conceptual frameworks vary considerably, but a common conceptualization is the rational actor model: an "actor," in some "situation," having "goals," and pursuing the goals through "action." This is a useful enough model if skillfully applied, but it presents serious analytic problems. Using "goals" to explain outcomes assumes rather than demonstrates a rational connection between outcomes and purposes. And focusing on "actor" behavior ties action so closely to individuals that generalizations about patterns are virtually impossible. Behavioral patterns may in fact exist, but this implicit conceptualization masks their presence. At the other extreme, many scholars work with conceptualizations so abstract that the behavior presumably associated with such patterns is ignored. Measures of various social or policy outcomes are manipulated to produce reported relationships, but the actions supporting the relationships are neither reported nor analyzed. "High income" states spend more on "welfare" than "low income" states, but the meaning of such a relationship or the mechanisms through which it may be achieved are typically unexplored.

In a book that proposes to offer general statements about federalism and public policy in the United States, it is important to move beyond the individual cases, but not so far that behavioral mechanisms are hidden from view. What are needed are concepts capable of supporting middle-range generalizations—that is, statements about observed phenomena that comprehend much, but not necessarily all, that is significant. To develop such concepts this chapter reviews three popular analytic perspectives: fiscal federalism, hierarchy, and public choice. Each of these perspectives offers important insights, but as I will argue, each is of limited relevance in understanding the complexities of modern federal relations. I borrow freely from them, however, in offering a more adequate analytic framework. This framework, built around the concepts of benefits and coalition, will be presented and justified later in this chapter.

FISCAL FEDERALISM

One popular model, derived from the work of Professor Richard A. Musgrave but developed further by a number of other social scientists, is the framework of *fiscal federalism* (Musgrave, 1959). Musgrave's contribution was to divide the functions of government into three classes that provided a clear rationale for the allocation of responsibilities in a multi-unit system. For Musgrave, appropriate governmental functions were stabilization, allocation, or distribution. *Stabilization* referred to the control of economic cycles through the use of monetary and fiscal policy. These activities obviously had to be applicable nationally to be effective and thus were clearly functions of the national government. *Distribution* referred to the provision of resources to the population, with particular emphasis on those segments of the population who were unable on their own to achieve a satisfactory level of resources. This too was an appropriate function for the national government, since subnational efforts to manage distribution were likely to be ineffective and inefficient. *Allocation* referred to the division of national resources between public goods, available to all, and private goods, available only to those who could pay for them. Since all governments produced public goods, all governments —including state and local governments—were legitimate participants in the allocation function. Here, then, was a clear rationale for state and local government action: to participate in the allocation function by providing public goods to satisfy the demands or tastes of state or local populations.

Fiscal federalism also offered a guide for appropriate interactions among federal, state, and local governments by building on the notion that the public goods provided by governments could be regarded as benefits, distributed to recipient populations. Many public goods are distributed entirely to people within the jurisdiction that produces them. Other public programs distribute benefits to people who live outside the producing jurisdiction—that is, the benefits "spill over" into other jurisdictions. From the point of view of the recipient jurisdiction, the benefits that "spill in" are pure gain; individuals obtain a public benefit for which they paid nothing.

From the point of view of the producing jurisdiction, however, the spillovers represent costs for which no benefit is received. The producing jurisdiction, accordingly, would be likely to cut back its production of the spilled-over benefits until its benefits more nearly matched its costs. Since the receiving jurisdiction has no similar incentive to produce goods it was not producing anyway, the availability of the good might then fall below desirable standards. In such circumstances, assistance from a higher level of government is appropriate in order to ensure that an adequate supply of the public good is available.

At what level should such assistance be provided? Within the framework of fiscal federalism, the answer is clear. Higher-level assistance should equal the portion of any given benefit that actually spills over into other jurisdictions. Thus, if 30 percent of the patrons of a city library are residents of other jurisdictions, a grant amounting to 30 percent of the library budget would be justified. If 20 percent of a state's health care services are provided to residents of other states, then a national grant amounting to 20 percent of the state's health care budget would be in order. The normative goal in fiscal federalism, obviously, is a system in which the beneficiaries of public benefits pay the costs of those benefits. But since the "fit" between benefit incidence and cost incidence is unlikely to be perfect in multi-unit systems, assistance from higher-level governments provides a vehicle for transferring some of the costs of desirable public goods to a larger tax base.

The same logic applies to spillovers that are not so pleasant. A city may dump untreated sewage into a nearby river that may provide water to several downstream communities. Since the benefits of city action are enjoyed only by city residents, but the costs are borne by many downstream communities, the logic of fiscal federalism would require that the cost of dumping be increased for city residents or, if such action proved unfeasible, that higher-level grants be awarded to downstream communities to assist in efforts to eliminate the pollution caused by the upstream city's action. For both positive and negative spillovers, in short, fiscal federalism offers recommendations premised on the desirability of matching benefits with an appropriate resource base.

The framework of fiscal federalism also recognizes that resource bases are not all the same. Quite apart from spillovers or spillins, some jurisdictions may be unable to offer services similar to those available in others because they do not have enough wealth, either in property values or personal income. Fiscal disparities of this kind often result in a lower level of public goods than is desirable, particularly in such basic services as education or public health. In such cases, adjustment of jurisdictional boundaries would increase wealth and produce a better match between resources and responsibilities. Since jurisdictional change is difficult to achieve in the United States, an alternative is higher-level grants to resource-poor jurisdictions designed to ensure that an acceptable level of essential public goods is available in all jurisdictions. Although the terms "acceptable" and "essential" are obviously defined in the political process, and thus subject to change, the important point is that for fiscal disparities, as for spillovers, the framework of fiscal federalism offers clear norms for linking jurisdictions in our federal system.

The norms of fiscal federalism are worth some emphasis. The most fundamental norm is that the beneficiaries of public programs should pay for them. If all benefits were paid only by beneficiaries, there would be perfect accountability: beneficiaries who chose not to pay would no longer receive benefits. Since this is seldom the case in federal systems, there is a need for mechanisms that retain a modicum of accountability while compensating for benefit-burden imbalances. Assuming that existing jurisdictions provide a satisfactory level of accountability, the major mechanism for overcoming benefit-burden imbalance is assistance from higher- to lower-level governments. Grants to lower-level governments promote efficiency in the provision of public goods by removing incentives to produce less than efficiency requires. Grants can also promote equity by increasing the resources available to poor jurisdictions. Without challenging the legitimacy of existing citizen preferences or existing governments, fiscal federalism seeks to promote accountability, efficiency, and equity through mechanisms that link the various units in our federal system (Oates, 1972, 1977).

Fiscal federalism is an attractive framework, sophisticated in its location of appropriate national and subnational governmental functions, parsimonious in its use of benefit and cost incidence as major tools of analysis, and clear in its recommendations for dealing with benefit-burden imbalances. Its main difficulty is a very poor fit between what the framework asserts—as fact or recommendation—and what occurs in the real political world.

To some extent the difficulty arises from conceptual ambiguity. As a practical matter, clear distinctions between allocation, distribution, and stabilization functions are often impossible to draw. Most major governmental activities, in fact, probably could be placed in more than one of these categories. Some, such as public welfare programs, obviously distribute resources, but they also allocate resources to these public services which are so large in monetary value that they clearly have an impact on economic stability. The apparently neat trichotomy that provides a basis for dividing public power thus turns out to be not so neat at all.

It is also clear that the major analytic tools used in fiscal federalism assume a level of measurement that is, for the most part, beyond our reach. Consider an assertion that might be made by a fiscal federalist: Policing is a necessary public good, and therefore cities should receive state or federal grants (or both) to support that portion of their police budgets devoted to servicing nonresidents. How would one measure the "nonresident" portion of police budgets? By the nonresident fraction of total arrests, or total citations? But doesn't an arrest or citation of a nonresident also provide a service to residents—indeed, would such actions not be a greater service to residents than to others? Or should one identify the number of nonresidents present in the city on a daily or weekly basis as a proportion of the resident population and use that figure to calculate an appropriate grant? The assumption here would be that both residents and nonresidents benefit equally, even though the benefits cannot be measured. But do residents and nonresidents enjoy equal benefits? If nonresidents are mostly workers in city firms, their stay in the city is limited to 8 or 9 hours, compared to residents' 24-hour presence. Or if the city is New York, many of the nonresidents may be tourists, who flock to the city for varying periods of time, including weeks of day-long residence, particularly in Manhattan. How do we account for such complications?

The answer, of course, is that we don't, because quite often we can't. Major public goods such as policing, education, the provision of clean water and clean air, or good public transportation cannot be allocated precisely—even in principle—among resident and nonresident beneficiaries, because providing the service to one class is providing the service to the other. Fuzzy estimates of the size of each class are possible, but to move beyond such estimates would require data that are not available now and that, in all probability, require inquiries quite distasteful to most Americans. "Beneficiaries should pay" is a fine principle, but it is more applicable to special services to distinct populations than to the public goods that are the staples of modern government. Compensation for spillovers is similarly a fine principle, so long as we remember that the measurement of spillovers is fuzzy at best, and nowhere close to the level of precision implied by fiscal federalism.

Despite its undeniable intellectual attractions, then, fiscal federalism remains more an ideal than a practice among American governments. Fiscal disparities between governments remain large and, in the case of many central cities and their surrounding suburbs in the North, are becoming larger. Yet neither the national government nor the states have yet adopted policies to equalize fiscal capacity among relevant jurisdictions. Many states have adopted equalization plans for their public schools, mostly under court order to do so, but even in these states public services are otherwise quite unevenly funded. Both the national government and the states have expanded their assistance programs quite dramatically in recent years, but compensation for spillovers or spillins has had little to do with the expansion. Program innovation to deal with serious problems, including environmental decay, energy, social services, and economic stimulation, have dominated national government actions, while tax relief has tended to dominate state actions (ACIR, A-86, 1981). The inescapable conclusion is that, in the United States, federal and state grant programs do not follow the prescriptions of fiscal federalism. Other theories will have to be found to analyze American federal politics and policy.

HIERARCHY

An alternative model that appears regularly in both political and analytic discourse is *hierarchy:* A system of authority, graded by rank, in which higher ranks exert control over lower ranks, following directives issued by the highest authority. Although it may seem surprising that this model is popular in a system with so many governments, few of which willingly accept a "subordinate" role, the idea of hierarchy has strong political and intellectual roots in the United States.

To begin with, we can easily view the whole structure of our governing system as a hierarchy. It is well established in law that local governments are creatures of the states and thus totally subordinate to them. Furthermore, the same Constitution that guarantees the continued existence of the states also asserts, in the famous Supremacy Clause, that both the Constitution and the laws of the United States ". . . shall be the supreme Law of the Land; and the Judges in every State shall be bound thereby, anything in the Constitution or Laws of any State to the contrary notwithstanding" (Article VI). Clearly, if national law takes precedence over state law, and state laws control local governments, the structure of our governing system seems quite hierarchical indeed. If the system actually worked this way, public policies would be promulgated by the national government, enforced by all the states, and implemented by the local governments. The states, rather than being autonomous units in a federal system, would be little more than the administrative arms of a centralized, national system.

Few politicians or analysts would argue for such a centralized system for the United States, but its intellectual appeal remains strong: It is both clear and straightforward. American scholars have been strongly influenced by the studies of bureaucracy done by the German sociologist Max Weber during the early decades of this century (Weber, 1947). Weber's images of officials—trained for their jobs, recruited on the basis of competence, and evaluated on the basis of performance within carefully graded systems of authority—have had a powerful appeal to American reformers, particularly those activated by outrageous scandals or evidence of waste. These images also fit nicely with our governmental ideologies, which value democratic participation but also, as Herbert Kaufman has demonstrated, executive leadership and nonpartisan competence (Kaufman, 1956). Indeed, strong leaders who have been able to resolve difficult problems or produce major accomplishments—Robert Moses in New York or Richard Daley in Chicago are examples—are often regarded as folk heroes, the people who can "get things done." They are the "fixers," to borrow a phrase from Eugene Bardach (Bardach, 1979), whose activities are necessary to overcome the inertia built into a system of many governments.

Hierarchy thus appeals to many intellectuals, and not a few politicians, as an alternative, one usually proposed in reaction to evidence of inefficiency or corruption. The diagnosis is usually the same: Duplication of services is rampant, causing waste of tax dollars; there is lack of coordination among different agencies that provide the same service; citizens are confused by the complexity of who is doing what and are thus unable to hold anyone accountable for waste and corruption. The hierarchical resolution to these problems is also usually the same: Centralize! Eliminate most of the duplicating agencies or programs; establish a central authority over the remaining units, with power to coordinate and evaluate their activities; establish procedures through which this centralized authority can be held accountable, and then hold it accountable.

Both the diagnosis of fragmentation and the prescription of hierarchical integration have a long history in American politics. These ideas were applied to city governments at the turn of the century, to state governments in the 1920s, to executive-legislative relations in the 1930s, to metropolitan areas in the 1950s and 1960s, and more recently to the organization of the federal government as a whole (Gulick and Urwick, 1937; Knott and Miller, 1987; Seidman, 1979). Although not always successful in reducing fragmentation, the ideas do remain powerful as an alternative model of government organization.

Hierarchy continues to be utilized as a model of reform at the state and local levels, largely because it provides a device for pursuing the values of efficiency and rationality that are so ingrained in the American political temperament. Applying the hierarchy model to relationships between the national government and the states, however, is more difficult. From a constitutional point of view, it would be difficult to argue that states derive their authority from the national government. The states not only pre- ceded the national government, but accepted doctrine holds that both the states and the national government derive their authority from the same source—the people (Corwin, 1978). If state authority originates in the people, it cannot come from the national government. The notion of a hierarchical relationship between Washington and the state governments thus appears impossible to reconcile with existing constitutional princi- ples. Even the Supremacy Clause, after all, applies only to national legislation that conflicts with state law. If there is no national law or if there is a national law but it is consistent with state laws, the Supremacy Clause does not operate.

Apart from constitutional principle, there is an insurmountable politi- cal defect in the idea of hierarchy: the absence of a national party system. American political parties are organized by state, and party ideologies tend to be organized by region, to the extent that they are organized at all. Although the labels Republican and Democrat are used nationally, eastern Republicans are very different from midwestern Republicans, southern Democrats are poles apart from northern Democrats, and western politi- cians are different from everybody else. Within states, strong political party organizations are rare. Instead, individual politicians choose an affiliation, mount their own campaigns with money they raise mostly by themselves, and push issues that may or may not have anything to do with national or state party platforms. Once elected to state or national office, therefore, these politicians have very little reason to accept party direction, except when it benefits them, and very little incentive to work hard at developing national agendas. Under these circumstances, it is impossible to imagine how national supremacy could work, since it would require unified support by a continuing majority of locally oriented legislators for actions that would result in some loss of local discretion. Political party decentralization, in short, completely undermines the political base neces- sary for a national hierarchy.

Finally, there is a practical matter to consider. National hierarchy implies a unified perspective that can be articulated and imposed on state and local governments. Congress, dominated by locally oriented politi- cians, cannot be expected to develop such unity. Can the executive branch do any better? The answer, almost certainly, is No. A strong president can occasionally marshall sufficient influence to develop a unified policy view among executive agencies, but the agencies and their programs have life spans that exceed any president's tenure by a wide margin. Those programs are so different from agency to agency, and supported by such different coalitions, that a unified executive branch view on any given policy is likely to be extremely rare. In this sense, the national government is no different than other American governments. Its executive agencies are as fragmented by purpose and personnel as are state and local governments, and overcoming fragmentation is no less difficult in Washington than it is in Chicago or Seattle. And so hierarchy, however much it may appeal to our desire for rationality and effective government action, does not describe, and cannot prescribe, the politics of federalism in the United States.

PUBLIC CHOICE

A third model of American federalism attempts to combine insights from both economic and political analyses into a public choice perspective. Like the fiscal federalism model, the *public choice* framework assumes the superiority of markets as mechanisms for producing and distributing benefits, and justifies government intervention only in cases of market failure. Externalities (or spillovers) for which the market would be unlikely to compensate, the use of common resources (like rivers), which a market could not control, or the need for public goods the markets would be unlikely to produce all justify government action in this model, as in the fiscal federalism framework (McKay, 1980).

The public choice model, however, does not assume that existing governmental structures are necessarily acceptable. Particularly in the work of Vincent and Elinor Ostrom and their colleagues, existing structures are challenged on both empirical and conceptual grounds. Empirically, evidence from a large number of studies is used to document the frequent failure of bureaucracies to perform effectively or to respond to citizen interests. Large governmental agencies are especially likely to be rigid in their adherence to established procedures, regardless of the effect of those procedures on the services or products these agencies were established to provide. The goods and services provided by government thus are likely to be quite standardized, even in situations where nonstandard products would be more effective in meeting agency goals. There is also lethargic delivery, even in situations where speedy response is vital.

Because the officials who make policy in public bureaucracies are often isolated from the recipients of public services by several layers of organization, adjustments in procedures are difficult to make. Officials who have the power to bring about adjustments often do not know what is going on, while those who know what is going on seldom have the power to bring about change. As a result, public bureaucracies often stumble along blindly, pursuing outdated policies without regard to either their effectiveness or their efficiency.

The conceptual weakness associated with these weaknesses in public bureaucracies, of course, is excessive reliance on hierarchy as the major alternative to the market. Since goods and services produced by government do not have a "price" like that attached to private sector goods, producers of government products have no easy way to estimate the demand for what they produce. And because careers in public agencies often depend on doing or producing more each year, public officials have an incentive to expand agency activities, regardless of consumer demand for them. The more public sector activities are organized as hierarchical bureaucracies, the fewer the units involved in those activities, the weaker the feedback or demand for those activities, and the greater the domination of producer rather than consumer interests in the production of public services. Reliance on large and centralized bureaucracies to produce the public goods made necessary by market failure, in short, can generate a cure far worse than the original disease (Ostrom, 1973).

If both markets and bureaucracies are marked by inherent weaknesses, what is the better solution? The answer, from a public choice point of view, is twofold: (1) Emphasize consumer sovereignty over public benefit; and (2) recognize that structures for the delivery of those benefits can be as varied as the benefits themselves.

If governments are viewed as producers of benefits demanded by consumers, then every good produced by government may be viewed as the product of the common interests of some group of citizens large enough to create a benefit to satisfy its need. In this sense, any governmental program may be viewed as an expression of some community of interest. Since communities of interest are likely to be diverse in a society as large as ours, public benefit programs are likely to be similarly diverse. They will often serve highly specialized communities of interest with programs specifically tailored to those interests. Individual citizens are likely to be members of many different communities of interest. In a consumer-driven system, however, multiple and overlapping service jurisdictions are benefits, since they permit these specialized interests to be served. So long as consumers demand and pay for such narrow programs, moreover, control over them can be exercised by the consumers themselves. Instead of large and distant bureaucracies exerting control over benefits, citizens as consumers exert political control directly by electing to support or not to support the benefits they receive.

Because basic services are provided in small packages, to specialized constituencies that often overlap other constituencies, the system requires a higher level of government. Disputes among the large number of primary constituencies are likely to be common, and a higher authority would be essential to resolve those conflicts. A higher level of government could also serve as a central production unit, taking advantage of economies of scale to offer some benefits at a lower unit cost. Or the higher-level unit might develop new services and "sell" them to the primary units. This kind of system would provide a large number of different services, some on a very narrow basis, some on a large-scale and centralized basis, depending on the kind of benefit and the demand for that benefit. Since some communities of interest would be broad, there would be a sufficient supply of public goods. But since many communities would be narrow, bureaucratic control would be unnecessary. Political control over service benefits, exercised through jurisdictions of various sizes and interests, would assure a variety of public programs, responsive to different interests and accountable through politics to the citizens served.

The public choice framework is appealing because it seems to move us away from the extremist formulations of the market as the only legitimate collective institution or monopolistic hierarchy. It also seems to come close to the American experience in its emphasis on demand as the source of governmental structure and activity.

But although the public choice framework seems to apply reasonably well to special district governments in the United States, which provide a single service to narrowly defined constituencies that pay for that service, its relevance for the more complex governments of our larger cities and states is not so clear. Citizens in more complicated environments may or may not have enough information to calculate their interests in supporting or not supporting certain services. Even with a great deal of information, citizens would have great difficulty making specific choices. Injunctions to "heed citizen-consumers" and "consider organizational alternatives to large bureaucracies" are sensible enough, but wholly lacking the detail that would be necessary to apply such advice in particular circumstances. Nor does the framework offer any clear guidelines for dividing responsibilities among jurisdictions, or among services that could be controlled directly by consumer choice and those that might require a more bureaucratic form of organization. In the end, therefore, the public choice framework amounts only to an argument for more market and fewer bureaucratic solutions to public problems; it contains no details or specific guidelines for actual change.

Toward Improvement

Fiscal federalism, hierarchy, and public choice are normative models; their strengths lie in prescribing what should be rather than in describing what is. They are valuable for the insights that allow us to understand general relationships. But because they are empirically weak, the frameworks leave open the question of how to describe and analyze actual patterns of intergovernmental behavior. This has proved to be an extraordinarily difficult question, precisely because the real world of federal politics is infinitely more complicated than any simple model. Nevertheless, by combining the view that government programs are benefits distributed to identifiable populations with the many detailed accounts of individuals coming together to pursue such benefits, it may be possible to develop conclusions that have empirical support. We turn now to the definition and justification of this alternative approach, the benefits coalition framework.

THE BENEFITS COALITION FRAMEWORK

American political thought has always emphasized a pragmatic conception of government. People exist before government exists, and collectivities of individual people come together to "create" governments whenever they find that some purpose can be better achieved through collective action. Government in the American sense is not some abstract essence, but an agency created to do something for specific groups of people. Should entirely new objectives become desired by citizens, governments can be eliminated, modified, or given new directions to pursue. In this context, government is a human artifact, to be designed and used only so long as its products fulfill the expressed wishes of individuals.

Purposes of Government

Given such a view, it seems plausible to conceptualize the purpose of American government as the creation and distribution of benefits to designated populations. As used here, the term *benefit* refers to any action or object that has value for some individual or individuals. Statements of purpose contained in early national documents such as the Constitution or the Declaration of Independence were primarily vague references to such benefits as "general welfare," "the blessings of liberty," the "pursuit of happiness." As time has passed and government activity has expanded, however, statements of purpose have become both more numerous and more precise. We can now identify three types of benefits that together comprise the bulk of government activity: economic, juridical, and symbolic.

Economic Benefits   The largest and most consistent focus of government activity in the United States is the promotion of economic well-being. However vague their rhetoric, the landowners and businessmen who led the American revolution and drafted its major documents clearly understood the uses of government to promote economic gain. This use of public action to promote private economic gain has been a consistent pattern in American public life, and lives today in the billions of dollars of public funds that are devoted to enhancing the economic welfare of individual citizens and corporations. National subsidies to corporations, to farmers and homeowners, plus military and civil service retirement pensions, and social security checks, food stamps, and other welfare payments to poor individuals constitute direct and tangible benefits to millions of people, all of whom have a continuing interest in such benefits. Other tangible economic benefits are distributed through the tax code, which provides billions of dollars of deductions and reductions in addition to direct subsidies.

State governments add billions more in tax and expenditure benefits, as do local governments, whose tax abatements and zoning regulations are often combined with state and federal benefits to stimulate local economies. Direct and indirect payments of cash to individuals and corporations, in short, constitute a major portion of all government activity in a nation dedicated to the use of government to improve economic well-being.

Not all recipients of government economic benefits are in the so-called private sector. Nearly 5 million people are employed by the national government; another 13 million work for state and local governments, and still another 4.5 million are paid employees of nonprofit organizations funded largely by government grants and contracts. The salary, fringe, and pension benefits paid to these 22 to 23 million workers are financially important. These benefits are also politically significant because the recipients are citizens as well as employees of governments, and as citizens often have opportunities to vote on policies that can increase or decrease the benefits they receive. As we will see in Chapter 4, the large number of public employees, together with their interest in maintaining salary and other economic benefits, are important factors in understanding a wide range of public policy issues.

Juridical Benefits   Although most common and most significant, economic benefits are not the only benefits distributed by American governments. A variety of legal benefits are distributed as well. They assign rights and obligations to individuals based on some defined status. All governments, for example, define the status of "voter," using age and residence to determine who is or is not eligible to participate in elections or hold public office within a particular jurisdiction. Similarly, governments authorize the performance of many activities by issuing licenses to individuals judged to be qualified to perform those activities. Doctors, plumbers, drivers of cars and buses, hairdressers, and lawyers are among the many individuals whose occupations are regulated by government license. Occupational licenses are juridical because they define legal rights and obligations, as well as performance standards; but in legitimizing income-producing activities, they must also be regarded as another form of economic benefit. By limiting entry to particular occupations, licensing helps to maintain the income of those who are allowed to pursue those occupations.

Symbolic Benefits   Finally, American governments constantly generate important symbolic benefits. Holidays that celebrate national independence, national heroes, or participation in the military provide repeated opportunities for public officials to reaffirm support for the symbols of national patriotism. State and regional commemorations of local events or individuals provide similar opportunities, as do athletic contests, particularly the well-attended football games between teams of the large state institutions of the Midwest, South, and West. Both national and regional celebrations are important because they help to maintain support for the political system, while regional events help to maintain support for diversity within national unity. Although the idea of "system support" is difficult to measure, it is increasingly recognized as a part of any government's capacity to rule effectively. Indeed, the New Jersey state legislature recently made special appropriations to Rutgers, the State University of New Jersey, for the purpose of developing a football team of national stature, precisely to generate a source of pride in and support for the state itself ("$3 Million for Rutgers Football," 1984). The idea may be less than precise, but politicians in a media age appear to recognize the need for system support and do what they can to develop it.

In addition to generalized symbols of support, governments create important symbolic benefits through the specific policies they choose to pursue. Government legislation or regulations that enunciate purposes such as "ending school segregation," "providing equal employment opportunities," or providing "a decent home environment for all Americans" offer public reassurance to large constituencies that their values are being addressed by responsive authorities. Reassurances of this kind often have less practical impact than the words imply, largely because the political majorities that are strong enough to enact the symbols are not strong enough to implement the required action in the face of determined minority opposition. But the symbols are nonetheless important, since they express publicly affirmed values that can be used in political debate. So while polluted water or employment discrimination or slum housing may continue to exist, the existence of official policy statements dedicated to the elimination of such conditions continues to motivate efforts to achieve these policy goals. Symbols can be important, in short, even when government actions fall far short of realizing them.

Benefit Coalitions

If the major products of government actions are benefits for designated populations, it seems reasonable to assume that the major sources of such benefits are the individual beneficiaries. A *benefit coalition*, accordingly, can be defined as any association of individuals, often representing other individuals, who mobilize to develop, support, and implement government benefit programs. *Coalition* is a simple enough concept, but there are subtleties that should be noted. The idea of coalition is often associated with a group politics framework, in which government action is viewed as a response to pressure exerted by groups outside the government itself. Within this framework, government officials are viewed as passive instruments, activated only when and if some external group or groups force them to act. Public action in response to pressure produces benefits primarily for the groups forcing the action; if the group weakens or falls apart, the benefits end.

This is an appealing idea expressing an important insight, but it tends to overlook a major development of the past half century. As governments have grown larger and assumed more comprehensive responsibilities, government officials themselves have become important sources of new program ideas, advocates for those ideas, and mobilizers of public support for proposals. It is no longer possible, if it ever really was, to see government officials as passive instruments, waiting for some external group to push them into action. My use of "coalition," accordingly, includes government officials as members of associations of individuals that propose and support public benefits.

Program as the Source of Benefits

Conceiving of government as a producer of economic, juridical, and symbolic benefits links government behavior to things and activities in which people place some value—a conception that fits nicely into the instrumental view of government that characterizes American political philosophy. To suggest that "government" produces benefits, however, is unclear. More than 82,000 separate governments are part of American government, and most of those separate jurisdictions are further divided into additional thousands of distinct departments, divisions, agencies, and offices. For some purposes, this huge and complex system can be simplified by relating benefits to agency. One might, for example, attempt to understand social policy by examining the benefits distributed by the federal Department of Health and Human Services. Or one might examine a state's education policy by examining the benefits produced by its department of education.

Such strategies are defensible, but they also pose problems. One problem is that agency responsibilities are seldom confined to a single policy arena and thus are bound to have a poor fit with abstract definitions of policy. HHS does indeed deliver social policy benefits, but so do HUD in its housing programs, Agriculture in its food programs, and even Defense, which fulfills housing and educational responsibilities. Studying any large agency is likely to produce a number of very different kinds of benefits. A more important problem for students of federal politics and policy is that an agency focus ignores the interagency activities that produce most federal benefits. The major HHS policies are administered jointly with state governments; the major education programs within states are administered jointly with local governments; the major HUD housing policies are administered jointly with local authorities; and so on.

A better alternative is to focus on the programs that generate and distribute government benefits. As used here, the concept of *program* refers to any repeated activity of public officials, directed toward some observable problem or objective, that is supported by measurable resources. This is a purposefully broad concept, but its qualifications are nevertheless important. Note, first, that attention is focused on the activity of people serving as public officials. Action is important simply because it can be observed, directly or indirectly; observing officials is important because no one has ever seen an "agency" or a "government" take action. *People* act, and this concept focuses on the actions they take when serving in some official capacity. Note, second, that unusual or one-time actions are excluded. Single events may be important, but understanding patterns of government requires us to look for action that is repeated. Third, this concept assumes that patterns of action are purposive, and uses problems or objectives to distinguish among programs. Finally, activities unsupported by measurable resources are excluded, on the assumption that no meaningful activity is possible without measurable financial or personnel support.

Viewing "program" as the source of government benefits has several advantages. By focusing on purposive activity rather than more abstract conceptions such as "the government," the concept of program encourages empirical precision as well as conceptual clarity. Adding modifiers such as "social" or "educational" allows analysis of similarly focused activity regardless of the organizational unit within which such activity may be found. Kramer's recent study, using "program" as the major analytic tool, discovered some 95 separate housing programs being operated by 14 different federal agencies (Kramer, 1985). Some of the programs he discovered are operated by national agencies, some by state and local agencies, and others by national, state, and local agencies. Clearly it is important to identify such administrative differences in order to begin to understand the major forms of public action and the social consequences they produce. It is particularly important to have a clear focus on such activities in a federal system complicated by large numbers of governments pursuing many different goals. Use of "program" as a conceptual tool allows us to cut through such complications, to identify and analyze groups of similar activities, organized by purpose, that flow through the federal system. Use of the concept also permits us to understand the differences between governments by focusing on the mix of different program activities carried out by any given government unit.

SUMMARY

The organizations we know as local, state, and national governments reflect characteristically different beneficiary interests through different patterns of public policy. The United Automobile Workers in Michigan and the tobacco farmers in North Carolina, for example, are both powerful coalition participants in their states, but the policy results reflect very different patterns of benefits. Coalition-based variety in public programs does not, however, imply an absence of pattern. Liebert has shown that the scope of local government activity varies systematically with age of government and region; Paul Peterson recently conceptualized the implicit structure of local, state, and national policies as predominantly developmental, allocational, and redistributive (Liebert, 1976; Peterson, 1981). There is considerable variety in interests present within jurisdictions, but there is a pattern within that variety as well.

Within the American structure, each governmental unit constitutes an interest that is part of the political environment of other governments. In addition to simple organizational maintenance, therefore, all American governments engage in political representation of organizational and constituency interests. From a local point of view, the state and federal governments provide much of the revenue and all of the regulations that govern local actions, while other local governments pursue interests or provide resources that often require sustained attention. From a state point of view, legal and financial responsibility for local government actions combine with localized legislative representation to determine much of state policy, while the administration of programs partially funded by the national government makes national agencies daily participants in state action. From a national point of view, localized representation in Congress and the locally specialized interests of national administrative agencies—HUD to service northeastern cities, Interior to service the joint federal-state interests of western states, Defense to interact largely with southern and coastal regions—give much of national policy its traditionally regional configuration. Shared responsibilities, in short, guarantee that many governments will be represented in political coalitions.

The fact that one government is always part of the relevant political environment of other jurisdictions implies that intergovernmental systems are inherently unstable. Since expenditures by one unit are often revenues for another, changes in taxing or spending policies have extensive ripple effects. Annual or biennial budget cycles guarantee that occasions for changes in budget policies will occur at least annually. Unanticipated events, such as unusually heavy snowstorms or floods, provide less predictable but repeated opportunities to adjust financial priorities. In a sense, therefore, coalitions that support existing financial priorities are constantly on guard against raids by new coalitions thrown up by unanticipated events or by the routinized questioning of budget cycles. Should new or different coalitions prevail in one jurisdiction, some effects will be felt and will cause actions in others. A shift in state expenditures may induce an increase in local taxes, or new national programs may bring substantial reductions in older state-funded programs. Despite the appearance of considerable structural stability, then, the intergovernmental system as a whole is inherently dynamic, constantly responding to changes in coalition structure.

Conceptualizing federal politics as patterned interactions among benefit-seeking coalitions, where the products of such interactions are benefits for members (including governments) of victorious coalitions, has several advantages. One is that the framework requires no heroic assumptions about individual knowledge or ability to calculate the costs and benefits of public action. What actors know and how they use or fail to use information in the process of building and maintaining coalitions are questions for investigation, not assumption. Use of the framework encourages a search for understanding without prejudging the rationality or effectiveness of coalition behavior. A second advantage is that this formulation can easily accommodate the rich empirical literature now available. Indeed, it is precisely this perspective that seems implicit in much of that literature, including the many recent studies of local implementation of, or reaction to, federal policies (Dommel, 1982; Nathan and Doolittle, 1983; Nathan, Manvel, and Calkins, 1975; Palmer and Sawhill, 1984; Pressman and Wildavsky, 1974; Stein, 1984). Use of the framework may permit us to develop interesting general statements simply by making explicit what seems implicit in many of these studies. A third very important advantage is that the framework is explicitly dynamic, encouraging a deeper exploration of sources and consequences of important actions, no less than the actions themselves. The benefits coalition model, in short, offers the promise of moving us some distance toward a better understanding of how American federalism works.

REFERENCES

ACIR, 1981. *The Federal Role in the Federal System: The Dynamics of Growth.* Washington, D.C.: Government Printing Office. Report A-86.

Bardach, 1979. Eugene Bardach. *The Implementation Game: What Happens After a Bill Becomes a Law.* Cambridge, Mass.: The Massachusetts Institute of Technology Press.

Corwin, 1978. Edward S. Corwin. *The Constitution and What It Means Today,* 14th ed., eds. Harold Chase and Craig Ducat. Princeton: Princeton University Press.

Davis, 1967. Rufus Davis. "The Federal Principle Reconsidered." In *American Federalism in Perspective,* ed. Aaron Wildavsky. Boston: Little, Brown.

Dommel, 1982. Paul R. Dommel and Associates. *Decentralizing Urban Policy: Case Studies in Community Development.* Washington, D.C.: The Brookings Institution.

Gulick and Urwick, 1937. Luther Gulick and Lyndall Urwick. *Papers in the Science of Administration.* New York: Institute of Public Administration.

Kaufman, 1956. Herbert Kaufman. "Emerging Conflicts in the Doctrines of Public Administration." *American Political Science Review* 50 (December): 1057–1073.

Knott and Miller, 1987. Jack H. Knott and Gary J. Miller. *Reforming Bureaucracy: The Politics of Institutional Choice.* Englewood Cliffs, N.J.: Prentice-Hall.

Kramer, 1985. Kevin L. Kramer. "Fifty Years of Federal Housing Policy: A Case Study of How the Federal Government Distributes Resources." Ph.D. dissertation, the University of Michigan.

Liebert, 1976. Roland J. Liebert. *Disintegration and Political Action: The Changing Functions of City Government in America.* New York: Academic Press.

McKay, 1980. David H. McKay. "The Rise of the Topographic State: United States Intergovernmental Relations in the 1970s." In *Financing Urban Government in the Welfare State,* ed. Douglas E. Ashford. New York: St. Martin's Press.

Musgrave, 1959. Richard A. Musgrave. *The Theory of Public Finance,* New York: McGraw-Hill.

Nathan and Doolittle, 1983. Richard P. Nathan and Fred C. Doolittle. *The Consequences of Cuts: The Effects of the Reagan Domestic Program on State and Local Governments.* Princeton, N.J.: Princeton University Press.

Nathan, Manvel, and Calkins, 1975. Richard P. Nathan, Allen D. Manvel, and Susannah E. Calkins. *Monitoring Revenue Sharing.* Washington, D.C.: The Brookings Institution.

Oates, 1972. Wallace E. Oates. *Fiscal Federalism.* New York: Harcourt Brace Jovanovich.

Oates, 1977. Wallace E. Oates, ed. *The Political Economy of Fiscal Federalism.* Lexington, Mass.: D. C. Heath.

Ostrom, 1973. Vincent Ostrom. "Can Federalism Make A Difference? *Publius* 3: 197–237.

Palmer and Sawhill, 1984. John L. Palmer and Isabel V. Sawhill, eds. *The Reagan Record.* Cambridge, Mass.: Ballinger.

Peterson, 1981. Paul Peterson. *City Limits.* Chicago: University of Chicago Press.

Pressman and Wildavsky, 1974. Jeffery Pressman and Aaron Wildavsky. *Implementation: How Great Expectations in Washington Are Dashed in Oakland.* Berkeley: University of California Press.

Seidman, 1979. Harold Seidman. *Politics, Position, and Power: The Dynamics of Federal Organization,* 2nd ed. New York: Oxford University Press.

Stein, 1984. Robert M. Stein. "Growth and Change in the U.S. Federal Aid System." Paper presented at the Southern Political Science Meetings, Savannah, Ga., November.

"$3 Million for Rutgers Football," 1984. *New York Times,* January 13.

Weber, 1947. Max Weber. *The Theory of Social and Economic Organization.* New York: The Free Press.

CHAPTER 3

THE DISTRIBUTION OF FEDERAL BENEFITS

If all Americans were under the authority of a single government, understanding the distribution of government benefits would be easy. Major public programs could be identified, program expenditures could be tabulated by various categories, recipients could be tracked down, and analyses of patterns of distribution could be performed. As we have seen, however, American governance is not so simple. Instead of a single set of programs, we have literally thousands of different combinations of programs. And instead of clear demarcation of responsibilities between units and levels of government, we have overlapping jurisdictions that confuse the issue of program responsibility. To appreciate who gets what from government in the United States, therefore, it is necessary to consider how federalism affects the distribution of public benefits.

BENEFIT DISTRIBUTION: AN OVERVIEW

The significance of federalism for benefit distributions can be quite dramatic, as illustrated by the Aid to Families with Dependent Children program. AFDC is jointly funded by national, state, and (in six states) local governments, but eligibility criteria and payment levels are largely determined by the states. A family of four could have received as much as $635 per month in 1985 if it were fortunate enough to live in Connecticut. If the same family lived in Mississippi, however, the maximum allowable monthly payment would have been only $120. Like other southern states, Mississippi prefers to rely more on the federally funded Food Stamps program rather than on AFDC, which requires substantial state funding. Even with Food Stamps, however, Connecticut and several other states pay twice as much or more as Mississippi and its southern neighbors (State Policy Data Book, 1986).

Part of the explanation for such dramatic differences in benefit distributions, of course, is environmental. We are a continental nation, with enormously varied climate conditions. Connecticut, a cold northern state, might well be expected to distribute larger AFDC benefits than Mississippi simply because residential heating costs are higher. Similarly, benefits for shipbuilders could be expected to be greater in Maine or Virginia than in Kansas or Wyoming, while tobacco farmers would certainly anticipate more help in North Carolina than in North Dakota. Very different physical environments, in short, structure very different opportunities for socioeconomic development. As those opportunities have been pursued, Americans have created a social system that is not only diverse, but regionally specialized. Environmental variety and the structure of economic interests erected upon that variety thus provide important stimuli for differences in benefits.

Important as they are, however, environmental conditions can provide no more than part of the explanation for differences. Environments can be and are altered by collective political action, particularly as new technologies permit previous physical barriers to be overcome—deserts have been transformed into productive farmland, for example. It is therefore essential to explore the social and political sources of variety that accompany environmental diversity. By definition, benefits are desired by someone, and preferences for public service levels and types fall into patterns that are relatively clear-cut. Some patterns are organized by state and are reflected in the mix of program activities conducted by states and their local jurisdictions. Others are organized by the interactions between states and the national government and can be observed in the flow of funds and legal obligations among levels. Both sets of patterns affect benefit distributions and thus require consideration. Before considering benefit differences, however, we should take a closer look at benefit growth.

THE GROWTH OF GOVERNMENT PROGRAMS

Broad public support for an instrumental view of government is a guarantee that public sector programs will change constantly in reaction to desires for new benefits. American governance as a whole is thus always in motion, becoming something else, from a base that is different from what it was. One measure of this dynamism is the vast expansion in the number and kinds of programs operated by government agencies at all levels.

It is important to distinguish between growth in programs, which has been substantial, and growth in governments, which has not occurred at all. Indeed, the total number of governments has declined from more than 155,000 as recently as 1942 to our present level of 82,000, largely because of state decisions to eliminate more than 90,000 local school districts during the past four decades. As Table 3.1 reveals, this remarkable transformation of American public education has been accompanied by a slight increase in municipalities and a dramatic threefold increase in the number of special districts in the same period.

Simple arithmetic will reveal that an average of nearly 3,000 structural changes were made each year during this time, a rough but useful measure of the level of governmental "tinkering" engaged in constantly by public officials. Although the United States remains the most "governed" nation on earth by quite a comfortable margin, these numbers show that a good deal of reform has occurred. Compared to a relatively recent past, public school governments are fewer and larger, some townships have been eliminated, and special districts have become a much more popular form of local governance.

But despite this substantial reduction in the number of governments, the activities actually carried out by governments have grown quite dramatically. One way to see this growth is to compare government spending to the economy as a whole. For much of American history, government expenditures were a relatively minor portion of the total economy, amounting to less than 10 percent of the gross national product as recently as 1929, and not reaching 20 percent until 1941. This fraction jumped to more than 40 percent during World War II, declined briefly after the war, and then began a steady upward march toward a present level that hovers around 35 percent of GNP. Increases in public sector spending have been accompanied by similarly dramatic increases in public sector employment. Wages and salaries paid to government employees consumed nearly 10 percent of total GNP by 1980, and the government labor force amounted to more than 15 percent of the total civilian labor force. Clearly, American government has been a growth industry for the past half century, in both absolute and relative terms (Break, 1982).

By definition, expansion of government's share of the total economy means that many activities formerly carried out in the private or household sectors have been shifted to the public sector. Although this shift is rooted in the long-term transition from an agrarian to an industrial-technological society, several periods can be identified as watersheds of new program development. The first great watershed era in this century undoubtedly was the Great Depression of 1929–1939, when national government expenditures as a percentage of GNP quadrupled.

Confronted by massive and continuing unemployment, bank failures, industrial failures, and the inability of state and local governments to cope with any of these problems, the national government gradually assumed a host of new responsibilities that grew into a major revolution in American

Table 3.1   Change in Governments, 1942–1982

TYPE OF GOVERNMENT	NUMBER OF GOVERNMENTS		CHANGE IN NUMBER
	1942	*1982*	
School districts	108,579	14,851	−93,728
Municipalities	16,220	19,076	2,856
Special districts	8,299	28,588	20,289

SOURCE: United States Bureau of the Census. *Statistical Abstract of the United States, 1986.* 106th ed. Washington, D.C.: Government Printing Office, p. 262.

federal politics. Efforts to provide immediate relief through job-creation programs or welfare assistance reflected a new willingness on the part of the national government to participate in activities traditionally thought to be state responsibilities. Even more revolutionary, however, were the new programs to subsidize agriculture and other industries, to guarantee the viability of the banking and housing industries, and to insure individuals against loss of income after retirement.

Such long-term programs were truly revolutionary because their effect was to socialize corporate and personal risk. No longer would individuals be expected to carry the heavy burden of income security alone; corporations would not be expected to suffer the accidents of the marketplace without some form of government assistance, either to prevent failure or to compensate for it. No longer, in short, was government to be viewed as merely a provider of services or a referee among competing interests. By the end of the Depression, national government programs had put into place an entirely new concept: government as guarantor of economic security. Later developments—especially the Full Employment Act of 1946, which announced a government responsibility to "promote maximum employment, production, and purchasing power"—added new and often voluminous detail. But the conceptual foundations of the guarantor state had been laid in the 1930s.

A second important watershed period began in the early 1950s, when local and state governments across the country began adding hundreds of thousands of new employees to engage in traditional activities suddenly given a new emphasis: education, social services, and physical planning and construction. Decaying cities, exploding suburbs, and rapid growth in the school-age population were the immediate causes of employment expansion among these governments, which averaged more than 200,000 new employees per year between 1951 and 1960. From 1960 to 1980, when new federal programs added further stimulation to state and local government payrolls, annual employment increases averaged more than 300,000 per year.

Since most of these new employees were well-educated teachers, engineers, health professionals, or managers, one major consequence was a vast improvement in the competence of government personnel. Another consequence, flowing in part from the changed quality of employees, was a growing effort to improve the quality of state and local institutions. Entirely new or revised state constitutions, increases in legislative pay and staffing, reorganized budget and management processes, and other reforms have spread across the country, eliminating many of the abuses formerly associated with state and local governments. The period from the early 1950s through the 1970s can fairly be described as an era of growing capacity in the state and local sector, producing competent local governments to complement the guarantor state initiated in the 1930s (Sabato, 1983).

A third watershed of program development, easily comparable in significance to the 1930s, was the decade 1965–1975. Although partially obscured by the tragedy of American involvement in Vietnam, this was a period of remarkable innovation. Beginning with President Johnson's War on Poverty and extending through President Nixon's New Federalism, hundreds of programs were enacted by the national government. Collectively, these new initiatives laid a foundation for a new conceptual premise—namely, that the purpose of government was not simply to insure against economic loss, but to promote social as well as economic gain. Programs to improve access to good education, from preschool through college, were enacted to enhance individual accomplishment. Community action programs were enacted to encourage a broader exercise of political power, and citizen participation requirements were attached to numerous other programs with the same purpose in mind. Medical care and nutrition programs enacted during this period helped to remove major barriers to social opportunity, while the most important barrier—low income—was attacked through major increases in welfare and pension programs, including automatic indexing to adjust for inflation. No single program summarized this new concept of government, but by the end of this remarkable decade it had become clear that the American concept of the general welfare to be promoted by government now included social as well as economic betterment (Rochefort, 1986; Schwarz, 1983).

There was one other important aspect to the programs enacted during this period. As the national government enunciated new social goals through new programs, the vehicle for achieving these goals increasingly became cooperative agreements with state and local governments. National officials articulated purposes and provided funds through grants, while state and local officials did the work of organizing and managing the new activities. In a sense, therefore, the conceptual shift from a negative to a more positive definition of welfare joined with the trend toward increased state and local capacity to produce not only new programs, but unprecedented policy patterns. Grants to state and local governments grew more rapidly than any other portion of the national budget. By 1975, national grants were the single largest source of state and local revenue, surpassing even sales and property taxes in significance (Anton, 1980a). More and more programs became clearly intergovernmental; fewer and fewer could be operated by a single level of government. And, as the federal presence became more important in state capitals and city halls, so did the state and local presence become far more significant in Washington. Representatives of governors, mayors, commissioners, and legislatures now became permanent residents (Haider, 1974). None of these developments was without historical precedent, but together they defined a federal politics of unprecedented interjurisdictional complexity.

Each of these program watersheds implied some adjustment in federal-state relationships. During the 1930s, when it assumed much of the financial burden of the Depression, the national government became the dominant financial force among American governments, accounting for more than half of all public sector spending. Since state and local governments had been responsible for three-quarters of all government spending as recently as 1929, the new dominance of Washington was a financial as well as conceptual revolution. National fiscal dominance became even more pronounced during World War II and continued thereafter, consistently accounting for two-thirds or more of total government spending since 1949. The national fraction declined somewhat during the 1950s and 1960s, when state and local governments were rapidly expanding programs and employees, but returned to previous levels in the mid-1970s, when national grants were reaching their peak and large increases in pension payments began to occur. Of course, national dominance in spending is not the same as dominance in actual delivery of services. The federal government operates some nineteen departments and a hundred or so other agencies, and it requires a large bureaucracy to send out social security and other pension checks, but delivery of virtually all domestic services is otherwise left in the hands of local and state governments. Washington increasingly has acted as a banker for state and local governments operating national programs; national government employment has been essentially stable for two decades, while state and local personnel have tripled in number. The confluence of the social empowerment state with the competent state has led to a practical, if not theoretical, division of responsibilities. Washington has been concerned with goal articulation, general administration, defense, and income security; state and local governments have assumed managerial responsibility for virtually all other public programs, including those funded largely by the national government.

The election and reelection of Ronald Reagan have made clear that the concept of a "social empowerment state" displayed in programs enacted during the 1965–1975 decade remains controversial. Unlike the guarantor state put into place in the 1930s, which enjoys broad public support, the use of public resources to promote social as well as economic gain continues to be opposed by an intense minority of Americans. Responding to that minority, President Reagan has attempted to undo or restrict many of the programs enacted during the empowerment decade. As a consequence, he has led the national administration away from a traditional function of national leadership: the articulation of national goals. The competent state put into place in the 1950s and 1960s remains, however, with the result that goal articulation for the nation as a whole has become more diffused than before, with a number of state governors joining senators and members of Congress in offering the nation political leadership. It is now clear that representatives of the competent state will continue to restrain presidential attacks on social empowerment programs. Whether that concept is abandoned, modified, or redefined to generate a broader national consensus is an issue for the coming decade.

THE STRUCTURE OF PROGRAM RESPONSIBILITY

State Tastes for Public Programs

Each of the fifty states is a separate political and legal system, operating very different administrative systems that include local governments of enormous variety. These legal differences are important, but it is equally important to recognize that financial and program responsibilities are distributed in patterns that are quite familiar. One such pattern is associated with age of government. In general, the governments of the original colonial states emphasized local rather than state responsibility for a comprehensive range of governmental services. Both the local emphasis and the comprehensiveness of public responsibilities reflected important colonial values that had less significance for people moving west to settle the new nation. As newer states were admitted to the Union from the Midwest, South, and West, therefore, different patterns of service responsibility developed. Single-function governments emerged, initially to separate education from the politics of other public services, and later to provide the same separation for a broad range of services from parks to mosquito control. In the South, state agencies were generally given greater emphasis than local governments. In the West, new state constitutions often provided innovative mechanisms for direct democracy, such as citizen ballot initiatives, that were rare in other parts of the country. Each new system was different, yet each was also partially a product of ideas prevailing at the time the new government was created (Elazar, 1972; Liebert, 1976).

Given massive recent increases in government responsibilities, state systems today are very different from what they were fifty or a hundred years ago. They nevertheless reflect the continuing influence of region in their division of governmental responsibilities. Roy Bahl recently presented a useful summary of these differences, based on work done in the Metropolitan Studies Program of Syracuse University. Bahl gathered 1980 data on the proportion of taxes raised and expenditures made by state and local governments in each of the fifty states and used those data to place each state into one of three major types of fiscal system: state government dominated, local government dominated, and mixed systems. The results, shown in Table 3.2, confirm the continued strength of regional patterns of taxing and spending. Eight of the fifteen states with high to moderate expenditure responsibility and six of the twelve states with high to moderate financing responsibility are in the southern tier; no southern state appears among those dominated by local taxing and spending. Bahl himself notes the interesting difference when he points out that "By contrast, only two of the fourteen northern tier states—Maine and Minnesota—may be classified as state dominated on the financing side. Eight of the fourteen northern tier states may be classified as locally dominated in terms of financing responsibility, and another five show a low state government expenditure responsibility. The western states are more of a mixture in the intergovernmental arrangements" (Bahl, 1984, p. 131).

These regional differences have some important consequences. Greater state responsibility for taxing and spending allows southern states to exert more influence over local governments than is possible in the North, where continued reliance on the locally controlled property tax allows a strong spirit of local independence. Thus most of the major reforms in metropolitan governmental systems have occurred in southern states, where regionwide financing of services can be used to induce cooperation, and where central cities have been more easily able to capture the

Table 3.2 Classification of State Fiscal Systems, 1980

STATE GOVERNMENT FINANCING RESPONSIBILITY	STATE EXPENDITURE RESPONSIBILITY[a]		
	High	*Moderate*	*Low*
HIGH[b,c]	Alaska Delaware Hawaii Kentucky New Mexico West Virginia Alabama Arkansas Maine South Carolina	Washington Idaho Mississippi North Carolina Oklahoma	California Minnesota
MODERATE	Rhode Island North Dakota	Maryland Wyoming Louisiana Utah Tennessee Virginia	Michigan Nevada Wisconsin Arizona Iowa Pennsylvania Indiana Florida Georgia Texas
LOW	South Dakota Vermont	Massachusetts Montana Oregon Connecticut Kansas Missouri New Hampshire	New York Colorado Illinois Nebraska New Jersey Ohio

[a.] State expenditure responsibility is the state share of total state and local direct expenditures.
[b.] High, moderate, and low designations for each category relate to whether the state placed in the top fifteen, middle twenty, or bottom fifteen among states.
[c.] State financial responsibility is the share of total state and local expenditures financed by the state.

SOURCE: Roy Bahl. *Financing State and Local Government in the 1980s.* New York: Oxford University Press, 1984, p. 130. Copyright © 1984 by Oxford University Press, Inc. Reprinted by permission.

proceeds of economic growth through annexation and consolidation authority provided by state law. As a result, cities in the South and West continue to be dominant within their metropolitan areas, whereas many cities in the Northeast and Midwest, unable to capture the wealth created in the movement of jobs and taxpayers to the suburbs, have lost much of their former economic influence. Northern states continue to spend more on public services in general, but because property wealth is so unevenly distributed, there is considerable disparity in spending levels among jurisdictions within a state. In northern and midwestern states that rely heavily on the property tax to fund public services, the real strength of local governance—as distinct from the legal powers of local governments —depends very much on the value of the property within jurisdictional boundaries.

State and Local Programs

In addition to the regional differences that characterize aggregate taxing and spending levels, there are characteristic differences in the programs carried out by state and local governments across the country. These differences have less to do with constitutional philosophy than with pragmatic political judgments about what kind of service can best be performed by what kind of government. Judgments of this kind never rest in concrete; they can be changed at any time to reflect new political preferences. In reviewing differences in program responsibilities across levels of government, therefore, it is important to bear in mind that the structure being observed is less stable than it may appear. Some change, large or small, is almost always being considered or implemented somewhere in the system.

It is also important to remember that changes may proceed in very different directions. For example, efforts to decentralize national government policies in housing, community development, labor, and education during the Nixon administration were accompanied by other efforts to centralize national policies in programs such as Food Stamps or Supplemental Security Income. More recently, the national government has attempted to divest itself of responsibilities, particularly in education, economic development, and housing. In a system as large and as complicated as the United States, we should never be surprised that some government actions appear to contradict other government actions.

With these caveats in mind, let us consider the major responsibilities of national, state, and local governments. As noted earlier, the fiscal and program revolution of the 1930s laid the foundation for national dominance of income security programs, to go along with well-established responsibilities for national defense and, in the current era of huge deficits, interest payments on the national debt. Most other programs are dominated by state and local governments, in patterns recently sketched out by the Advisory Commission on Intergovernmental Relations (ACIR, 1984).

ACIR attempted to identify the "dominant service provider" for each of nineteen governmental services, defining a dominant service provider as "one that accounts for more than 55% of the direct general expenditure" for a particular service. Table 3.3 reports the ACIR results for 1967 and 1977 to show changes in existing patterns of service delivery.

In 1967 state governments were the dominant service providers in the areas of natural resources, corrections, public welfare, and highways and somewhat less dominant as providers of health and hospital services. Between 1967 and 1977, however, state dominance declined by ten states in highways, and by seven states in hospitals, reflecting increased local participation in these activities. On the other hand, seven more states became the dominant welfare providers between 1967 and 1977, as states assumed a burden too heavy for many local units to carry. None of these changes suggest any fundamental reshaping of traditional state responsibilities, but they do suggest the continuous nature of system reform.

Local governments were dominant service providers throughout the decade in fire, police, sanitation, education, airports, and parking, but some aspects of local services deserve to be noted. One is that localities became considerably less dominant as providers of police services during the decade. State and county governments, through enhanced police services of their own, reduced the number of states in which local units funded the bulk of police services from 33 to 27. An even more substantial shift occurred in park and recreation services. Municipalities were dominant providers of such services in 44 states in 1967; by 1977, shortly after the Supreme Court had emphasized the significance of this "traditional" local service in the Usery decision, municipalities were dominant in only 24 states. In this area, as in housing, highways, and hospitals, service provision had become significantly more intergovernmental.

Comprehensive data for more recent years are not yet available, but journalistic reports and various government documents suggest that the years since 1977 have been marked by two prominent developments. The first is a continuing centralization of state responsibilities, especially for education. Proposition 13 in California and other tax limitation referendums have limited the taxing powers of local governments and forced state governments to assume a larger share of the financial burden. Though not aimed at local service authority, the result of many of these referendums has been to restrict that authority in favor of greater state dominance. The second recent trend, noticeable in health, housing, sanitation, and even police, is the privatization of service delivery. Partly in response to new financial restraints, and partly in reaction against the high cost of unionized services, local and state governments have found a variety of ways to use private sector organizations to manage or deliver services that formerly were considered to be public. These experiments raise important issues of ethics, accountability, and responsibility that continue to be debated with great vigor (see Chapter 7). As the debate continues, the experiments themselves add further dynamism to an already dynamic system.

The data provided in Table 3.3 can be read as a series of probability

Table 3.3 Dominant Service Provider by Type of Government and Function, 1967 and 1977

	Education	Highways	Public Welfare	Hospitals	Health	Police	Fire Protection	Sewerage	Other Sanitation	Parks and Recreation	Natural Resources	Housing/ Renewal	Airports	Water Transport[b]	Parking	Correction	Libraries	General Control	General Public Buildings
1967																			
State	1	49	36	31	31	—	—	—	—	—	49	3	3	17	—	49	1	4	5
County	3	—	10	6	2	—	—	—	—	1	—	—	6	15	—	—	6	7	7
Municipality	—	—	2	—	1	33	50	38	48	44	—	22	27	—	47	—	21	—	1
Township	—	—	—	—	—	—	—	1	1	—	—	—	—	—	1	—	—	—	—
School district	37	—	—	—	—	—	—	—	—	—	—	—	—	—	—	—	—	—	—
Special district	—	—	—	1	—	—	—	3	—	2	—	23	5	8	1	—	2	—	—
More than one provider[a]	9	1	2	12	16	17	—	8	1	3	1	2	7	2	1	1	20	39	37
1977																			
State	1	39	43	24	30	—	—	—	—	3	48	3	6	16	—	46	2	7	5
County	2	—	1	4	4	—	—	1	1	1	—	—	9	3	—	1	9	1	8
Municipality	—	—	1	—	—	27	48	33	44	24	—	16	26	20	47	—	19	—	1
Township	—	—	—	—	—	—	—	—	2	—	—	—	—	1	—	—	—	—	—
School district	37	—	—	1	—	—	—	—	—	—	—	—	—	—	—	—	—	—	—
Special district	—	—	—	—	—	—	—	4	—	2	—	21	5	6	1	—	2	—	—
More than one provider[a]	10	11	5	21	16	23	2	12	3	20	2	10	4	1	2	3	18	42	36

[a] A dominant service provider is one that accounts for more than 55% of the direct general expenditure in a particular function. "More than one provider" indicates there is no dominant service provider.

[b] Only 42 state-local systems exhibited this function in 1967, and 47 in 1977.

SOURCE: Advisory Commission on Intergovernmental Relations. *The Question of State Government Capability.* Washington, D.C.: Government Printing Office, 1985, p. 22.

estimates, based on actual behavior, allowing us to predict the kinds of activities likely to be conducted by state and local governments. Some estimates approach certainty. Thus, no matter what state is considered, it is virtually certain that fire protection will be dominated by local governments, or that state agencies will be the dominant providers of natural resource programs. Other estimates are less certain, but still impressive. Anyone guessing that states are the most important providers of welfare or highways or health services would be far more often right than wrong, as would anyone guessing that local governments dominate in the provision of school, sanitation, or police services. There is considerable variety in the particular responsibilities assigned to different levels of government from one state to another, and the assignments can change quickly. But there is also a clear structure, defined by governmental actions, that remains relatively stable and thus amenable to observation.

STATES AS SYSTEMS OF BENEFIT DISTRIBUTION

Cultural Diversity

Despite the social homogeneity implied by the penetration of national television into all corners of the United States, regional differences in culture continue to thrive. The tense aggressiveness often displayed by residents of northeastern states contrasts sharply with the polite courtesies of the South, the friendliness of the Midwest, or the relaxed life styles of the West Coast. In politics, as in culture, regional differences are easily observed, but differences between states are even more prominent. Scholars who have studied several states are quick to note obvious differences. Consider the variety of images evoked in one recent study, which refers to

> Iowa as pragmatic, non-programmatic, and cautious; Virginia as distinctive in its sense of honor and gentility; Louisiana and Mississippi as dominated by the demagogic-horatory style; and Massachusetts, Pennsylvania, and California as primarily ideological in style. . . . A strong disposition of compromise pervades Oregon; hard work and a general conservatism are obvious features of Kansas; Indiana is intensely partisan, Wyoming mainly individualistic, and Ohio fundamentally conservative; and ethnicity—the dominance of the Japanese in Hawaii, the influence of the Irish in Massachusetts, and the Mormon ascendancy in Utah—shapes the style in other states. (Rosenthal and Moakley, 1984, p.10)

These characterizations make clear that state politics and state governments seem very different to observers who are fortunate enough to examine more than one state. Why should this be so?

One reason is that different mixes of people are found in each state, with characteristically different values and orientations to public life. In his very useful analysis, Elazar has identified these population mixes and tracked their movements all the way back to the earliest American settlements (Elazar, 1972). The English Puritans who originally settled New England established a dominant "Yankee" culture and then, as the frontier opened, moved west across New York and northern Pennsylvania to the Great Lakes states. Joined by Scandinavians and other northern Europeans in the mid-nineteenth century, the Yankees moved on to settle Colorado, Utah, and portions of Oregon, Washington, and California. The mid-Atlantic colonies were settled by rather different groups, largely from non-Puritan England and Germany. These groups, later reinforced by other settlers from western Europe, moved west across Pennsylvania and the central portions of Ohio, Indiana, and Illinois, before jumping across the Mississippi to Nevada and northern California. English and western European farmers interested in traditional styles of agriculture were attracted to the southern states and later carried their ideas westward across a southern route extending from South Carolina and Virginia through Louisiana and Texas to southern California. With increasing urbanization, these streams of migration were enriched by new population groups from southern and eastern Europe, producing new and dynamic mixtures of peoples and cultures. Very different thought patterns were associated with each of these groups, producing very different political cultures. Three types of political culture have been identified as especially significant: the moralistic, the individualistic, and the traditionalistic.

The *moralistic* culture brought by English Puritans and shared by Scandinavian and north European settlers assumes the existence of common interests that bind individuals together in the good society, or commonwealth. Government is prized as the vehicle for pursuing this public interest, and participation in politics is a civic obligation to be shared by as many citizens as possible. The more heterogeneous groups that settled the mid-Atlantic area were more interested in economic prosperity for themselves than in visions of a good society. For them, government was a mechanism for promoting individual success. In this context, politicians were expected to use government just as individuals might use other forms of employment—as a means to achieve personal gain. Tolerance for both individual and group utilization of public office to achieve private gain was thus built in to this *individualistic* political culture.

The agrarian values of southern settlers, based on models of aristocracy derived from the European experience, produced a culture Elazar labels as *traditionalistic*. Preservation of existing relationships based on elite control over essentially passive populations was the major thrust of this culture. Maintenance of elite control implied opposition to citizen participation in public affairs, opposition to institutions that might challenge that control (such as professional officials), and opposition to expanded government in general.

As people bearing these orientations spread across the country and settled in communities, distinctive cultural configurations emerged in each state. However, the extent to which one or another of these orientations dominated a state varied considerably. In the southern states the "traditional" culture was relatively homogeneous, sustained by the continued control of white elites. In midwestern states such as Indiana or Illinois, on the other hand, the moralistic culture carried by settlers of northern portions of the state contrasted sharply with the individualistic orientations brought from West Virginia and Kentucky by settlers in the southern portions. In these states, and others like them, a distinctive culture emerged from a mixture of different perspectives rather than from a single perspective. Table 3.4, based on Elazar's classification, shows each state's dominant culture, or dominant mix of cultures.

Elazar's original formulation of moralistic, individualistic, and traditionalistic cultures was an interesting conceptualization, but it lacked the empirical data normally used by social scientists to document assertions. Both the identification of different cultural patterns and statements about the policy preferences associated with these patterns were initially regarded as no more than interesting hypotheses. It is a measure of Elazar's insight that other scholars, having transformed his conceptualizations into testable propositions, have been able to establish their general validity.

Among the most sophisticated of these efforts is Richard A. Joslyn's effort to use survey data to determine whether patterns of public opinion conform to Elazar's typology (Joslyn, 1982). Drawing upon data from three national surveys conducted by the Survey Research Center of the University of Michigan, Joslyn selected 68 separate measures of political attitudes, using factor analysis and multidimensional scaling techniques to examine variation in state public opinion. From the discovery that ". . . Minnesota, Oregon, Washington, Iowa and South Dakota are the most like one another and are the most unlike Georgia, Louisiana, Tennessee and Mississippi," Joslyn concludes that ". . . in general, the moralistic states cluster at one end of the dimension, the individualistic states cluster in the middle, and the traditionalistic states cluster at the other end" (p. 69).

These different clusters of ideas have some very important political consequences. For one thing, they structure the attitudes citizens bring to everyday political life. As Joslyn notes, for example: "Citizens in moralistic states tended to be more efficacious, more participatory, more trusting, and more prone towards governmental intervention than citizens in individualistic or traditionalistic states" (p. 76). More important, perhaps, these ideas also appear to structure the attitudes of political elites. Analyzing data on various political attitudes expressed by 441 state senators from 24 states, Susan Welch and John G. Peters conclude:

> . . . those from the moralistic political cultures were most likely to favor social change, support government intervention on the economic welfare issues, be self-declared liberals, and believe political corruption to be a substantial political problem. . . . Legislators from the traditionalistic states were the most conservative across all three issues that had a liberal-conservative bent, and

Table 3.4 State Political Cultures: The National Configuration

SECTION	M	MI	IM	I	IT	TI	T	TM
New England	Vt.	Me. N.H	Conn. Mass. R.I. N.Y.					
Middle Atlantic			Del. Md.	Penna. N.J.				
Near West	Mich. Wis.		Ohio[a] Ill.[a]	Ind.				
Northwest	Minn.	N.D. Colo. Iowa Kansas Mont. S.D.	Neb. Wyo.					
Far West	Utah Ore.	Calif. Wash. Idaho		Nev.				
Southwest					Mo.	Tex. Okla. N.M.		Ariz.
Upper South					W.Va. Ky.	Va.	Tenn.	N.C.
Lower South					Fla.	Ala. Ga. Ark. La. S.C. Miss.		
Pacific				Alaska	Hawaii			

[a] Illinois and Ohio have strong traces of M in their northern counties and T in their southern counties.

Key: M: Moralistic dominant.
MI: Moralistic dominant, strong individualistic strain.
IM: Individualistic dominant, strong moralistic strain.
I: Individualistic dominant.
IT: Individualistic dominant, strong traditionalistic strain.
TI: Traditionalistic dominant, strong individualistic strain.
T: Traditionalistic dominant.
TM: Traditionalistic dominant, strong moralistic strain.

Note: The eight columns in the table should be viewed as segments on a forced continuum that actually has elements of circularity. The specific placing of the individual states should be viewed cautiously, considering the limits of the data.

SOURCE: Daniel J. Elazar. *American Federalism: A View from The States*, 2d ed. New York: Harper & Row, 1972, Table 15, p. 118. Copyright © 1972 by Harper & Row, Publishers, Inc. Reprinted by permission of Harper & Row, Publishers, Inc..

were the least likely to see corruption as a problem. Correspondingly, then, the individualistic legislators occupied an intermediate position on all four measures. (Welch and Peters, 1982, pp. 157–158)

Given these shared political attitudes, defined and distributed very much as Elazar had suggested, it is understandable that public policies also differ by political culture. In an imaginative paper, Sharkansky converted Elazar's concepts into a linear scale, with moralism scored low and traditionalism scored high, and then correlated that scale with 23 different measures of policy, including 3 measures of actual participation, 4 measures of government size, and 16 measures of program scope and expenditure. Statistically significant relationships were found between the culture scale and 15 of the 23 measures of state policy (Table 3.5), leading Sharkansky to conclude:

> The states that place high on the Traditional end of the scale (and therefore low on Moralism) tend to show low voter turnout and illiberal suffrage regulations, underdeveloped government bureaucracies, and low scores on

Table 3.5 Coefficients of Simple Correlation Between the Scale of Political Culture and Dependent Variables

Measures pertaining to participation:	
1. Percent voting for governor	$-.59^a$
2. Percent voting for U.S. representative	$-.79^a$
3. Liberality of suffrage regulations	$-.54^a$
Measures pertaining to bureaucracy:	
4. Number of government employees	$-.44^a$
5. Salary of government employees	$-.57^a$
6. Employees covered by health insurance	$-.31^a$
7. Employees covered by life insurance	$-.11$
Measures pertaining to government programs:	
8. Tax effort	$-.43^a$
9. Total expenditures per capita	$-.62^a$
10. High school graduations	$-.74^a$
11. Exam successes	$-.82^a$
12. Total road mileage	$.17$
13. Municipal road mileage	$-.01$
14. Rural road mileage	$-.24$
15. Completed I-system	$-.30^a$
16. AFDC payment	$-.75^a$
17. OAA payment	$-.67^a$
18. AB payment	$-.56^a$
19. APTD payment	$-.42^a$
20. AFDC recipients	$-.25$
21. OAA recipients	$-.11$
22. AB recipients	$.14$
23. APTD recipients	$-.21$

[a] significant at the .05 level.

SOURCE: Ira Sharkansky. "The Utility of Elazar's Political Culture: A Research Note." *Polity* 2 (Fall 1969): 66–83, p. 79. Reprinted by permission from *Polity*.

several measures of tax effort, government spending, and public services. (Sharkansky, 1969, 78)

In an analysis using somewhat more sophisticated measures of both culture and policy outputs, Charles A. Johnson comes to similar conclusions:

> Indices of moralistic, individualistic, and traditionalistic political cultures were constructed, using religious census data for each state. Discriminant analysis grouping the states according to the three cultural indices produced results quite congruent with the classification set forth by Elazar. . . . Expected relationships between political culture and eight state political characteristics were examined. Statistically significant correlations in the predicted directions were found for six dependent variables: government activities, local emphasis and administration of programs, innovative activity by the government, encouragement of popular participation in elections, and party competition. Importantly, the relationships remained significant when controlling for state socioeconomic variables. (Johnson, 1976, p. 507)

These analyses all suggest that the beginning of wisdom in understanding American benefit distributions is recognizing the different cultural patterns that structure the contexts within which benefits are distributed. These contexts are quite varied, particularly if local as well as state areas are taken into account. Still, scholars have identified three major perspectives that, singly or in combination, help to define the scope and magnitude of state benefit distributions. (1) Traditionalist states, many in the South, tend to have less popular participation in governmental affairs, less government spending, fewer public officials, fewer programs, less interest in innovation, and more limited mixes of public benefits in general. (2) Moralist states, many in the North, tend to have more citizen participation, larger governments, more public officials paid higher salaries, more programs, more interest in developing new programs, and more expansive mixes of public benefits in general. (3) Individualist states, many distributed throughout the nation's middle, are likely to have more participation and more government than traditionalist states, but less interest in innovation than moralist states.

The important point is that these cultural patterns are not merely historical artifacts. Property acquisition and sale, family relationships, level of education, public health and safety, and a host of other matters affecting daily life continue to be guided by state government actions. State boundaries thus continue to define the relevant political environment and state capitals continue to provide forums within which each state develops its distinctive approach to public problems.

Political Culture and Program Outcomes

The continuing political significance of these state cultures has been demonstrated effectively in an intriguing study by Arthur R. Stevens.

Stevens imagined that state boundaries could be thought of as ". . . invisible walls keeping people apart from one another" and channeling their behavior in different directions. To test the validity of this "wall effect," Stevens observed behavior and interviewed residents in three small border communities at the junction of Michigan, Ohio, and Indiana. The towns were similar in size and socioeconomic characteristics; they were all within the same 25-square-mile area; and there were no rivers, mountains, or other natural barriers between them—they were just in different states. Did the invisible walls of state boundaries have any impact on individual behavior?

According to Stevens, the boundaries were indeed significant. Across a variety of indicators, a clear state bias was evident. Residents of border towns ". . . worship in their own state. They want their state university to go to the Rose Bowl. The students plan to attend college in their own state. The families subscribe to newspapers published in their own state. The school children plan to live in their own state when they are grown up." Interviews with prominent citizens in each town proved equally revealing. Answers to identical questions put to the banker, the mayor, the newspaper editor, the school superintendent and the chief of police persuaded Stevens that the wall effect was quite obvious:

> The clearest indicator of this was that none of these men had ever met their counterparts in the other two states though only a few miles distant from each other. They did not even know their names. Yet every one of them was widely acquainted with men in similar occupations in their own state. This was true, for example, of government officials. The school superintendents of these border schools might . . . be pictured as standing close together, but with their backs to one another. One looks to Lansing, another to Columbus, and the third to Indianapolis. (Stevens, 1982, pp. 164–165)

State political cultures do live and find expression in the daily activities of millions of politically active people, but as different individuals become more or less active, and as new problems emerge, cultural orientations adjust accordingly. State cultures today are thus different from what they were fifty or a hundred years ago, and the nationalization of perspectives encouraged by television has blurred regional distinctions to some extent. Nonetheless, careful students of state politics, from journalists to systematic empirical researchers, agree that state boundaries continue to define important differences of substance as well as style in American politics. Depending on which culture they live in, Americans will pay more or less in state and local taxes, for more or fewer benefits, delivered by larger or smaller numbers of officials, whose training is more or less adequate. States, in short, do make a difference.

One way to see the impact of state differences is provided in Table 3.6, which lists the top ten and bottom ten states on selected measures of policy and policy outcomes. These listings suggest some clear patterns in public tastes as well as some interesting exceptions. Total state and local spending per person obviously conforms rather closely to the cultural typology, with the moralistic states of the northern tier dominating the top ten and the traditionalistic southern states dominating the bottom ten, as would be expected. Similarly, average salaries paid to full-time state and local employees, another good indicator of expansive or restrictive preferences for government services, reveal the same cultural cleavage. Quite clearly, the moralistic—and some individualistic—states of the North prefer larger public programs and higher public salaries than the traditionalistic states of the South.

Higher levels of public spending generally permit states to offer more generous levels of support for those in need. Columns III and IV of Table 3.6, which report average per person spending for welfare and unemployment compensation, can be thought of as measures of state compassion. By these measures, big spenders such as New York, Michigan, or Minnesota do a great deal to assist the poor or those who are out of work, while the smaller spenders of the South are far less compassionate, particularly to those who are out of work. Interestingly enough, Wyoming and Nevada are both big spenders in general but very low in payments to the less fortunate—their priorities obviously lie elsewhere. From the opposite point of view, Louisiana emerges as the leading payer of unemployment compensation, although hardly a big spender in general. These examples underline the need to view any assertions regarding patterned behavior, whether attributed to culture, environment, or economic status, as statements of probability rather than as laws.

That caveat is equally applicable to the data displayed in columns V and VI of Table 3.6, which list high and low states on prisoners per 100,000 population and the extent to which state operations have been computerized. Taken together, these listings can be thought of as a rough index of administrative modernity. Incarceration reflects the traditional "punishment" approach to law enforcement rather than newer theories that stress rehabilitation, often in non-prison settings. Similarly, states that have been slow to adopt computerized technologies, even for routine activities such as checkwriting, can fairly be thought of as clinging to more traditional administrative methods. In a general sense, columns V and VI again confirm the differences between more traditional states such as South Carolina, Alabama, and Georgia, which utilize prisons extensively, and more innovative states such as Iowa or Minnesota, where alternatives to prison are obviously more important components of state policy.

Iowa and Minnesota also are among the leaders in computerization, along with other northern states such as Michigan and Washington. Note, however, that South Carolina is among the leaders in both lists, pursuing traditional correction policies and modern administrative practices simultaneously. Nebraska, on the other hand, lies near the bottom of both lists in its simultaneous use of innovative corrections policy and more traditional administrative methods. The traditional-modern dimension is real enough and states generally fall into expected patterns, but the exceptions again

Table 3.6 Highest and Lowest in State Policy Outcome

	I TOTAL STATE AND LOCAL EXPENDITURES PER CAPITA (1983–1984)	II AVERAGE EARNINGS OF STATE AND LOCAL FULL-TIME EMPLOYEES (1984)	III STATE AND LOCAL SPENDING FOR WELFARE PER CAPITA (1983–1984)	IV AVERAGE WEEKLY UNEMPLOYMENT COMPENSATION BENEFIT (FEBRUARY 1986)	V PRISONERS PER 100,000 RESIDENTS (JUNE 1985)
Highest:					
	Alaska $9,917	Alaska $35,496	New York $539	Minnesota $170.19	Nevada 397
	Wyoming 4,327	California 27,156	Alaska 455	Wyoming 160.26	Louisiana 308
	New York 3,665	Michigan 24,888	Michigan 452	Alaska 158.98	South Carolina 291
	Washington 3,263	New York 24,744	Rhode Island 419	New Jersey 158.48	Delaware 290
	Minnesota 3,014	Minnesota 23,940	Minnesota 395	Pennsylvania 156.90	Maryland 283
	Utah 2,961	Washington 23,400	Massachusetts 383	Connecticut 156.79	Alabama 265
	Nebraska 2,952	Connecticut 22,980	California 360	Texas 154.82	Georgia 262
	California 2,891	Arizona 22,764	Wisconsin 356	Utah 154.30	Oklahoma 255
	Oregon 2,871	Illinois 22,680	Maine 347	Colorado 152.60	Alaska 252
	Nevada 2,815	Rhode Island 22,572	Connecticut 309	Massachusetts 152.49	North Carolina 251
Lowest:					
	Virginia $2,022	Kentucky $17,628	Missouri/Utah $171	Arizona $110.85	Iowa 96
	Kentucky 1,984	Tennessee 17,496	New Mexico 169	South Dakota 110.39	Rhode Island 96
	New Hampshire 1,952	Maine 17,484	West Virginia 167	Missouri 106.94	Massachusetts 91
	Indiana 1,944	Louisiana 17,472	Arizona 163	Georgia 106.82	Utah 90
	Idaho 1,922	West Virginia 17,004	Wyoming 162	Kentucky 106.59	West Virginia 87
	North Carolina 1,920	Georgia 16,932	North Carolina 161	Alabama 99.62	Maine 85
	Mississippi 1,919	South Carolina 16,836	Alabama 148	Idaho 98.99	Vermont 78
	South Carolina 1,896	South Dakota 16,824	Idaho/South Carolina 133	South Carolina 97.22	New Hampshire 64
	Missouri 1,849	Arkansas 15,684	Texas/Nevada 132	Mississippi 92.73	Minnesota 55
	Arkansas 1,645	Mississippi 14,244	Florida 127	Tennessee 91.21	North Dakota 50

	VI	VII	VIII	IX	X
	PERCENTAGE COMPUTERIZATION OF STATE GOVERNMENT (1982)	PER CAPITA STATE AND LOCAL SPENDING FOR EDUCATION (1983–1984)	HIGH SCHOOL GRADUATION RATE (1984)	STATE AND LOCAL SPENDING FOR HEALTH & HOSPITALS PER CAPITA (1983–1984)	INFANT MORTALITY (PER 1000 LIVE BIRTHS) (1983)
Highest:	Michigan 88%	Alaska $2,309	Minnesota 89.3%	Wyoming $374	Mississippi 15.1
	Minnesota 88	Wyoming 1,526	North Dakota/Nebraska 86.3	Georgia 340	South Carolina 15.0
	Alaska 82	Delaware 952	Iowa 86.0	New York 301	Louisiana 13.5
	Florida 82	New Mexico 939	South Dakota 85.5	Alaska 284	Georgia 13.4
	Washington 79	North Dakota 929	Wisconsin 84.5	Mississippi 282	North Carolina 13.2
	Iowa 76	Montana 916	Vermont 83.1	Nevada 266	Alabama 13.1
	Ohio 76	Wisconsin 903	Montana 82.1	Louisiana 263	Tennessee 12.8
	California 74	Oregon 902	Kansas 81.7	Alabama 261	Alaska/Illinois 12.4
	Illinois 74	Minnesota 893	Ohio 80.0	Michigan 244	Florida 12.2
	New Jersey 74	New York 885	Connecticut 79.1	South Carolina 231	Virginia 11.9
Lowest:	Nebraska 53%	Idaho $630	Kentucky 68.4%	Maryland $133	California 9.7
	New Hampshire 53	Florida 617	Nevada 66.5	Illinois/Montana 131	Wisconsin/Oregon 9.6
	Vermont 50	Georgia 613	Texas/Arizona 64.6	Pennsylvania/North Dakota 128	Washington/Arizona 9.5
	Alabama 47	Nevada 610	South Carolina 64.5	Utah 123	Hawaii 9.4
	Indiana 47	Kentucky 609	California 63.2	Arizona 121	Massachusetts 9.1
	Missouri 38	Missouri 602	Georgia 63.1	Delaware 118	Montana 9.0
	Mississippi 35	New Hampshire 597	Mississippi 62.4	Vermont 107	North Dakota/Iowa 8.9
	New York NA	Mississippi 593	Florida/New York 62.2	Kentucky 106	Utah 8.8
	Pennsylvania NA	Arkansas 592	Alabama 62.1	New Hampshire/South Dakota 100	Vermont/Maine 8.7
	Utah NA	Tennessee 540	Louisiana 56.7	Maine 97	New Hampshire 8.6

SOURCE: *State Policy Data Book*, 1986.

make clear that state actions are chosen by politicians, and thus are variable rather than predetermined.

Variations in total spending, spending for individual programs, or administrative style do more than allow us to characterize the actions of state governments; state policies have important consequences for the life chances of individuals within each state. Columns VII to X of Table 3.6 demonstrate some of these consequences by comparing spending with outcomes. Here too familiar regional patterns emerge, with southern states generally spending less per person on education than northern states. Perhaps not surprisingly, southern states lag behind the rest of the nation in high school graduation rates, while the states that spend more, graduate more. Rankings are more mixed in health and hospital expenditures per capita, as well as in the relationships between health spending and infant mortality. Georgia, Mississippi, Louisiana, and Alabama unexpectedly appear among the top ten spenders, along with states such as New York and Michigan. However, high levels of spending seem less effective in the South than elsewhere: Eight of the ten states with the highest rates of infant mortality are in the South. Other states with high health spending do much better. Nevada, Iowa, and Wyoming, for example, appear in the top ten in health expenditures and in the bottom ten for infant mortality. Differences in environment, as well as political culture, obviously influence these outcomes.

In a nation as diverse and dynamic as the United States, no statement about relationships among culture, politics, and outcomes should be interpreted as law, controlling all such relationships at all times. It is far more useful to think of such statements as probability estimates, suggesting what is likely to be true within a given time frame. Seen this way, the evidence reviewed here can be helpful. That evidence suggests that popular and official tastes for public services differ from one state to another, and that the differences often fall into cultural and regional patterns. Depending on whether individuals live in moralistic, individualistic, or traditionalistic cultures in different regions of the country, they will not only have access to more or fewer services, but their opportunities for healthy and productive lives will be enhanced or diminished. State boundaries structure different patterns of politics and public services, and those political and service differences are themselves important components of the life styles and life chances of individual Americans.

THE NATIONAL INFLUENCE

The Scope of National Policy

Differences among people and political elites in the states in their tastes for public programs are important sources of influence on the distribution of public benefits, but they are not the only sources. National government programs have played a significant role from the outset, and many observers believe that the national role has become even more important in the past half century. In a recent commencement speech at the University of South Carolina, Lane Kirkland, President of the AFL-CIO, painted a vivid verbal portrait of the impact of national programs in his native state:

> . . . I remember a South Carolina that was too poor to paint and too proud to whitewash. Nothing in my experience has contradicted what I absorbed in my youth in South Carolina, and I remember it well.
> . . . I remember when the destitute aged were sheltered not in the bosom of a warm and loving family but in county poorhouses. Then Social Security came and tore those poorhouses down, freeing young and old alike of that specter.
> . . . I remember when some fine little colleges were one jump ahead of the sheriff, were hard-pressed to put meals on the students' tables and couldn't meet their payrolls. They were rescued and made solvent by the National Youth Administration, wartime training programs and the G.I. Bill of Rights.
> . . . I remember when the Broad, the Wateree, the Bush and the Saluda ran brick-red from the erosion of farms and deforested uplands. The Soil Conservation Service and the millions of trees planted by the 30 or so Civilian Conservation Corps camps placed in South Carolina had something to do with the improvement.
> . . . I remember when kerosene lit the farms until the Rural Electrification Administration electrified and humanized them, bridging the cultural gap between town and country—and, incidentally, creating new markets for the appliance industry.
> . . . I remember things that used to happen in this land, the treatment of people by people. While we still have a way to go, does anyone think we would have approached our present level of equity and civility without the intervention of the Federal Government? I have met no South Carolinian who has expressed to me any desire to return to the old days of racial cruelty and exclusion. (Kirkland, 1986, p. 21)*

From income security to education to environmental protection to civil rights, the national government has actively shaped the quantity and quality of benefits available in South Carolina and other states. Kirkland's statement is also interesting, however, because his final paragraph makes clear that national efforts to shape benefit distributions often have been opposed by state populations and state political elites. To appreciate the national influence on benefit distribution, therefore, it is necessary to understand not only national government programs, but the political mechanisms through which conflicting state and national purposes are accommodated. As a first step toward that appreciation, let us look at recent trends in national government spending.

National Spending

National government spending increased progressively through two watershed periods from less than 10 to more than 33 percent of GNP. The first watershed occurred during the 1930s, when programs such as social security, unemployment compensation, and Aid to Families with Dependent Children were enacted to protect individuals against loss of income. The second watershed was the decade 1965–1975, when hundreds of new programs were enacted, and existing programs expanded, to promote social and economic gain. These two periods of national expansion, sandwiched around a period of expansion in state and local responsibilities, expanded the role of government in general and gave the national government a greater financial influence than it had ever before had. By the early 1970s the social insurance policies enacted forty years earlier had matured into multibillion-dollar programs that, combined with the socioeconomic programs of the 1960s, drove much of the federal budget.

During the 1970s, therefore, national spending became more focused on social assistance, with expenditures for entitlement programs such as social security or Medicare increasing from 41.5 to 48.6 percent of total expenditures, and defense spending declining substantially, from 28.1 to 20.2 percent of the total. During this period as well, national government grants to state and local governments expanded even more rapidly than the budget as a whole, from $24 billion in 1970 to more than $91 billion in 1980 (Anton, 1983). President Carter's effort to increase defense spending while reducing the rate of increase for social assistance and grants-in-aid was given a more pronounced emphasis by President Reagan, causing the defense share of the total budget to increase during the early 1980s. It is worth noting, however, that grants-in-aid suffered no more than a temporary setback, climbing back to nearly $98 billion by 1984 (OMB Special Analyses, 1986, p. H19).

Perhaps the most notable achievement of the Reagan administration, however, was its elevation of interest payments to one of the very largest programs in the federal budget. The president's inability to reduce total expenditures, coupled with the loss of tax revenues caused by his 1981 tax reform legislation, created huge budget deficits and vast expenditures on interest to service the new debt. By fiscal 1986, interest payments alone were close to $200 billion, or roughly the same as total outlays for the entire social security program. This was and remains a development of truly startling proportions.

Observing national spending totals in this way allows us to draw some useful conclusions about national-state priorities. Although the Reagan administration has tried hard to limit the growth of social assistance expenditures, they remain the dominant portion of the national budget. Social security and Medicare are major components of national social assistance, but it is worth pointing out that programs such as Food Stamps or Supplemental Security Income have contributed to what I have referred to elsewhere as "a trend toward welfare nationalization" (Anton, 1985). To a very considerable extent, therefore, the national budget deserves to be regarded as a social assistance budget. The other major component, apart from interest, is defense, which grew rapidly during President Reagan's first term. Given the relative—although not absolute—decline in grants to state and local governments during the past few years, it seems fair to conclude that national priorities are becoming more dominated by social assistance, defense, and debt service, whereas state policies reflect the greater variety implicit in the need to deliver a broad range of services to populations whose tastes for those services are very different.

The dominance of social assistance benefits is a very important clue to the distribution of national government benefits. Social assistance benefits are delivered largely to individuals, rather than to governments or other organizations, and they are delivered largely according to predetermined formulas. The result, not surprisingly, is that more populous areas receive more national government dollars. Although individual social assistance payments are the major influence on this pattern, it is also true that more populous states receive larger amounts of all kinds of benefits as well. A recent analysis of 46 different national programs classified as "soft" (social assistance) or "hard" (capital investment) revealed that both kinds of benefits were distributed in about the same way, with the more populous states receiving more of both than the less populous states (Anton et al., 1980). Moreover, since population changes slowly, the aggregate distribution of national benefits appears relatively stable from one year to the next, or even one decade to the next.

Surprisingly enough, even national grants to state and local governments reveal patterns that are remarkably stable across time. This is "surprising" because grants have fluctuated so much in recent years, increasing dramatically from 1960 to 1970, and again from 1970 to 1978, before entering a period of relative decline that continues today. Despite these fluctuations, the structure of recipients has been relatively stable for decades:

> Since at least the mid-1920's most federal grants have been concentrated in a handful of states, typically those with the largest populations, and these have generally been the same states. . . . Thus when the distribution patterns of federal grants are correlated across years, the relationships show a powerful stability within periods of a single decade, and surprisingly powerful stability across half a century. States receiving the largest amounts of federal aid decades ago, in short, are the states receiving the largest amount today. Since total grant funds distributed have increased so much, one consequence of this stability is a much larger dispersion, in per capita dollars, around the state average per capita grant. In 1924 the difference between the biggest state "winner" and biggest state "loser" was only $21 per person. By 1960 this difference had increased to $200, and it expanded further to . . . $759 in 1978 (Anton et al., 1980, pp. 10–11)

To note the close relationship between population and national benefit distributions is not to suggest that the largest states are receiving more than they should. On the contrary, when total national dollars are divided by population to obtain per capita expenditure totals, we discover striking disparities among the states, with many large states receiving far less than the smaller states. These disparities too seem quite stable, as is apparent in

Table 3.7   Correlations of Federal Grants Received by State, 1924–1978

TIME PERIOD	CORRELATION	TIME PERIOD	CORRELATION
1924–1930	.77	1924–1930	.77
1930–1940	.87	1924–1940	.65
1940–1950	.93	1924–1950	.72
1950–1960	.98	1924–1960	.76
1960–1970	.94	1924–1970	.55
1970–1978	.98	1924–1978	.55

SOURCE: Thomas J. Anton et al. *Moving Money.* Cambridge, Mass. Oelgeschlager, Gunn and Hain, 1980. p. 11. Reprinted by permission of the publisher.

Table 3.8, which shows per person spending compared to the national mean in each of the fifteen least benefited states for both 1971 and 1980. A review of these lists will show that thirteen of the 1971 "winners" are also winners in 1980. Among the "losers," Illinois and Louisiana are replaced by New Hampshire and New York, but the losing states are otherwise the same. The dollar disparity between winners and losers, however, becomes more extreme. Even if we exclude Alaska on the grounds that its special circumstances constitute an extreme case, the difference between expenditures in winning states such as New Mexico or Nevada and midwestern losers such as Indiana, Michigan, or Ohio exceeds $2,000 per person. As far as national dollars are concerned, this clear pattern of stable disparity means that states are definitely not given equal access to national government dollars (Anton, 1983).

No more than a quick glance at the "winners" and "losers" is required to see that most of the winners are the sparsely populated states of the Great Plains and the Far West, where even relatively small sums can appear large when divided by a tiny population. The older and more populous states of the East and the Midwest actually receive very large amounts of dollars from the national government, but because these dollars are divided by much larger populations to achieve per person data, the data consistently show below-average receipts. This does not mean that per capita calculations are invalid, or that they are unimportant. It does suggest that an evaluation of those calculations should be sensitive to the environmental and social differences that produce them. In the aggregate, the largest amounts of national government dollars go to the states with the largest populations. On a per capita basis, however, the largest amounts tend to go to states with smaller populations. Whichever measure is used, disparities among the states are both large in size and stable in duration.

An important source of disparity in national government benefit distributions, of course, is the variety of environmental conditions that exist within states—a variety clearly reflected in the organizational structure of the national government. Although it is often useful to speak of a national "government," it is also misleading, since the "government" is in reality no more than a collection of different agencies, doing very different things, supported by very different constituencies. Because these constituencies tend to be specialized within the states, the activities of

Table 3.8   Net Domestic Winners and Losers

WINNERS 1971			WINNERS 1980		
		Difference from Mean			*Difference from Mean*
Alaska	$2,251	$1,393	Alaska	$5,096	$2,802
North Dakota	1,446	588	New Mexico	3,835	1,541
New Mexico	1,444	586	Nevada	3,830	1,536
Nevada	1,337	479	Wyoming	3,561	1,267
Hawaii	1,268	410	Hawaii	3,284	990
Colorado	1,188	330	Colorado	3,186	892
Maryland	1,183	325	North Dakota	3,161	867
Montana	1,152	294	South Dakota	3,030	736
Washington	1,137	279	Montana	2,890	596
Arizona	1,110	252	Maryland	2,879	585
South Dakota	1,107	249	Washington	2,874	580
Oklahoma	1,080	222	Virginia	2,844	550
Wyoming	1,078	220	Tennessee	2,833	540
Utah	1,056	198	Idaho	2,833	539
Virginia	1,054	196	Arizona	2,801	507
Idaho	1,054	196			

LOSERS 1971			LOSERS 1980		
		Difference from Mean			*Difference from Mean*
Connecticut	$ 552	$−306	Indiana	$1,638	$−656
Indiana	574	−284	Michigan	1,672	−622
Wisconsin	575	−282	Connecticut	1,680	−614
Ohio	616	−242	Wisconsin	1,717	−577
Michigan	618	−240	Ohio	1,777	−517
Pennsylvania	674	−184	New Jersey	1,820	−474
Illinois	677	−181	North Carolina	1,883	−411
New Jersey	686	−172	Delaware	1,936	−358
Delaware	717	−141	Massachusetts	1,974	−320
North Carolina	717	−141	Pennsylvania	1,984	−310
Vermont	721	−137	Vermont	2,001	−293
Massachusetts	739	−119	Iowa	2,022	−272
Louisiana	762	− 96	New Hampshire	2,028	−266
Iowa	772	− 86	Rhode Island	2,032	−262
Rhode Island	774	− 84	New York	2,084	−210

1971 average: 858   1980 average: 2,294

SOURCE: Thomas J. Anton. "The Regional Distribution of Federal Expenditures, 1971–1980." *National Tax Journal* 36 (December 1983): 429–442, p. 432. Reprinted by permission of the publisher.

national agencies are equally specialized and reflected in patterns of expenditure concentration.

Such patterns are evident in the proportion of each national department's total expenditures allocated to a given state for any given year. In 1978, for example, there was no case in which more than six states were required to accumulate at least one-third of agency outlay totals for any of the fifteen major national agencies; only three were required to reach that level for EPA disbursements. For NASA, California alone accounted for nearly 40 percent of agency spending, and nearly 67 percent of the annual total was achieved by adding Texas, Maryland, and Florida. For Commerce, three states received nearly 40 percent of agency spending; for HUD, four states received more than a third of all spending; for SBA, it was five states, and so on.

In many cases these patterns are relatively stable, leading to long-lasting relationships between national and state officials that give a distinct regional bias to national agency activities. For years HUD has been dominated by officials drawn from the northeastern states that were pioneers in housing programs, just as Agriculture Department officials have been attracted from the Farm Belt states, or Interior Department leaders drawn from the mountain and western states in which the national government owns most of the land. These agencies are "national" in scope and responsibility, but often quite regional in the perspectives on their work.

In other cases, patterns of agency spending change from year to year in response to new conditions or new policies, or both. EPA, SBA, or Commerce tend to fall into this class of agencies. In 1978, for example, SBA spent a larger fraction of its resources in Georgia and Iowa than in bigger states such as New York or Pennsylvania. The causes of this unusual pattern included the coincidence of severe drought in farm states and a change in national legislation that removed a previous restriction against SBA assistance to farmers. The result, documented by Oppenheim, was that agricultural assistance as a proportion of total SBA assistance jumped from 13 percent in 1977 to 73 percent in 1978. A review of these results led to further legislative changes that reduced this proportion to 34 percent in 1980, and a consequent return to more traditional patterns of agency spending (Oppenheim, 1983, pp. 91–97, 148). In the case of SBA, the more traditional pattern included concentrations that changed from year to year, depending again on interactions between events and policy adjustments.

State and Local Influences on National Spending

When we speak of "national" government spending, therefore, it is important to realize that much of it either reflects or is determined by state and/or regional influences. The very large transfer payments to individuals are distributed more according to the location of those individuals than by any conscious national policy, just as payments for harbor improvements or national parks are spread unevenly because such environmental features are distributed unevenly. In programs more subject to the discretion of national officials, state influence is often powerful because national officials have state and regional perspectives derived from years of interaction with particular regions of the country. Or regional coalitions in Congress may propose national legislation that provides for unusual concentrations of benefits in designated areas. In short, a great many benefits distributed by the national government reflect either state influence or state conditions, or both.

How do we best understand state influence over benefits that are presumably products of national government activity? One clue, documented in several studies, is the strong statistical relationship between the number of state and local public employees and the number of national program dollars that flow into a state (Anton et al., 1980; Oppenheim, 1983). This relationship makes sense intuitively, since more employees mean more officials available to lobby for outside funds, more programs to absorb them, and more agencies to house the programs. The recent expansion of national-local programs, in fact, encouraged local officials to join with state colleagues in pursuit of national benefits, creating a much larger corps of regional representatives in the nation's capital (Haider, 1974). If state income is taken into account as a measure of a state's economic resources available to support the activities of public officials, then it becomes possible to think about and develop crude measures of state capacity—the extent to which states and their local jurisdictions are able to achieve public objectives, including the receipt of national government benefits.

Oppenheim's recent analysis provides an intriguing explanation of the difference made by variations in state capacity. In an effort to account for the distribution of emergency disaster assistance from two national agencies, the Farmers Home Administration and the Small Business Administration, Oppenheim demonstrated impressive statistical relationships among state public employment, state wealth, and the receipt of emergency assistance for the past several decades. To illustrate, he offered a discussion of emergency assistance in Michigan, Ohio, and Indiana, the same states in which a "wall effect" had been documented earlier by Stevens (Stevens, 1982).

Oppenheim found that Michigan and Wisconsin consistently received larger amounts of disaster assistance in the period 1951–1978 than either Ohio or Indiana, but that there was very little correlation between the actual damage from natural disasters and the amount of disaster assistance received. Indeed, when he mapped assistance dollars by county, Oppenheim discovered that the southern Michigan counties immediately adjacent to Ohio and Indiana received twenty times more assistance than the neighboring Ohio counties and as much as a hundred times more assistance than neighboring Indiana counties! Stevens had described this area as without natural boundaries: ". . . no mountains, no rivers of any consequence—nothing to inhibit movement or to channel it in any particular direction. The land and the natural features—the small lakes, streams, woods, open fields—are similar everywhere" (Stevens, 1982, p. 161). As Oppenheim drily observes: "Either disaster events (such as tornadoes or floods) are affected by state boundaries or these boundaries structure different allocations of federal assistance" (Oppenheim, 1983, pp. 105–106).

Pursuit of differences in political-administrative processes led Oppenheim to some useful observations. For one thing, both agencies required that a national official—the president or the secretary of agriculture —designate a state or region as a disaster area before national funds could be allocated. However, an official request from a state official (usually the governor) was required before national officials could act. Thus, state politicians and processes had to be activated before national assistance could be received: the effectiveness with which demands for assistance were given political voice; the willingness of state executive agencies to seek national aid; the ability of state agencies to provide the information necessary to justify national action. Although Oppenheim did not develop a model of state capacity elaborate enough to capture all the relevant variables, his study makes clear that state capacity varies, and that it matters. In this case, the more aggressive and better prepared Michigan system delivered far more national assistance to its citizens than was available to individuals in Ohio or Indiana. The dollars were national, but their distribution was significantly influenced by state action.

States, of course, are not the only non-national sources of influence on national benefit distributions. Programs such as General Revenue Sharing, Community Development Block Grants, or Urban Development Action Grants deliver substantial sums of money from national agencies directly to the 40,000 American local governments. Thousands of government installations, from post offices to military bases, are located in these jurisdictions, and hundreds of thousands of national government workers, earning millions of dollars in wages, help to sustain local economies. It is not surprising, therefore, that cities play an active role in shaping the distribution of federal benefits. Nor should it be surprising to learn that both the level of activity and its effectiveness are largely determined by local government capacity.

In examining participation in federal assistance programs among 145 local jurisdictions, for example, Stein discovered many communities that failed to receive assistance, even though they were clearly eligible for various forms of aid. The reason for the lack of aid was not the absence of need—indeed, these were often the very kinds of needy communities for which federal assistance programs were designed. Why, then, were they not receiving the assistance for which they were clearly eligible? The answer, quite simply, was that they had not applied for it. More than half of the communities examined, in fact, ". . . failed to make a single application for federal assistance" during the six years covered in Stein's study (Stein, 1979, p. 11). Since four of every five communities that did apply received assistance, it was clear that the application process was the crucial factor. It was also clear that applications were far more likely to be made if communities had planning agencies staffed by people with the necessary writing and technical skills. As Stein concluded: ". . . planning is a major factor in translating need into effective demand behavior for all categories of federal grant assistance" (Stein, 1979, p. 15).

In another impressive study, Rich has shown that local demand was an important factor in the allocation of federal grant-in-aid funds during the period 1950–1983. Measuring local demand by the number of grant applications submitted and the presence or absence of a lobbyist in Washington, Rich discovered that ". . . cities with greater demand for federal aid . . . received larger program allocations than cities with lesser demand" (Rich, 1985, pp. 264–266). Like Stein, Rich emphasized the importance of the application process by noting that 90 percent or more of all applicant cities received assistance from each of the six programs he examined. Rich also observes that prior participation in federal aid programs had an important impact on the amount of current allocations. These discoveries, derived from a careful analysis of all available data for six large programs, led Rich to suggest that we

> . . . remember that policymaking in the United States takes place in a federal system with state and local governments playing an important role in the development and implementation of domestic public policies. For many programs, including several examined in this study, decisions made by state and local officials have more of an impact on the distributional impacts of federal programs than those made by congressmen and bureaucrats. In sum, mayors, congressmen, senators, bureaucrats, and presidents are all important governmental actors seeking to influence the distribution of benefits. The element that brings all these participants together is the federal program. (Rich, 1985, pp. 293–294)

In emphasizing the significance of state or local capacity it is important to remember that capacity is itself partly a product of actions taken by the national government. Without section 701 of the 1954 Housing Act, for example, it is doubtful that many local jurisdictions would have developed the planning structures that Stein and others have identified as crucial components of local capacity. Moreover, as many recent studies have shown, past participation in federal programs improves local capacity substantially (Friedland and Wong, 1983; Kramer, 1985; Rich, 1985). In this respect the General Revenue Sharing program enacted in 1972 may have been one of the most profoundly significant public actions in our history. By distributing several billion dollars to every general purpose local government in the country through a predetermined formula, this program sent funds to thousands of local jurisdictions that had never before participated in national programs. And sure enough, having been given a taste of easy federal dollars, many of these new entrants into the federal aid system expanded their interest to other federal programs (Stein, 1981). This obviously contributed to the vast expansion in federal assistance programs that occurred during the 1970s (Anton, 1980a), but the more important long-run consequence may well be a significant improvement in local capacity to govern.

It is therefore important to remember that much of what appears to be "local" or "state" influence may well reflect the activities of national government agencies in local or state jurisdictions. Local or state participation in a national government program often requires the creation of new agencies to receive and manage national dollars. To receive urban renewal or low-income housing assistance, for example, cities have had to create local agencies authorized to receive and spend national program dollars. Such requirements in housing, economic development, transportation, and other national programs have spurred the growth of what Yin has referred to as "counterpart bureaucracies"—that is, local or state agencies created to work with their national government counterparts in the administration of federal programs (Yin, 1980). The growth of national benefits thus has been accompanied by a flowering of new agencies that are deeply enmeshed in a wide range of governmental activities in state and local jurisdictions, and that sometimes provide direct channels of access to a variety of national agencies. To speak of "local" or "state" influence in such circumstances, without recognizing the substantial national presence in subnational governance, would be inaccurate. Local and state governments help to determine what is or is not "national" policy, but the national government is also deeply involved in what are conventionally regarded as "local" or "state" actions.

Earlier I borrowed an image of three school superintendents standing with their backs to one another to summarize the effect of state boundaries on the organization of political life. A complementary image might be useful in summarizing the effects of state and local influence on national government benefit distributions. Imagine three individuals representing the local, state, and national governments, standing in a circle, with arms extended and hands joined. Each individual takes benefits from the others, but each also gives benefits to the others. Each stands alone and can act alone, but each also influences the others. Together they support the larger society through unending exchanges of benefits, which provide more collectively than any of them could provide alone. Because of the linkages, it is never entirely clear who is gaining or losing, but periodic changes in the size of each individual suggest periodic shifts in the balance of benefits. It is a somewhat fuzzy relationship, but it manages to continue, and it manages to distribute public benefits to a large and growing population of Americans.

SUMMARY

Although each level of American government can act independently in some areas, many government benefits in the United States are a product of joint interactions among two or more levels and are thus properly regarded as "federal" benefits. Distribution of such benefits is influenced by many forces, of which the most important are state desires for public services and national and state policy priorities. State and local tastes, reflecting different mixes of population, range from traditionalistic state cultures that emphasize limited government and social stability to moralistic cultures that seek positive uses of government to enhance individual welfare and the public interest. Traditionalistic, moralistic, and individualistic cultures constantly change, but they also exhibit a continuity based on the continued significance of the states as separate political systems.

National and state policy priorities reflect the emergence of characteristically different governmental interests. During the past two decades, the national government has increasingly concentrated its funds on social insurance and assistance benefits, national defense, and interest payments on the national debt. These benefits are generally distributed according to population, although particular programs are often concentrated in just a few states. State (and local) governments have focused their energies on education, health, transportation, and housekeeping programs, with a recent flurry of new activities designed to promote state economic development. These differences in policy interests do not preclude one level of government from entering another's sphere of interest, but they do help to restrain such entry and thus reduce to some extent the opportunities for intergovernmental conflict. Along with characteristically different preferences for public benefits, policy specialization helps to maintain the flow of public benefits through an extraordinarily complex governmental system.

REFERENCES

ACIR, 1984. Advisory Commission on Intergovernmental Relations. *Regulatory Federalism: Policy Process, Impact and Reform*. Washington, D.C.: Government Printing Office. Report A-95.

Anton, 1980a. Thomas J. Anton. "Federal Assistance Programs: The Politics of System Transformation." In *National Resources and Urban Policy*, ed. Douglas E. Ashford. New York: Methuen.

Anton, 1980b. Thomas J. Anton. *Administered Politics: Elite Political Culture in Sweden*. Boston: Martinus Nijihoff.

Anton, 1983. Thomas J. Anton. "The Regional Distribution of Federal Expenditures, 1971–1980." *National Tax Journal* 36 (December): 429–442.

Anton, 1985. Thomas J. Anton. "Decay and Reconstruction in the Study of American Intergovernmental Relations." *Publius* 15: 65–97.

Anton et al., 1980. Thomas J. Anton, Jerry P. Cawley, and Kevin Kramer. *Moving Money*. Cambridge, Mass.: Oelgeschlager, Gunn, and Hain.

Bahl, 1984. Roy Bahl. *Financing State and Local Government in the 1980s*. New York: Oxford University Press.

Break, 1982. George F. Break. "Government Spending Trends in the Postwar

Period," in Boskin and Wildavsky, eds., *The Federal Budget: Economics and Politics*. San Francisco: Institute for Contemporary Studies.

Elazar, 1972. Daniel J. Elazar. *American Federalism: A View from the States*, 2d ed. New York: Harper & Row.

Friedland and Wong, 1983. Roger Friedland and Herbert Wong. "Congressional Politics: Federal Grants, and Local Needs: Who Gets What and Why?" In *The Municipal Money Chase*, ed. Alberta M. Sbragia. Boulder, Colo.: Westview Press.

Haider, 1974. Donald H. Haider. *When Governments Come to Washington. Governors, Mayors, and Intergovernmental Lobbying*. New York: Free Press.

Johnson, 1976. Charles A. Johnson. "Political Culture in American States: Elazar's Formulation Examined." *American Journal of Political Science* 20 (August): 491–509.

Joslyn, 1982. Richard A. Joslyn. "Manifestations of Elazar's Political Subcultures: State Public Opinion and the Content of Political Campaign Advertising." In *Political Culture, Public Policy and the American States*, ed. John Kincaid. Philadelphia: Institute for the Study of Human Issues.

Kirkland, 1986. Lane Kirkland. "A Reminder of the Government's Bounty." *New York Times*, January 26.

Kramer, 1985. Kevin L. Kramer. "Fifty Years of Federal Housing Policy: A Case Study of How the Federal Government Distributes Resources." Ph.D. dissertation, University of Michigan.

Liebert, 1976. Roland J. Liebert. *Disintegration and Political Action: The Changing Functions of City Government in America*. New York: Random House.

OMB Special Analyses, 1986. Executive Office of the President. Office of Management and Budget. *Special Analyses, Budget of the United States Government FY 1986*. Washington, D.C.: Government Printing Office.

Oppenheim, 1983. John E. Oppenheim. "Federal Response to Natural Disasters: A Spatial Political Analysis." Ph.D. dissertation, University of Michigan.

Peterson, 1981. Paul Peterson. *City Limits*. Chicago: University of Chicago Press.

Rich, 1985. Michael Rich. "Congress, the Bureaucracy and the Cities: Distributive Politics in the Allocation of Federal Grants-in-Aid for Community and Economic Development." Ph.D. dissertation, Northwestern University.

Rochefort, 1986. David A. Rochefort. *American Social Welfare Policy: Dynamics of Formulation and Change*. Boulder, Colo.: Westview Press.

Rosenthal and Moakley, 1984. Alan Rosenthal and Maureen Moakley, eds. *The Political Life of the American States*. New York: Praeger.

Sabato, 1983. Larry Sabato. *Goodbye to Good-time Charlie. The American Governorship Transformed*. Washington: C Q Press.

Schwartz, 1983. John E. Schwartz. *America's Hidden Success: A Reassessment of Twenty Years of Public Policy*. New York: W. W. Norton.

State Policy Data Book, 1986. Alexandria, Va.: State Policy Research, Inc.

Stein, 1981. Robert M. Stein. "The Allocation of Federal Aid Monies: The Synthesis of Demand-Side Explanations." *American Political Science Review* 75 (June): 334–343.

Stein, 1984. Robert M. Stein. "Growth and Change in the U.S. Federal Aid System." Paper presented at the Southern Political Science Meeting, Savannah, Ga., November.

Stevens, 1982. Arthur R. Stevens. "State Boundaries and Political Cultures: An Exploration in the Tri-State Area of Michigan, Indiana and Ohio." In *Political Culture, Public Policy and the American States*, ed. John Kincaid. Philadelphia: Institute for the Study of Human Issues.

Welch and Peters, 1982. Susan Welch and John G. Peters. "State Political Culture and the Attitudes of State Senators Toward Social and Economic Welfare and Corruption Issues." In *Political Culture, Public Policy and the American States,* ed. John Kincaid. Philadelphia: Institute for the Study of Human Issues.

Yin, 1980. Robert K. Yin. "Creeping Federalism: The Federal Impact on the Structure and Function of Local Government." In *The Urban Impacts of Federal Policies,* ed. Norman J. Glickman. Baltimore: The Johns Hopkins University Press.

CHAPTER 4

FEDERAL COALITIONS FOR FEDERAL PROGRAMS

Rationalism has been the dominant mode of thinking about public policy in the United States for most of the twentieth century. During the 1960s and 1970s, when large numbers of professional economists moved into prominent positions in Washington and other centers of government, rationalist interpretations of public sector behavior became even more pronounced. Program and performance budgeting were developed for use within Planning-Programming-Budgeting (PPB) systems. Cost-benefit and cost-effectiveness studies provided criteria for evaluating the desirability of new or existing programs. New techniques of analysis, emphasizing quantitative and mathematical methods, provided evidence to support judgments made by the new mandarins of rationalism. Within an environment dominated by a pervasive optimism that we could devise precise means to achieve clearly defined ends, it was easy to understand policy as purpose, and to measure success by matching purpose to result.

In the rationalist paradigm, policy arises from the identification of some condition as a "problem," the specification by policymakers of alternative solutions to that problem, the estimation of the costs associated with various solution alternatives, and finally, the selection of a particular policy after considering the tradeoffs between benefits and costs. In this paradigm, "analysis" is the vehicle through which alternatives are selected and evaluated and, often enough, the source of the original problem definition. Since the analysis is done by well-educated analysts, this view of the origins of public policy may be thought of as the "wise men" paradigm.

But the development of policy is seldom so neat. Unfortunate social conditions often persist for decades before they are classified as "problems," and decades more may pass before such problems are thought to be a proper focus for public action. Changing popular standards of good and bad as well as changing conceptions of government responsibilities affect the way "conditions" are translated into "problems." From this point of view, public problems do not simply exist; they are created. The creators are individuals who experience some need or want and press for public action to satisfy the need or want. Advocacy rather than analysis is the core of policy development in this paradigm, and benefits for designated groups are among its most important results.

Although effective advocacy is sometimes achieved by individuals acting alone, it is more typical for those seeking influence over public action to join with other individuals in coalitions. So if advocacy rather than analysis is at the core of policy development, understanding policy development requires understanding the coalitions that come together to define, support, and sustain public benefit programs. In the American polity, these coalitions necessarily are federal in focus and operation. Understanding these various coalitions is the purpose of this chapter.

THE STRUCTURE OF ACCESS

Beneficiaries with Interests

By definition, the objects or actions produced by various police, welfare, highway, and other public programs are *benefits;* that is, they are valued by some individual or group of individuals. Individuals for whom program products are benefits may be said to have an interest in the program both because they value the products and because they are often implicated in the generation of the products. At a minimum, once they have begun, program beneficiaries prefer that benefits be continued into the indefinite future. More typically, beneficiaries prefer that benefits be improved across time in order to increase their value. For any given program, therefore, there are individuals who have a continuing and often growing interest in the program. Individual interest, multiplied many times to account for the thousands of programs delivering benefits to millions of beneficiaries, provides both a motivation and a mechanism for access.

Who are the individuals whose interests motivate a quest for access? Conventional analysis tends to emphasize a single group, citizens who receive something from government, and a single benefit, cash or an equivalent in-kind payment (such as food stamps or means-tested housing assistance). This is assuredly a large group, encompassing retirees who receive social security or pension checks, workers who receive unemployment compensation or disability checks, families who receive child assistance or welfare payments, farmers who receive payments for crops that are grown or not grown, and many other primary beneficiaries. But the beneficiary group is much larger than many people suppose, for it includes many individuals who benefit from the processes of delivering government benefits to other individuals. We may think of these persons as secondary beneficiaries.

One prominent group of secondary beneficiaries is government employees—some 15 million of them. Although terms and conditions of employment differ greatly by jurisdiction and agency, most public employees receive salary payments every week or month; most enjoy substantial additional fringe benefits such as medical insurance or paid vacations; and most are involved in systems that provide both job security and defined pathways to government "careers." These individuals clearly have a substantial interest in what government does, since as a practical matter, they *are* the government. Quite apart from concepts of purpose or mission that are typically used to describe government agencies, then, it is useful to remember that every such agency can also be said to have an interest which inheres in the various benefits enjoyed by agency employees. Agency executives recognize the significance of that interest by frequently acting as advocates for the agency cause in budget discussions, in negotiations over policy proposals, and in public discussions of agency activities.

A less visible, thus often overlooked, group of secondary beneficiaries includes employees of the private sector and nonprofit organizations that participate in government programs. Banks that charge fees for processing government loans, or that profit from packaging such loans for sale in other markets, are direct economic beneficiaries. Hospitals that derive much of their revenue from Medicaid and Medicare are direct economic beneficiaries. Corporations that profit from defense and other government contracts, universities that impose fees on government-sponsored re-search, nursing homes whose revenue is derived from social service programs, are all examples of organizations whose employees benefit directly from government programs. Indeed, public spending is so large and so all-embracing that it is difficult to imagine any activity in modern America which is free of some form of government participation.

The task becomes even more difficult when we consider the cash benefits derived from our tax system. All the benefits mentioned to this point are derived from direct government spending. Some public agency pays a salary, buys something, or mails a check to an individual or firm. The benefit, in other words, is provided by the dollar paid out. Precisely the same benefit can be achieved by *not taking* a dollar from an individual or firm that otherwise would pay a dollar in taxes to the government. Such benefits, technically referred to as *tax expenditures*, have become increas-ingly important as government has attempted to accomplish more and more goals through tax rather than expenditure policies. At the national level, for example, tax expenditures have increased much more rapidly than the budget as a whole during the past decade (Anton et al., 1980).

Examination of some of the more prominent tax expenditure programs suggests how pervasive such tax assistance has become. Table 4.1 lists the value of national taxes foregone in the 1986 fiscal year for just a few of the many tax expenditures available from the national government. For purposes of comparison, Table 4.1 also shows expenditures for other major portions of the national budget, as well as all federal spending for means-tested welfare programs.

It is apparent that national tax policies are extremely generous to both corporations and middle- to upper-income individuals. Tax expenditures for accelerated depreciation, investment credits, and capital gains all exceed $30 billion, and even a relatively small corporate benefit such as the reduced tax on the first $100,000 of income is larger than the largest

Table 4.1 1986 Tax Expenditures and Outlays ($ billions)

TAX EXPENDITURES		1986 OUTLAYS	
Accelerated depreciation	$ 32.6	Medicaid	$ 23.7
Investment tax credit	30.1	Food Stamps	12.7
Capital gains	32.0	Housing assistance	12.3
Mortgage interest deduction	27.6	SSI	9.9
IRAs	19.6	AFDC + child support	9.0
Consumer credit	16.0	Social services	6.7
Property tax deduction	10.9	Child nutrition	6.2
Reduced corporate income	10.0	Title I	3.8
Homes sales deferrals	2.7	Guaranteed student loans	3.3
		Energy assistance	2.1
TOTAL	$181.5		$ 89.7
		Defense outlays	$285.7
		Social security	202.2
		Medicare	67.2
		Interest on debt	199.4
		Net interest	142.6

SOURCE: Thomas J. Anton. Figures prepared for a presentation given at Brown University, Providence, R.I., 1986.

federal cash assistance program, AFDC. Nearly $40 billion is put into the pockets of homeowners through deductions for mortgage interest and local property taxes—deductions claimed by more than 25 million taxpayers in 1982, who represented more than three-quarters of all taxpayers who filed itemized returns (Dye, 1985). Individual Retirement Accounts alone cost the national government about as much as Food Stamps and AFDC combined. Clearly, our system offers better rewards by far to "them that has." But the important point is that both the haves and the have-nots are recipients of public largesse. Whether it is the one-third of all American families who participate in means-tested assistance programs, or virtually all other individuals and corporations that profit from both spending and tax programs, Americans today live in a society in which government benefits are an important part of the fabric of everyday life.

The comprehensiveness of these government benefit programs is an enormously important political fact: Since so many people and organizations receive benefits, the number of individuals who are active in the development of program benefits is quite large. Since secondary beneficiaries are as interested as primary beneficiaries in the flow of benefits, the constituencies available to support programs are much larger than is often perceived. Farmers and manufacturers of processed food products are interested in programs such as Food Stamps or Child Nutrition (Hadwiger and Talbot, 1982); local banks and financiers are interested in the loans made available by the Small Business Administration (Rozoff, 1985); hospital administrators, manufacturers of medical supplies, nurses, doctors, and social workers are all interested in Medicaid (Morone and Dunham, 1984); contractors, real estate developers, and bankers are all interested in UDAGs (Rich, 1985); and so on. The comprehensive and pervasive presence of government benefits in American life motivates both a need and a search for access across a broad spectrum of social and economic groups.

Barriers to Access

The search for access is constrained by the two dominant principles of government organization in the United States: territoriality and fragmentation. By organizing several layers of public authority according to different territorial boundaries, the American system provides several points of initial access, depending on the type of program. As we have seen, the various territorial authorities are to some extent specialized in the programs they carry out. Citizens and others seeking access are able to use that specialization to select the agencies and officials to be contacted. For example, a parent seeking assistance on some educational matter would probably approach a local agency—school board or school department— but, given the strong financial and supervisory role of state governments, might find it necessary to approach a state agency as well. A contractor seeking to make a bid on a highway construction project would almost certainly make contact with a state highway agency, but in many states a contractor might also be in contact with a county official. A doctor seeking to solve a health policy problem would be most likely to approach a state agency; but for many problems, federal officials would have to be contacted as well. These examples suggest that the territorial system is structured tightly enough to allow interested parties to choose appropriate targets of influence, but loosely enough to fit many targets within the "appropriate" range.

No territorial authority, of course, is a unified governmental system. Instead, public authority is normally fragmented among two or three separate branches for any given jurisdiction, and the branches are often fragmented among subunits. The result is a profusion of potential access points, divided among various bureaucratic, legislative, and judicial agencies. In addition to a choice among levels, therefore, individuals seeking access can choose among types of officials. A local council member, state legislator, or member of Congress can be used to pursue a political approach; various program administrators offer bureaucratic routes; and state and federal judicial systems offer legal alternatives. Fragmentation in the organization of territorial public authority, in short, offers a multitude of opportunities to search for and exert influence.

These *multiple cracks*, as they have been called, imply a certain confusion in the system of access. But here too there are organizing principles at work, of which the most significant are program and jurisdiction. Program-based access organizes influence around the benefits distributed by some program. Since so many programs are joint products of several governmental levels, program-based access often assumes a decidedly vertical form. Program administrators and beneficiaries at one level interact primarily with beneficiaries at higher and lower levels, rather than with other program beneficiaries at the same level of government. Repeated across a number of programs, from education to highways to health, this vertical form links functional constituencies in what some writers have called "picket fence federalism" (Wright, 1982).

Cross-level political interactions allow localized constituencies to become allies of state and national program managers in campaigns to increase resources, and they also allow national or state officials to become allies of beneficiaries in pursuit of localized policy goals. Pursuit of vertical influence requires knowledge of many different local environments, as well as state and national policies regarding program benefits. Program-based access patterns, accordingly, have led to a vast increase in the number of officials and other beneficiaries who reside in a local jurisdiction but who are equally at home in Washington or various state capitals. These can truly be called "federal" politicians.

Jurisdiction-based access organizes influence horizontally, around the benefits distributed by a single level of government. This form of access is more typical, in part because different levels emphasize characteristically different kinds of services, and in part because many of the services that require multilevel coordination are operationally focused at a single level. For example, the national government provides funding for many programs—Community Development Block Grants is an example—whose day-to-day operations are entirely in the hands of state or local officials.

Horizontal access is not necessarily focused on a single government unit, however. It is common for several separate governments, such as a school board, city, town, or sewer district, to exercise jurisdiction in the same territory. Moreover, contractual service agreements between such jurisdictions are becoming more common. Two or more cities, for example, may agree by contract to jointly support a common library, or school system, or police services. Jurisdiction-based access may be focused on a single unit, but it is equally likely that horizontal access patterns will include multiple jurisdictions.

THE CONCEPT OF COALITION

Defining Terms

Those who use these various access points typically are organized into *coalitions*, by which I mean two or more individuals, each of whom represents some other individuals who agree to promote and support some benefit program or programs. This definition is useful for several reasons. First, it refers to individuals, rather than to the more abstract notion of group that is most often used in discussions of coalitions. This is important because it is individuals who take action and who can be observed in action. Establishing a "group" source of individual actions is difficult in any case because the concept of group is itself ambiguous: Does it refer to numbers of people, to a particular cause, to a particular allegiance, to some bond between individuals, or to something else? Rather than attempt to resolve such muddy issues, the definition proposed here focuses on individuals and their actions, if and when those actions represent multiple individuals. Actions that do not represent others are excluded, since exclusive self-representation requires no agreement with others and thus no coalition at all.

The definition is also open-ended with respect to both numbers and types of individuals. Since small coalitions are often quite powerful, it is important to avoid the assumption that size and influence are necessarily related. For example, a three-person coalition made up of the president, the Speaker of the House, and the Senate majority leader would have considerable influence, despite its size. Larger coalitions are often influential because of their numbers, but whether coalitions are influential, and whether influence arises from sheer numbers or some other source, should always be matters for investigation, not assumption.

It is equally important to have a definition of coalition that allows for participation by many different types of individuals, including government officials. Many previous definitions of coalition have been built upon theories of "group politics" that located groups outside the government itself (Truman, 1971). In the group politics model, government action occurs only when and if officials are pressured by nongovernmental groups. Public officials themselves are viewed as essentially passive, as waiting for someone or something else to push them to action, much as a billiard ball is moved when struck by the cue ball.

Finally, note that the definition is focused on benefit programs, rather than social structures. Although it is true that individuals often share interests with many other individuals of similar social position, it is also true that similarly situated persons often have very different interests, and that individual interests change. The result is nicely summarized in the popular saying "Politics makes strange bedfellows." Labor and management, whose views differ on so many issues, may come together on the desirability of import quotas to protect jobs and profits. Food manufacturers and poor people, so different in economic status and political outlook, may come together on the desirability of food programs to promote sales and reduce hunger. Insurance companies and consumer groups, at odds on so many issues, may come together on the desirability of air bags for automobiles. These examples are common enough to suggest that a definition of coalition based on the characteristics of members is likely to overlook much behavior that is important in understanding public programs. For that reason, the definition offered here is based on what individuals want from government, rather than who they are. In this sense too, the definition is open-ended, allowing for any combination of partners that emerges to support some particular government benefit.

As used in this discussion, then, "coalition" is concrete rather than abstract in its focus on individuals, open-ended with respect to number and type of participants, and oriented to program benefits rather than social characteristics. It assumes nothing about individuals except their occasional interest in joining with other individuals to obtain a benefit from government. No assumptions about size are made, nor are government officials excluded; in fact, the definition specifically allows officials to be included among the many types of individuals who participate in benefit-oriented coalitions. The definition, in short, is both empirically clear and analytically neutral, identifying phenomena to be observed without imposing predetermined conclusions about those phenomena. For all these reasons, the definition should serve us well in examining federal benefit coalitions.

USING THE COALITION CONCEPT

Horizontal and Vertical Dimensions   American governments are all partially autonomous in the sense that they can take certain actions without consulting other governments. But they are also entwined with higher and lower governments that can constrain their behavior. How can the coalition concept help us to understand policy development in such complex systems of interaction?

The answer is implicit in the previous discussion. If policy is a product of coalition behavior and governments are defined by the policies they pursue, then governments themselves can be viewed as coalitions of individuals pursuing government benefits. Benefits derived from those programs in which a government has autonomous control are pursued by coalitions that can be thought of as horizontal; that is, their activities focus on a single level of government. Benefits derived from programs jointly controlled by several levels of government are pursued by vertical coalitions; that is, their activities focus on the several levels of government involved in delivering the benefit. It is generally agreed that vertical coalitions are more numerous today than ever before because of the vast expansion of national government assistance programs during the 1960s and 1970s. Increasingly, however, state and local governments have been setting policies in areas long thought to be national responsibilities—local "nuclear free" zones or state government "treaties" with other nations to promote state exports are prominent recent examples. Pressures from both top and bottom have therefore expanded the number of vertical coalitions without eliminating the horizontal ones. Fortunately, we know enough about both kinds of coalition behavior to generate useful insights into federal program development.

Vertical Coalitions Monypenny's brilliant papers of a quarter century ago, initiating a research approach that has been followed by many other scholars in recent years, give us important insights into the nature and sources of vertical coalitions (Anton, 1985; Monypenny, 1958, 1960). Monypenny set out to explain the existence and growth (in 1960, well before the later explosion!) of federal grants, as well as their characteristically ambiguous designations of purpose. His explanation began by noting the variety and narrowness of interests spawned in a society as large and as diverse as the United States. When these narrow interests produce specific policy goals that are widely shared (such as providing basic elementary education or police protection), individuals easily form coalitions to support government programs to achieve these purposes. Most interests are too narrowly defined to attract support from large numbers of people, however, particularly if support is sought for direct action by a government.

To gain such action through legislation or administrative action, the narrow interest must be defined with sufficient specificity to make clear what it is that the government will do. Once drafted, such a statement has two significant political effects. By making clear that the number of beneficiaries is limited, political support for the program is weakened. At the same time the opposition, which before lacked a firm base of coalition, is now given a clear target to attack. Except for the few core programs that reflect widely shared interests, developing a coalition strong enough to secure direct government action toward a narrow goal is unusually difficult.

The situation is entirely different if those who seek narrow goals seek to act through grants to another government. Groups too weak to secure their ends in local or state jurisdictions may, by joining with similar groups from other local or state jurisdictions, mobilize sufficient support to gain assistance from another government. Since it is financial support that is proposed to other governmental units, the details of the program that inhibit political success elsewhere need not be addressed. Grant purposes can be stated in general terms, allowing the granting unit to be supportive but at the same time allowing recipient units to pursue interests that typically vary considerably. Thus, as Monypenny writes of state educational grants to local units, "a minimum state program is assured, but wide room may be left for differences of local emphasis."

In seeking funds from another unit rather than a program from one's own unit, it becomes possible to pursue localized interests at little local expense—political or financial. Monypenny argues:

> . . . if this is so in the states, where there is an extensive legal power of regulating the policy, as well as the structure and finance of local units, it is the more so in the federal government. The fiscal power of the federal government can be invoked without bringing to play its policymaking powers, except for that minimum on which those desiring the fiscal assistance can agree. . . . It is

possible to get unemployment compensation on a virtually national basis without battling to the wall every combination of employers determined to pay for no more than a minimum program, and yet get a more extensive program in those states where there is support for it. It is possible to get the semblance of a national highway program while still enabling each state to decide whether it will support a more extensive program of highway construction.

It can be asserted therefore that politically speaking, federal aid programs are an outcome of a loose coalition which resorts to a mixed federal-state program because it is not strong enough in individual states to secure its own program, and because it is not united enough to be able to achieve a wholly federal program against the opposition which a specific program would engender. (Monypenny, 1960, p. 15)

Placing coalition behavior at the center of his analysis enables Monypenny to show the inherently political nature of government programs in general as well as in the particular case of federal grant programs. This may seem too banal a statement, but many analysts continue to frame studies of government activity as rationalistic inquiries into program goals rather than as political inquiries into program beneficiaries. Monypenny not only calls attention to the significance of political support; he also shows dynamic interactions between coalition behavior and program design that are quite consistent with federal programs such as aid to aviation, through which tiny local minorities, unable to secure local support for their specialized interest, have been able to secure large national subsidies for 2,224 general aviation airports that have been described by the Congressional Budget Office as facilities "of primarily local interest" (CBO, 1983). His explanation of why grant programs typically have vague objectives anticipates many recent studies that document ambiguous legislative language (Larkey, 1979), as well as other studies that document the diverse local or state uses of federal program dollars, or the diverse local uses of state program dollars (Derthick, 1975; Dommel et al., 1982; Wirt, 1980).

Monypenny's formulation is interesting because it emphasizes the weakness rather than the strength of local coalitions to explain the emergence of multilevel programs. Coalitions strong enough to achieve their desired benefits at a local level presumably need not appeal to higher jurisdictions. So long as other jurisdictions exist to which appeals can be made, however, weak local coalitions can take on strength by banding together with others of similar interest to exploit the multiple points of access available in the American federal polity.

Nevertheless, the strength of vertical coalitions need not derive from policy agreement. Vertical coalitions are "loose," according to Monypenny, and they are seldom "united enough" to secure a wholly federal or wholly state program. It is precisely the weakness of vertical coalitions that leads to the use of dollars as the major program medium. Lacking sufficient strength to determine what to do, vertical coalitions typically focus on higher-level dollars, whose uses can be determined "in the field" by the local or state officials who receive them. The result is what I have elsewhere referred to as the "spend some money and see what happens" syndrome:

> If the coalition seems powerful enough, and the demonstration of "problem" persuasive enough, funds are provided [by the higher-level government]. Mechanisms for distributing dollars to individuals are relatively efficient, and less efficient but serviceable mechanisms for allocating money to governments or groups are also available. Since cause and effect are so unclear, funds distributed to organizations cannot be severely constrained at the outset. Instead, funds are allocated in support of a generally defined cause or problem, with the intention of discovering the uses of those funds at some later point in time. Discovery occurs after a year or two of expenditure experience, usually in the form of a congressional [or legislative] hearing, to which program administrators and selected beneficiaries are invited in order to describe accomplishments achieved with program dollars. Depending on who says what at such hearings, programs can be adjusted by introducing tighter (or less tight) use constraints—again with the purpose of discovering what consequences are produced by such adjustments. (Anton et al., 1980).

But why should higher-level officials respond to such entreaties? If vertical coalitions are loose and too weak to secure passage of carefully defined programs, why should these officials agree to provide support for their programs? One answer, of course, is that the weak local coalitions often appear much more powerful if many of them are active at a higher level. A more important reason, however, is that higher-level officials can generate substantial benefits for themselves by responding to or even joining vertical coalitions. Legislators can appear to be responsive to societal needs and at the same time take credit for new program dollars that flow into their own districts. Administrators can also appear to be responsive while simultaneously expanding budget and staff to deliver the new benefits. Lower-level officials who receive the benefits have new resources to be devoted in various ways to the problem or problems that originally motivated their search for assistance. When vertical coalitions are successful, in short, everyone benefits (Fiorina, 1977).

Horizontal Coalitions and the Mix of Programs

In addition to vertical coalitions, built on locally weak interests, every level of government has horizontal coalitions that reflect local strength—that is, individuals who are sufficiently powerful to achieve their benefits through local or state action, without resorting to higher-level assistance. Because they are organized around benefits, the major participants in horizontal coalitions can be identified through the principal programs carried out at different governmental levels.

Provision of basic housekeeping services such as streets, sewers, and refuse collection; public safety services such as police and fire protection; education; real estate; and commercial development define a collection of public benefit programs that are provided everywhere by local governments. The coalitions in support of these basic or core services are similarly ubiquitous, including homeowners, downtown and neighborhood merchant associations, city and school employees, taxpayer associations, and others interested in maintaining each municipality's image as "a good place to live and work" (Peterson, 1981). Older and larger cities, with more diverse populations, often generate coalitions in support of still other services such as hospitals, museums, colleges and universities, and various social services (Liebert, 1976). Depending on size and age, therefore, there can be considerable variety in the services supported by local coalitions in addition to the core housekeeping responsibilities (Fossett, 1983).

Coalitions in support of state government benefits are similarly varied around a group of core programs. Powerful and continuous coalition support for highways, health care, higher education, parks, and criminal justice services exists in all states, alongside equally powerful coalitions representing the interests of local governments. Because states provide legal frameworks for the taxation and regulation of business enterprise, moreover, corporate and labor organizations are also powerful coalition partners in every state. With these basic state coalitions exist numerous others that reflect different historical and cultural development. New Hampshire's tradition of Yankee thrift continues to be reflected in low state taxes and the absence of many services provided by other states (Winters, 1984). New York, on the other hand, traditionally has been an activist innovator state, leading the way in social programs such as low-income housing, as well as the more recent development of industrial policies (Anton and Reynolds, 1985; Smith, 1984). Kentucky, for years dominated by a highway mentality, recently has used increases in coal prices and coal taxes to fund active social policies (Herbers, 1986; Landy, 1984).

At the national level, powerful horizontal coalitions mix with developing coalitions to produce a similar benefit structure. This structure includes a number of long-lasting programs, supported by stable coalitions, that represent agreed-upon political commitments. Core programs of this kind are relatively few in number, but they represent a large fraction of distributed funds. And because they reflect a stable political agreement, core programs are likely to be extremely resistant to anything but incremental change. Fund levels will increase as the national budget increases, but major program changes will seldom occur, and then usually as a result of some crisis, or perhaps a political realignment. When such changes occur in core programs, the terms of coalition support are renegotiated in order to ensure stability for the revised program (Light, 1985). Core programs, in short, represent institutionalized political settlements that are durable as well as purposive. Programs such as social security, national defense, highway grants, or mortgage interest deductions are good examples.

In addition to core programs, national expenditures support a wide variety of benefits that reflect current political concerns but are not yet fully institutionalized. These concerns change from one year to another. When successful, coalitions organized around new issues produce new programs to service newly recognized constituencies, some of which may be organized as vertical coalitions. At any given time, therefore, the full range of programs at any level can be viewed as a political barometer of sorts, measuring the developing concerns of the political system as well as its lasting settlements.

Success in initiating a new program, however, is no guarantee that the program will become institutionalized; concern over the issue may weaken, coalition members may be unable to sustain cooperative action, or new concerns may arise with stronger claims on national resources. Thus, around the core programs we can observe a fluctuating variety of barometer programs, only some of which will achieve stable support: General Revenue Sharing did not achieve this support, but AIDS testing programs apparently will. Viewed horizontally, then, the benefit system at any level is both "structured" around core commitments and coalitions, yet constantly changing to accommodate the interests of new or developing coalitions. From this point of view, structure and change are both amenable to observation, measurement, and analysis.

Winners and Losers

The distinction between strong horizontal coalitions and weak coalitions that gain strength through vertical alliances implies the possibility of identifying which coalitions exhibit strength at each level. For some time, conventional analysis has held that business and commercial coalitions dominate local and state policy, while more "liberal" urban, ethnic, labor, and low-income coalitions have ascended to power in Washington as their role in presidential electoral politics has grown (Reagan and Sanzone, 1972). These speculations certainly seem plausible, but until recently evidence to support them has been largely anecdotal rather than systematic. An interesting recent paper by Wolman and Teitelbaum, however, offers an innovative examination of state "winners and losers" that helps to clarify the issue (Wolman and Teitelbaum, 1984).

Wolman and Teitelbaum were interested in measuring the relative influence of different social groups, but instead of imprecise estimates of "group" strength, they measured influence directly by focusing on "the extent to which the interests were served by favorable public policy." Treating program benefits such as AFDC payments, maximum disability payments, or average teacher's salary as indicators of the success of various interests, Wolman and Teitelbaum developed ". . . an output measure of interest success rather than an input measure of interest-group influence" (p. 325). All states were ranked from high to low in various payment categories. In addition, the level of benefit payment was compared to state income to provide a measure of the influence of each interest relative to other interests in the state. The authors suggest that the latter measure can

Table 4.2 Correlation Between Measures of Interest and State Characteristics

INTEREST	STATE PER CAPITA IN-COME (1983)	PERCENTAGE OF STATE POPULATION IN POVERTY (1980)[a]	PERCENTAGE MINORITY POPU-LATION (1980)
POOR			
Adjusted AFDC payment, 1983	.58	−.68 (−.67)	−.44
Percentage of poverty population receiving AFDC, 1983	.48	−.39 (−.35)	.14
Adjusted Medicaid payments per recipient, 1982	−.04	−.21 (−.24)	−.34
Percentage of poor receiving Medicaid, 1982	.41	−.34 (−.29)	.01
AFDC effort score, 1983[b]	.22	−.55 (−.56)	−.52
Medicaid effort score, 1982[b]	−.15	−.14 (−.13)	−.30
Difference between tax rates for middle income people and the poor, 1980	.22	−.20	−.09
LABOR (BUSINESS)[c]			
Maximum disability payment, 1983	.53	−.30 (−.25)	−.12
Disability effort score, 1983[d]	.44	−.25 (−.17)	−.09
BUSINESS			
Business taxes as % of business income, 1979	.37	−.33	−.13
TEACHERS			
Adjusted average teacher's salary, 1983	.70	−.19 (.16)	.25
Teacher salary effort[e]	−.12	.11 (.23)	−.01
PUPILS			
State-local per pupil revenue, 1983	.76	−.50 (−.56)	−.23
Pupil effort score, 1983[f]	−.35	−.39 (−.40)	−.40
BIG CITIES			
State general support to big cities: state general support to all municipalities, 1981	−.01 (1980)	.24	.64

SOURCE: Harold Wolman and Fred Teitelbaum. "Interest Groups and the Reagan Presidency." In *The Reagan Presidency and the Governing of America*, ed. Lester Salamon and Michael Lund. Washington, D.C.: Urban Institute Press, 1984. p. 328. Reprinted by permission of the Urban Institute Press.

[a] Figures in parentheses in this column represent the correlation between 1980 values of the row variables and the column variable.
[b] AFDC and Medicaid effort scores are calculated by dividing state AFDC benefit levels and state Medicaid expenditures per recipient, respectively, by state per capita income.
[c] Business interests can be interpreted as the inverse of labor interests on this measure.
[d] Disability effort score is the state maximum disability payment divided by state average weekly earnings.
[e] Teacher salary effort score is the state average teacher salary divided by state per capita income.
[f] Pupil effort score is state-local revenue per pupil for each state divided by the state's per capita income.

be thought of as ". . . an 'effort score,' measuring the extent to which a state provides a policy output relative to its capacity to do so" (p. 326). These measures were then correlated with three standard measures of state characteristics: per capita income, percentage of population in poverty, and percentage of minority population. The results are shown in Table 4.2.

The authors note that these data are broadly consistent with other studies in demonstrating that ". . . the interests of the poor, labor, pupils and teachers are inadequately served in states with low per capita income and in states with a high percentage of poor people or minorities." What they find both surprising and interesting, however, is that ". . . with the exception of teachers, the interests of these groups also are weak relative to other groups within these states—that is, states with low per capita income, high poverty, and high minority populations provide lower benefits relative to their income to the poor, labor, and students than other states do. By contrast, the interests of business are best served (and stronger relative to other groups) in these same states" (p. 327). Not surprisingly, if we recall the discussion of state "tastes" in Chapter 3, southern states were least favorable to the interests of the poor, labor, students, and minorities and most favorable toward business, while the reverse was true in the states of the Northeast. And while the authors made no attempt to measure state tastes, their results are quite consistent with those of other studies that have included cultural variables.

It appears, then, that the received wisdom regarding business domination of state politics and strong liberal-labor strength at the national level may be too simplistic. Liberal coalitions have been strong nationally for the past several decades, and weak in many states, particularly those that are both poor and southern. But they also have been powerful in wealthier states such as Michigan and Massachusetts, where unions and allied organizations have built effective coalitions. Indeed, the really striking finding in the Wolman-Teitelbaum analysis is that liberal coalitions are strong not in states with large numbers of minority or poor populations, but in states with coalitions that can effectively represent liberal interests. Similarly, business coalitions are powerful in some states but weak in others, particularly the wealthier states of the Northeast and Midwest, where liberal coalitions have been able to gain program benefits for poor and minority communities. Business coalitions have also been extraordinarily powerful at the national level during the years of liberal ascendancy in Washington.

At any given time, therefore, one alignment may appear to be dominant at the state or national level, but such appearances mask considerable variety among the states, as well as the increasing difficulty of maintaining national dominance for a lengthy period of time. Liberal coalitions, in retreat at the national level under the Reagan administration, have become more influential in the states; conservative forces have assumed more national influence. But no one should expect the present alignments to remain unchanged. Instead, as coalitions shift their targets and redefine their interests, current alignments will assume new and perhaps surprising shapes.

CHANGES IN COALITION COMPOSITION

The Erosion of Political Parties

Most observers agree that new and surprising coalition shapes are already present in the political environment. Traditionally, political parties have been thought of as ideological coalitions that bring together a number of different interests around a common set of shared values (Eldersveld, 1982). To accommodate the number of votes necessary to win elections, however, the different interests within a party must be reconciled around priorities that all can accept. As a result, "shared values" are stated in purposefully vague terms, designed more to mobilize supporters than to provide blueprints for action. Nevertheless, the process of accommodating various interests within the party framework encourages practical compromises that enhance the ability to govern, when in power, and encourage party unity during electoral campaigns. In this sense, political parties in the United States have been properly regarded as coalitions of interests, loosely organized around characteristically different but vaguely defined principles. In both mobilization and governance, they have been regarded as integrative rather than narrowly dogmatic.

This view of American political parties, however, has been eroding for several decades, as scholars first noticed and then began to explain a widespread loss of party allegiance among voters. As increasing affluence and new communications technologies eroded the previous functions of party organizations, voter allegiance shifted from party to person, with more and more citizens preferring to think of themselves as independents rather than partisans. One result has been a noticeable loss of party discipline within legislative bodies, leading to less predictable and more haphazard decision processes. Another result has been the decay or even elimination of party organizations as political actors. Even the legendary Chicago political machine, led for many years by Mayor Richard J. Daley, was so consumed by internal strife in 1986 that it neglected to publicize all of its candidates for statewide political office. The result was the nomination of two members of a neo-Nazi group as candidates for lieutenant governor and secretary of state to run on the Democratic ticket alongside the party nominee for governor, Adlai E. Stevenson, Jr. Stevenson promptly announced his refusal to run with these individuals who, he complained, ". . . are not Democrats, nor are they remotely qualified to hold public office." Stevenson's complaints notwithstanding, it is difficult to find more dramatic evidence of the decline of party organization than the election of two non-Democrats in a primary conducted by what had once been the most powerful Democratic organization in the country (Malcom, 1986, p. A14).

But however weak they may have become, political parties are far from dead. Indeed, there is considerable recent evidence that state and national party organizations have assumed new and increasingly significant roles in recent years. As campaign costs have increased, national and state party committees have become important sources of funds for candidates. They have also become major service providers, offering candidates expert advice on topics such as polling, media management, utilization of direct mail techniques, and campaign organization (Cotter, 1984). Political party allegiance may have been eroded among the electorate, but political party organizations continue to exert a powerful influence among more active citizens and politicians.

The Iron Triangle

As party allegiance, cohesion, and organization have declined, other types of coalitions have emerged as powerful influences on public programs. Perhaps the most significant of these, with deep roots in American history, is the so-called iron triangle, sometimes referred to as a *subgovernment.* The *triangle* refers to the alliance among a legislative committee, a bureaucratic agency responsible for distributing some benefit controlled by the committee, and the beneficiaries or client groups that receive the benefits. It is *iron* because such alliances have been found to endure for many years and to be relatively impervious to influence from outside agencies or actors. As scholars have examined more and more programs, usually at the national level but often at local or state levels as well, they have repeatedly discovered that such triangles not only control many programs, but that the control lasts for years or even decades. It is precisely this durability of control that has led observers to think of these iron triangles as subgovernments, clothed with authority from the public at large, but devoted to the preservation of benefits for narrowly defined constituencies. From this point of view, American governance is best characterized as a large number of subgovernments, each of which controls some small piece of the public pie, and relatively free from other influences, including the more general ones of presidents, governors, and mayors.

Issue Networks or Policy Communities

The iron triangle remains a useful metaphor for government policymaking in the United States, but observers increasingly have wondered whether the triangle is the most appropriate shape and whether iron should be replaced by something less durable. These questions have been stimulated by a realization that, in the fragmented world of federal policymaking, participation is not confined to bureaucrats, politicians, and beneficiaries. Other participants have assumed increasingly prominent roles in defining issues and making decisions. One major reason for this expanded participation is the technological complexity of many policy problems. As governments have assumed new responsibilities in environmental protection or family care, and as new scientific discoveries in areas such as medical care or space exploration have expanded the boundaries of possible government action, more and more scientists and other professional experts have been brought into the policy process.

Since government agencies often lack sufficient expertise or prefer not to hire their own expert employees, much technological work is contracted out to consulting firms whose technical skills often allow them to dominate discussions of complicated policy issues. The growth of consulting firms in Washington—sometimes called "beltway bandits" because they operate within the highway system that rings the city—has been so striking that few major areas of national policy are free from consultant influence, and major Washington thoroughfares such as K Street are identified as centers of consultant activity. Consultant growth has been no less remarkable among state and local governments, most of which are pursuing more technologically complicated activity than ever before and thus require as much or more assistance from consultants as does the national government.

Apart from private consulting firms, the growing demand for specialized scientific competence has brought greater numbers of academics into positions of influence. Like consultants, university professors often possess the specialized knowledge and information sources required to make intelligent program assessments. In addition to these qualities, however, university-based researchers often carry with them an aura of prestige arising from the prominence of the institutions in which they are employed. Government use of academics as consultants, therefore, can be an effective way to improve the political saleability of some proposal, as well as providing academic access to the policymaking process.

The increasing complexity of policy issues implies a need for more specialized legal knowledge as well. Government expansion has led to a vast expansion of rules and regulations, which increased by six times between 1955 and 1980 at the national level alone, to say nothing of rule expansion in the states, where agencies and personnel were growing very rapidly during the same period (Heclo, 1978). Special interest or public interest law firms have emerged all over the country to interpret and litigate the regulations that accompany new programs. As in the case of consultants and academics, such firms often include individuals who have served in government agencies responsible for the programs they later deal with from positions outside the government. Not infrequently, therefore, law firms rather than government bureaus become the sources of authoritative interpretations of the law, just as consultants often become the most authoritative sources of information on program history or purpose.

Increased participation in policy development by consulting firms, university-based academics, law firms, and other professional specialists means that many "public" decisions are in fact made by a variety of "private" specialists. Conceptually, these developments suggest rather strongly that the so-called triangle of policymaking should be supplemented by images that contain more sides and more angles. In his analysis, Heclo abandons the geometric imagery entirely, proposing instead that we think of "issue networks" as sources of policy (Heclo, 1978). Kingdon has suggested that the various public and private individuals involved in policy determination be conceptualized as "policy communities" (Kingdon, 1984). Although obviously somewhat fuzzy, these notions have three distinct advantages: One is that they capture the new realities of multiple-participant decision processes. A second is that they retain a focus on "policy" or "issue" that is specific enough to guide empirical analyses. And third, they are open-ended with respect to the individuals who are included in "networks" or "communities." That is, membership in these coalitions is determined by observation rather than by definition.

The latter quality is particularly important, because patterns of participation that structure access by issue or policy are inherently fluid. Since participation is often determined by professional interest rather than membership in an established structure, access costs are minimized. A professional expert may gain access simply by writing a knowledgeable letter to an official, or perhaps to a newspaper. A lawyer with no government experience at all may gain access by representing a client in a legal action involving a policy question. A scholar may gain access by doing nothing more than she or he might have done anyway—publishing a book or an article in a scholarly journal. The low cost of access to issue networks means that such networks are not only broadly based, but subject to considerable shifts in participation, as various individuals decide to invest more or less time in some particular problem, or as entrepreneurs in public office reach out to other officials and individuals to mobilize support for some action. As a result, policy communities or issue networks expand and contract continuously, and often unexpectedly. Clearly, their connecting tissue is not "iron" at all, but rather something closer to rubber in composition.

Single-Issue Coalitions

The movement away from the rigidity of iron triangles to the fluidity of issue networks is clearly reflected in the large number of single-issue coalitions that have emerged in recent years, primarily to promote new government action. International issues such as the prevention of nuclear war or apartheid, morality issues such as abortion or school prayer, or even more pragmatic issues such as tax reform all have attracted individuals who believe that one issue is more important than any other and who are willing to devote all their political energies to that issue. Single-issue coalitions are often "computer coalitions" in the sense that they make use of computer technology to mobilize support, usually through the development of specialized mailing lists that can be used to raise funds, disseminate information, or coordinate action.

Such coalitions also can be quite sophisticated in their use of the mass media to publicize causes. Through careful staging and the cooperation of the media themselves, a small group can appear to be a large crowd— nothing more is required than the right television camera angle or suitably ambiguous phrasing in a newspaper account. Careful preparation also can allow a spokesman to generate attention with a 20 to 30 second statement that fits easily into the typical television report or newspaper headline. To some extent, therefore, many single-issue coalitions can also be thought of as media coalitions. Indeed, the media are often the most important and influential participants in such coalitions.

The Rise of the Topocrats

Single-issue coalitions can be important because they often exert consider- able influence on the national political agenda. From a federal policy point of view, however, other coalitions have a more pronounced impact on policy. Associations of senior public officials, for example, have become much more active in seeking to shape domestic policy. Organizations such as the National Association of Counties, the U.S. Conference of Mayors, the National Association of State Budget Officers, and the National Conference of State Legislatures, among others, have grown enormously in size and sophistication to a point at which they are now routinely involved in national policymaking. Among the newer and more fluid forms of coali- tion, these associations of senior public officials, or *topocrats*, to borrow a term from Beer, have become increasingly significant (Beer, 1978).

Many trace their origins back a half a century or more, but their political influence has more recent roots. The general expansion of state and local government activities that occurred in the 1950s and 1960s did not just increase the number of state and local employees; service expansion also increased the level of professionalism among those employ- ees. As new programs stimulated demand for new academic programs in areas such as planning or financial analysis, more and more public employees earned degrees in order to obtain positions or earn promotions. By the 1970s large numbers of state and local officials had earned advanced degrees that gave them professional as well as organizational status. Greater activity by the national associations organized around these professional specialties thus became a natural outgrowth of higher levels of professional competence among state and local employees.

It is also important to note that, as American subnational governments were becoming more professionalized, the governmental stakes became greater. Stimulated initially by the Great Society programs of President Lyndon Johnson and later by the social policy initiatives of the Nixon administration, federal financial aid to state and local governments rose rapidly. By 1975, national funds represented the largest single source of state-local revenue, exceeding sales, property, and income taxes in financial significance (Anton, 1980). With much more to gain or lose, state and local officials went to Washington to promote their interests and established themselves as permanent participants in Washington politics (Haider, 1974).

Finally, it seems essential to underline the role of the Advisory Commission on Intergovernmental Relations as both an informational resource for the new intergovernmental coalitions and a symbol of their growing influence in national policymaking. Created by Congress in 1959 to monitor the operations of the federal system, the commission is a permanent agency of 26 members representing executive and legislative branches of national, state, and local governments, as well as the general public. With its headquarters in Washington, the commission has provided an obvious symbol of the national significance of subnational governments. And with a small but experienced staff of analysts, supplemented by visiting academics on temporary appointment, the commission has been able to produce a variety of influential studies, ranging from analyses of specific programs, to studies of structural problems, to continuing analyses of taxing and spending patterns among all American governments.

During its early years, ACIR provided much of the information available to the developing intergovernmental coalitions. As these coalitions have developed their own information resources, the commission has become less dominant as a resource, but it continues to help shape the federal policy agenda through its research and the recommendations derived from that research. Its fiscal studies have produced widely used standards such as its "representative tax system" measure. The commission's continued promotion of its proposals to "sort out" national, state, and local responsibilities have had a strong influence on President Reagan's domestic policy agenda. Indeed, ACIR provided much of the analysis used by all parties to debate the president's proposals to swap Food Stamps and AFDC for Medicaid and to turn back a number of other programs to the states. Many of the commission's studies have been more polemical than analytic, but that is precisely the point: ACIR has provided an important political forum for intergovernmental topocrats to debate federal program priorities.

Inevitably, the confluence of more people with better training spending more money has led to a much higher level of sophistication in the pursuit of federal program benefits. The Hall of the States in Washington provides a permanent home for many of the intergovernmental associations, whose staffs provide expert analyses of federal policy proposals. One of the best examples of this new expertise is the Federal Funds Information for States Newsletter, published monthly from the Hall of the States with support from the National Governors Association and the National Conference of State Legislatures. In its first issue, dated August 1983, the Newsletter announced its purpose:

> WELCOME TO THE FFIS NEWSLETTER! This newsletter will be issued regularly with information and analysis on the distribution of federal funds. While the newsletter will deal with a range of issues, each month will focus on a specific area. The theme of this month's issue is elementary and secondary education funding.

The newsletter went on to report state-by-state and regional distributions of funds from five major education programs (Handicapped Education, Vocational Education, Impact Aid, Compensatory Education, and the Education Block Grant), changes in these distributions resulting from the supplementary appropriations bill, and a comparison of state-by-state distributions from different House and Senate bills to improve science and math education.

Merely reporting such patterns was interesting, in part because the capacity to do so had not been available previously. Thus readers learned that "The distributions for the handicapped education basic state grant and the education block grant (Chapter 2) are the most similar, since both are distributed on the basis of demographic factors. . . . Impact aid spending for "3a" children is the most concentrated, focusing on those states with large military or Indian populations." But such information clearly is practical as well as interesting. In reporting on new funding for removal of architectural barriers for handicapped children, for example, the Newsletter notes: "While no information has been made available on the distribution of funds, FFIS expects that the distribution will not be dissimilar from that of the Education for the Handicapped basic state grant. That distribution is displayed in Table 1 of this newsletter, and states can gauge their potential share from this distribution."

Subsequent issues have explored other major programs in health, employment, and defense, in each case providing information on current and proposed legislation, and in each case providing state and regional information on current and proposed legislation, and in each case showing state "winners" and "losers" from policy changes. Clearly, state officials are now much better prepared to understand their stake in federal programs and much better equipped to participate in debate on program change.

The availability of program benefit data on a state-by-state or city-by-city basis has brought a transformation of policy debates. More and more, the distributional consequences of present or proposed policies have become central issues in determining the desirability of such policies. Since virtually all taxing and spending policies have distributional effects that benefit some states and regions more than others, the number of proposals that are potential sources of state or regional conflict is very large. And since politicians can now easily develop and disseminate knowledge about those distributional consequences to potential coalition partners, the costs of coalition formation have been substantially reduced.

While it would be too much to suggest that traditional regional cleavages based on culture and economic structure have been supplanted, it is nevertheless true that the new sophistication has opened up new possibilities for regional coalitions built around the predicted consequences of specific programs. The coalitions that reflect the new regional consciousness in American public policy are far less predictable in structure and far more fluid in operational style than ever before. In their unpredictability and fluidity, their reliance on computerized information technology, and their use of mass media for formation, the new regional coalitions clearly reflect the emergence of a more sophisticated generation of topocrats who are ready, willing, and able to participate in determining national priorities.

SUMMARY: COALITIONS AND FEDERAL POLICY

Because public policies typically are clothed in statements of purpose, scholars often find it easy to explain policies simply by referring to the statements. Policy goals reflect problems to be solved, and policies are the means to solve problems; hence policies are "explained" as means aimed at ends. Attractive as it may be in our rationalist culture, this formulation is seriously deficient. Policies are purposive, but the pursuit of policy also distributes benefits. Few policies, furthermore, are neutral: Some allocate gains; some allocate losses; some allocate both. Potential winners and losers are important sources of support or opposition as well as shapers of program design. Failure to appreciate the distributional consequences of policies can seriously overestimate the role of rational analysis in policymaking and seriously underestimate the significance of advocacy in shaping solutions to public problems.

Advocates typically organize into coalitions that have horizontal and vertical components. Coalitions that are strong enough at one level of government to achieve their desired benefits operate primarily at that level. Coalitions that are too weak to achieve the desired benefits at one level, however, have other options. By seeking allies at higher or lower levels, these coalitions can gain sufficient strength to achieve some or all of the benefits they seek—often in the form of financial grants from a higher- to a lower-level unit. Financial aid often helps to avoid political problems by expressing agreements in dollars rather than clear statements of purpose. Political disagreements over purpose are replaced by agreements on dollar sums, leaving recipients of the dollars relatively free to use grants for their own purposes, while allowing contributing governments to claim credit for their "responsive" allocation of funds. Financial assistance programs are thus built on coalitions whose dimensions are both vertical, to aggregate the interests of multiple levels of government, and horizontal, to integrate those interests into a politically acceptable program. Problems that arise in the implementation of such programs often can be traced to inadequate consideration of one or both of these dimensions (Nathan, 1983).

For many years, scholars and journalists described the most common form of coalition as an iron triangle, sometimes referred to as a subgovernment. Triangular relationships among administrative agencies, congressional committees, and clientele groups controlled many federal programs for long periods of time, protecting both benefits and beneficiaries from interference. Although the iron triangle model continues to be relevant, newer forms of coalition have emerged in recent years. Single-issue coalitions, often using new communications and computer technologies, have become significant forces in setting the national political agenda.

As public policies have become more numerous and more complex, professional and technical experts from academia, law firms, and consulting firms have been drawn into the policy process, forming loosely structured issue networks or policy communities. Perhaps more important from a federal policy point of view, new coalitions of public officials have developed, some organized around local or state jurisdictions, others organized around geographically defined regions of the country. Originally stimulated by perceived imbalances in the flow of federal expenditures between the so-called Sunbelt and the Snowbelt, regional and jurisdictional coalitions have become established in national policymaking. Indeed, the professional and information resources available to these new coalitions, including sophisticated computer technology, now easily rival the resources available to national government agencies.

The spread of information processing capacity has dramatically reduced the costs of coalition formation. Information about the current or projected consequences of policy proposals is now routinely gathered by agencies such as the National Governors Association and distributed to state and local governments. Depending on whether the projected consequences are good or bad, states and their localities can determine their political strategies, including whether or not to seek allies to promote or prevent some policy. Since policies affect states in very different ways, coalitions can be very different from one issue to another.

More accurate and easily available information fuels the fluidity of federal policy coalitions by revealing distributional differences that can promote a search for new allies for each new issue. Thus, while there is clearly a new regionalism in federal policy coalitions, there is also a new sophistication, driven by new information technology, that promotes a state-centered coalition process. Tension between region and state, no less than tension between region and nation, continues to provide a strong source of political cleavage in the American polity.

REFERENCES

Anton, 1980. Thomas J. Anton. "Federal Assistance Programs: The Politics of System Transformation." In *National Resources and Urban Policy*, ed. Douglas E. Ashford. New York: Methuen.

Anton, 1985. Thomas J. Anton. "Decay and Reconstruction in the Study of American Intergovernmental Relations." *Publius* 15: 65–97.

Anton et al., 1980. Thomas J. Anton, Jerry P. Cawley, and Kevin L. Kramer. *Moving Money*. Cambridge, Mass.: Oelgeschlager, Gunn and Hain.

Anton and Reynolds, 1985. Thomas J. Anton and Rebecca Reynolds. "Old Federalism and New Policies for State Economic Development." Providence, R.I.: Taubman Center, Brown University, unpublished manuscript.

Beer, 1978. Samuel Beer. "Federalism, Nationalism, and Democracy." *American Political Science Review*. 72 (March): 9–21.

CBO, 1983. Congressional Budget Office. *Public Works Infrastructure Policy Considerations for the 1980's*. Washington, D.C.: Government Printing Office.

Congressional Record, October 1, 1982, S13020.

Cotter, 1984. Cornelius P. Cotter. *Party Organizations and American Politics*. New York: Praeger.

Derthick, 1975. Martha Derthick. *Uncontrollable Spending for Social Services Grants*. Washington, D.C.: The Brookings Institution.

Dommel et al., 1982. Paul R. Dommel and Associates. *Decentralizing Urban Policy: Case Studies in Community Development*. Washington, D.C.: The Brookings Institution.

Dye, 1985. Thomas R. Dye. "Federal Tax Reform: The View from the States." *Policy Studies Journal* Vol. 13, No. 3 (March): 547–567.

Eldersveld, 1982. Samuel Eldersveld. *Political Parties in American Society*. New York: Basic Books.

Fiorina, 1977. Morris Fiorina. "The Case of the Vanishing Marginals: The Bureaucracy Did It." *American Political Science Review* 7 (March): 177–181.

Fossett, 1983. James W. Fossett. *Federal Aid to Big Cities: The Politics of Dependence*. Washington, D.C.: The Brookings Institution.

Hadwiger and Talbot, 1982. Don F. Hadwiger and Ross B. Talbot. *Food Policy and Farm Programs*. New York: The Academy of Political Science.

Haider, 1974. Donald H. Haider. *When Governments Come to Washington: Governors, Mayors, and Intergovernmental Lobbying*. New York: Free Press.

Heclo, 1978. Hugh Heclo. "Issue Networks and the Executive Establishment." In *The New American Political System*, ed. Anthony King. Washington, D.C.: American Enterprise Institute for Public Policy Research.

Herbers, 1986. John Herbers. "States Forced into Lead on Housing for Poor." *New York Times*, March 24.

Kingdon, 1984. John W. Kingdon. *Agendas, Alternatives, and Public Policies*. Boston: Little, Brown.

Landy, 1984. Marc Landy. "Kentucky." In *The Political Life of the American States,* ed. Alan Rosenthal and Maureen Moakley. New York: Praeger.

Larkey, 1979. Patrick D. Larkey. *Evaluating Public Programs: The Impact of General Revenue Sharing on Municipal Government.* Princeton, N.J.: Princeton University Press.

Liebert, 1976. Roland J. Liebert. *Disintegration and Political Action: The Changing Functions of City Government in America.* New York: Academic Press.

Light, 1985. Paul Light. *Artful Work: The Politics of Social Security Reform.* New York: Random House.

Malcom, 1986. Andrew Malcom. "Stevenson Bars A Campaign with 2 Extremists on Slate." *New York Times,* March 21.

Monypenny, 1958. Phillip Monypenny. *The Impact of Federal Grants in Illinois.* Urbana: University of Illinois.

Monypenny, 1960. Phillip Monypenny. "Federal Grants-in-Aid to State Governments: A Political Analysis." *National Tax Journal* 13 (March): 1–16.

Morone and Dunham, 1984. James A. Morone and Andrew Dunham. "The Waning of Professional Dominance: DRGs and the Hospitals." *Health Affairs* 3 (Spring): 73–87.

Nathan, 1983. Richard P. Nathan. "State and Local Governments: A Political Analysis." *National Tax Journal* 13 (March): 1–16.

Peterson, 1981. Paul Peterson. *City Limits.* Chicago: University of Chicago Press.

Reagan and Sanzone, 1972. Michael D. Reagan, and John G. Sanzone. *The New Federalism,* 2d ed. New York: Oxford University Press.

Rich, 1985. Michael J. Rich. "Congress, the Bureaucracy and the Cities: Distributive Politics in the Allocation of Federal Grants-in-Aid for Community and Economic Development." Ph.D. dissertation, Northwestern University.

Rozoff, 1985. Jonathan M. Rozoff. "The United States Small Business Administration: Reaction and Redundancy." B.A. Thesis, Brown University.

Smith, 1984. Paul Smith. "New York." In *The Political Life of the American States,* ed. Alan Rosenthal and Maureen Moakley. New York: Praeger.

Truman, 1971. David B. Truman. *The Governmental Process: Political Interests and Public Opinion,* 2d ed. New York: Knopf.

Winters, 1984. Richard F. Winters. "New Hampshire." In *The Political Life of the American States,* ed. Alan Rosenthal and Maureen Moakley. New York: Praeger.

Wirt, 1980. Frederick Wirt. "Does Control Follow the Dollar? Value Analysis, School Policy and State-Local Linkages." *Publius* 10: 69–88.

Wolman and Teitelbaum, 1984. Harold Wolman and Fred Teitelbaum. "Interest Groups and the Reagan Presidency." In *The Reagan Presidency and the Governing of America,* ed. Lester Salamon and Michael Lund. Washington, D.C.: Urban Institute Press.

Wright, 1982. Deil S. Wright. *Understanding Intergovernmental Relations.* Monterey, Calif.: Brooks/Cole.

CHAPTER 5

DYNAMICS OF SYSTEM BEHAVIOR

Coalitions that come together to mobilize support for program benefits pursue a variety of strategies to achieve their objectives. Some strategies arise from early calculations of intent; others emerge from reactions of coalition partners or opponents; still others develop as unanticipated events force coalition members to adjust to circumstances that often change quite rapidly. This bumping around of coalitions and strategies usually appears quite chaotic, but in fact there are several distinct patterns of action in the development of federal policies. In this chapter we review the structural conditions that give rise to these patterns before proceeding to a consideration of the patterns themselves. The chapter concludes with a discussion of the difference between "change" and "reform" in order to appreciate why reform is so difficult in a system characterized by continuous change.

PERMANENT INSTABILITY

Scholars sometimes describe American political institutions as a "separation of powers," but that description is quite misleading. As John P. Roche has pointed out recently, our system is more accurately described as a separation of institutions, in which most powers are in fact shared by a multitude of agencies (Roche, 1986). Viewed horizontally, executive agencies exercise legislative power through devices such as the veto; legislatures exercise executive power when they approve or reject appointments; and courts exert judicial review over both executive and legislative actions. Viewed vertically, constitutional ambiguity (see Chapter 1) permits the national government to intervene in matters such as traffic regulation or public education that are not typically regarded as national responsibilities. Both authority—the right to act—and power—the ability to act—are thus diffused among numerous governmental units. Funding for public action is also typically shared among numerous units, encouraging the provision of many services that might be unavailable in the absence of funds from several separate governments. The organizations are separate and in many respects autonomous, but they share powers and funding in a system of extensive overlapping responsibilities.

These characteristics of American federalism imply that actors seeking public benefits have several avenues of access and influence. Executive hostility to some proposal may be countered by legislative warmth. Legislative reluctance may be overcome by recourse to court action. A benefit unobtainable from local authorities may be obtained from a state agency if allies can be found to add weight to a request. If even more allies can be found, national action can be organized to overcome local preferences. With so many areas in which to promote interests, those who know something about the variety of organizational preferences and rules clearly have an advantage. A sophisticated knowledge of this variety can maximize the probability of success in a given arena, and can convert local weakness into state or national strength, as Monypenny has shown (Chapter 4).

Apart from offering multiple opportunities for political access, the intermingling of powers and finances in American federal politics has another consequence of enormous significance: Power sharing guarantees that relations among governments will be permanently unstable. Because several governments share authority for police services, or education, or highways, government organizations frequently bump into one another. With each bump, an opportunity is provided to challenge or affirm existing understandings regarding who should do what, on whose budget. Even if routine bumping were less frequent than it is, annual budget cycles provide opportunities to question current understandings.

Budgets for virtually all major general purpose governments contain substantial amounts derived from other governments. Budget adjustments made by one unit thus can have major impacts on other units—for example, an increase or decrease in state aid for local schools can be the occasion for joy or despair among local school administrators. Such occasions arise with great frequency not only because budgets are mingled, but also because budget cycles are often different. The national fiscal year begins on October 1; some state and local governments have the same fiscal year, but most begin their fiscal years on July 1, while others begin on January 1, April 15, May 1, or other dates. Overlapping budgets that operate according to different cycles make certain that existing arrangements are always in question and always subject to change. Organizational and programmatic instability, in short, are built into the structure of American federal policymaking.

POLICY DYNAMICS: MODELS OF CHANGE

The Bottom-Up Model

Responses to permanent instability can take a variety of forms, of which the most common might be thought of as the *bottom-up* model. In this model a problem becomes identified at the local level, is gradually seen to have broader implications, before it is ultimately dealt with by some higher authority. One of the clearest statements of this model was provided by James L. Sundquist in his important study, *Making Federalism Work:*

> As a major internal problem develops—or comes to public attention—public attitudes appear to pass through three phases. As the problem begins to be recognized, it is seen as local in character, outside the national concern. Then, as it persists and as it becomes clear that the states and communities are unable to solve it unaided (partly because the same political groups that oppose federal action want to oppose state and local action too), the activists propose federal aid, but on the basis of helping the states and communities cope with what is still seen as their problem. Finally, the focus of basic responsibility shifts: the problem is recognized as in fact not local at all but as a national problem requiring a national solution that states and communities are mandated, by one means or another, to carry out—usually by inducements strong enough to produce a voluntary response but sometimes by more direct, coercive means. (Sundquist, with Davis, 1969, p. 11)

Bottom-up processes of this kind have been associated with many notable public programs. During the early part of this century, for example, many states enacted programs of assistance to mothers who lacked sufficient resources to care for their children. Later, when the Depression vastly increased the number of poor people in general as well as the number of needy mothers, the national government accepted some of this responsibility by enacting the Aid to Dependent Children program as part of the 1935 Social Security legislation. Now known as Aid to Families with Dependent Children, or AFDC, the program has become one of the largest social assistance programs in existence.

National housing assistance programs have similar origins, arising from innovative programs in states such as New York that were copied by the national government once housing became accepted as a national responsibility. Very similar histories define the development of many other programs, from child labor laws to social insurance to highway construction. All began as local responses to perceived problems before growing into accepted national responsibilities. Cities and states, in short, frequently have provided policy laboratories in which new ideas have been tested before being adopted for the entire nation.

Although bottom-up processes typically are initiated by public officials, citizens or representatives of nongovernmental organizations often provide initiatives that spread from local to state or national agendas. In states where extensive opportunities for citizen initiatives are provided by law, citizens are able to use established legal channels to help shape policy. Even in states without such provisions, normal political processes allow citizens to promote ideas that can be spread to wider jurisdictions. In Illinois, for example, a coalition of neighborhood groups recently persuaded the state legislature to enact a law limiting heating costs for the elderly to 12 percent of income (Herbers, 1985). Not infrequently, citizens who act as policy entrepreneurs of this kind are able to use their activities as a springboard to local or even higher-level public office.

Particularly in recent years, local policy experiments have been organized with the explicit purpose of assessing the state or national utility of some proposed program. Nonprofit foundations as well as other private agencies have provided considerable support for such efforts to give direction to national policy. One interesting example is the Manpower Development Research Corporation of New York City, which was founded in 1974 with support from the Ford Foundation to evaluate public job development programs. Among its more ambitious studies is an effort to evaluate "workfare" programs that require welfare recipients to take public service jobs as a condition of receiving welfare benefits. Workfare programs are politically controversial, but MDRC's analyses of their operation in several state and local jurisdictions has had a considerable impact on the way national policymakers think about the problem of the chronically unemployed. By serving as both supporters and chroniclers of local program initiatives, foundations provide other avenues through which local program experiences become sources of national policy.

The Top-Down Model

From time to time, events occur that produce a broad consensus for national action to deal with certain issues. Such occasions are characterized by widespread agreement that some set of observed conditions constitutes a national "problem," that the problem is serious enough to warrant public action, and that one or more solutions to the problem are both plausible and acceptable as national policy.

Because they are designed to stimulate national debate between competing political views, presidential elections often provide the vehicles through which national policy agreement is developed. Candidates for president offer different assessments of the national condition, based on their own perspectives on that condition. Normally, candidates also offer different program priorities to deal with the problems they have identified. After an exhaustive year-long campaign in which these alternative agendas are debated repeatedly in the national and regional media, voters choose both a president and the policy preferences he has expressed. Having shaped a national debate by articulating his own policy agenda, and having received enough popular support to be elected to office, a new president is entitled to believe he has a mandate to promote the program objectives articulated during the campaign (West, 1984).

Particularly during his first year in office, therefore, when campaign ideas are fresh and his mandate strong, a newly elected president often becomes the source of new federal programs (Light, 1982). New programs are devised, legislation is drafted, and congressional approval is sought by the new presidential team, often with minimal or no consultation with either Congress or the state and local officials who will later be expected to implement the programs. The initial results of this "top down" approach can be quite dramatic. Within months of assuming office, for example, President Reagan had cut more than $80 billion from President Carter's budget proposals, pressed Congress to enact the largest tax cut in American history, and begun moving toward his notion of a "new federalism" by consolidating some 57 federal grant programs into just 9 block grants.

While less successful than President Reagan, other recent presidents have been no less lofty in their aspirations. Within weeks of his assumption of office in 1964, Lyndon B. Johnson declared his Great Society, which included dozens of the programs later eliminated, reduced, or consolidated by Ronald Reagan. Similarly, Richard Nixon entered office with an ambitious program to rationalize, coordinate, and initiate federal grant programs that he also referred to as a New Federalism. Newly elected presidents, in short, try very hard to implement a perceived electoral mandate by initiating programs derived from the campaign agenda. Instead of bubbling up from below, these programs originate in Washington and are then handed to state and local governments for implementation.

Top-down programs, of course, are not solely a product of presidential initiative. Indeed, the notion of "presidential" initiative is itself ambiguous, since the presidency as an institution includes many career and appointed officials who serve as staff to the president. Many proposals initiated by a president, therefore, turn out to be proposals made by agency heads or political appointees that are part of the president's overall program. Often enough these are ideas with a long lineage; earlier studies, in past administrations, had examined some problem and offered the same solution. Most of President Reagan's budget reduction plans, for example, were considered in previous administrations (Stockman, 1986). To say that presidential initiative is an important source of top-down programs is to say that the officials who serve the president, and not the president alone, must be regarded as an important source of such proposals.

We should not assume, however, that the executive branch is the sole, or even the major, source of top-down policy. Much recent scholarship has underlined the significance of Congress, rather than the president, as policy initiator. Pious, for example, has argued that Congress has taken the initiative on many pieces of major legislation, such as social security, collective bargaining arrangements, public housing, atomic energy, the space program, the environment, and manpower training. In only a few domestic areas, such as civil rights and antipoverty legislation, have presidents played the leading role in policy initiation. And even in these fields Congress eventually dominates the process (Pious, 1975).

Whether Congress always "dominates" seems unclear (Rockman, 1984), but it is true that Congress is a major participant. Indeed, the ability of individual members of Congress to initiate new laws appears to have increased considerably in recent years with the erosion of both the seniority system and the control of party leaders over their congressional followers. New patterns of congressional behavior are characterized by greater activity by individual policy "entrepreneurs," who specialize in some policy issue, who often use their positions on subcommittees as platforms to generate publicity, and who skillfully exploit the media in pursuit of their objectives (Roberts, 1986).

In a fragmented institutional environment, individual legislators can have a major impact on national policy. Thus John Blatnick in the House or Edmund Muskie in the Senate were dominant figures in the shaping of national legislation to attack water and air pollution (ACIR, A-83, 1981), while Representative Lenore Sullivan was almost singlehandedly responsible for the Food Stamp program (Berry, 1982). Top-down policy, in short, has been as much a product of congressional entrepreneurship as executive initiative.

Nor should it be assumed that presidential elections are the only occasions that generate a national consensus for action. Unusual or unexpected events often create a pressure to act—to "do something"— that can lead to virtually instant policymaking. Consensus on the need for action in such situations typically confines advocacy to a search for solutions in the vicinity of existing problem areas, or to quick acceptance of the first proposal that seems reasonable. Actions taken under such pressure are likely to require renegotiation once the original source of pressure has abated. Thus, barely five years after enacting a substantial program for the production of synthetic fuels in the aftermath of the 1973 oil crisis, the entire program had been abandoned (Hershey, 1985). Sometimes pressure for public action grows more slowly, accumulating as a series of events gradually create both a national "mood" and latent coalitions in support of new policies.

Observers of the environmental protection legislation enacted in 1969 and 1970 often point to a new public mood that had been shaped by a series of events. "The Santa Barbara spill had just occurred, the Cuyahoga River had caught fire, and the news was laden with stories of environmental trauma" (Liroff, 1976). A nationwide celebration of Earth Day on April 22, 1970, helped to dramatize and focus these events, and create even more pressure for some form of public response. As Charles O. Jones has noted: ". . . in 1970 a majority seemingly awaited unspecified strong action. Thus, instead of a majority having to be established for a policy, a policy had to be constructed for a majority. Much that occurred within Congress as proposals escalated toward various actors' perceptions of what was necessary to meet public demands" (Jones, 1975).

Top-down policies, whether a result of political initiative or political response, often suffer from coalition fragility. The groups and individuals who come together quickly in response to some dramatic event may find there is little to hold them together once the event has faded from memory. Or a presidential mandate that seems clear the day after an election may begin to seem fuzzy when efforts are made to translate it into specific proposals. These problems are often exaggerated by the tendency of state or local governments to view top-down programs as "their" rather than "our" programs. Instead of incorporating them into ongoing routines, lower-level governments often make such programs into separate units, with separate budget accounts that can be abandoned if necessary. As the details of top-down programs become clear over time, state or local governments may withdraw their support and thus contribute to coalition collapse. Both the Law Enforcement Assistance Administration and the Comprehensive Employment and Training Assistance program, two innovations of the Nixon administration, suffered precisely this kind of loss and were terminated barely a decade after they began ("LEAA: The End Is Here," 1982; Franklin and Ripley, 1984). Top-down programs, in short, are not always easy to institutionalize, despite the drama that often attends their birth.

Scholars and politicians occasionally engage in heated arguments over the increasing prominence of the top-down pattern, which is alleged to be creating a far more centralized system than had existed in the past. Although it is true that the top-down pattern was prominent in the thirties and again in the sixties, it is also true that the bottom-up pattern has continued to flourish. At any given time, therefore, both patterns are likely to be active. Over time it appears that periods of top-down prominence are often succeeded by periods of bottom-up prominence, creating cyclical patterns of federal policymaking. The notion that an increasingly centralized policy system is inevitable because of social and technological trends continues to be popular, but it is contradicted by the cycles that have marked our history. Indeed, by making information available nationally on a virtually instantaneous basis, modern technology appears to have encouraged policy initiation through processes that are neither top-down nor bottom-up.

Diffusion Models

It is often very difficult in practice to distinguish between programs that are initiated from the bottom up and those that flow from the top down. Some programs emerge from processes in which national, state, and local actors are equal participants. Others emerge only after one level of government, then another, assumes the initiative. Still others appear to emerge in bunches, with a number of different government agencies taking similar actions, for similar reasons, at about the same point in time. Communication technologies which provide virtually instant reports of problems and solutions across the entire nation allow policy "bunches" to form more and more frequently. Neither top-down nor bottom-up, these kinds of processes can be regarded as products of *policy diffusion*.

Jack L. Walker's pathbreaking analysis of policy innovation in the states has given us a valuable insight into diffusion processes (Walker, 1969). Walker was interested in identifying and explaining patterns of policy initiation that he believed characterized the behavior of different states. By recording the time of enactment of state legislation in 88 different policy areas, for all states, across a period of several decades, Walker was able to document some interesting patterns. Some states were consistently early in adopting new programs, others were consistent laggards, and others varied in their receptivity to new programs depending on the nature of the program, political developments, and other factors.

Walker's explanation for these patterns was ingeniously simple: States copied what other states were doing. Walker found that state officials across the country tended to place themselves in "leagues" made up of states they thought were similar to their own. Confronted by some new issue or request for action, officials usually contacted other states in their league to see what they were doing. A program operating in a comparable state thus became a model that could be copied by others in the same league, and eventually by other states as well. Over a wide range of policy areas, therefore, a politics of emulation was apparent, structuring patterns of innovation of considerable complexity:

> The process we have been describing is extremely complex; many influences shape decisions to adopt innovations and no two ideas diffuse in exactly the same way. In all cases, however, the likelihood of a state adopting a new program is higher if other states have already adopted the idea. The likelihood becomes higher still if the innovation has been adopted by a state viewed by key decision makers as a point of legitimate comparison. Decision makers are likely to adopt new programs, therefore, when they become convinced that their state is relatively deprived, or that some need exists to which other states in their "league" have already responded. (Walker, 1969, pp. 896–897)

Although not without flaws (Gray, 1973), Walker's analysis seems as sound intuitively as it is persuasive empirically. Faced with situations that lack precedent, it makes sense for officials to find out what other jurisdictions have done, and it makes equal sense to focus the search on states that are most like one another. Twenty years later, of course, emulation has become easier. Television can transmit a sense of policy urgency almost immediately, new computer technologies can transmit information just as quickly, and the new professional organizations that have developed to service state and local officials provide a guarantee that these new technologies will be used.

During the 1980s, policy searches routinely canvass all the states, not just a few, and policy ideas diffuse quite rapidly. In the aftermath of the severe recession of 1981–82, for example, states rushed to enact a variety of new economic development policies, often copied from other states, including some 1,300 "enterprise zones" established by 524 local jurisdictions in some 25 states (Anton and Reynolds, 1985; Hansen, 1983). An even more dramatic example of diffusion was the virtual explosion of legislative interest in laws requiring hospital officials to solicit organ donations from families of dead or dying patients. No state had enacted such a law prior to 1986. Between January and June of 1986, however, some fifteen states enacted "routine request" laws, legislation had been introduced in sixteen other states, and the drafting process was under way in two others (Malcolm, 1986). The desirability of organ donation clearly was an idea whose time had come—an "idea in good currency," to borrow Donald Schon's phrase—and the states virtually jumped at the opportunity to make new laws (Schon, 1971). Similarly rapid diffusion processes have been documented by Savage for policies as different as sunset laws, child passenger restraint laws, and defective product laws (Savage, 1985).

The diffusion model is interesting not just because it seems to capture the ability of new technologies to reflect public desires quite rapidly; policy diffusion also says something important about the quality of leadership in American federal politics. Innovation in any governmental unit requires political leadership, and to the extent that the enactment of new policies is diffused, so too is the capacity for political leadership. In reflecting on the recent spate of economic development policies enacted by states, for example, Anton and Reynolds state:

> The emergence of states as leaders in articulation, mobilization and innovation in economic development policy suggests that we need something like a "magnet" model to account for leadership patterns in American federal politics. That is, on issues for which there is agreement for action, that action will move to the political units whose energy generates the most activity and thus the greatest claim to leadership. Policy leadership, in short, is attracted to officials who try to make policy. Since it is activity rather than position that defines leadership, local and state agencies are as able to assume leadership as federal agencies, particularly since states and localities now have the professional and financial resources necessary to perform leadership functions persuasively. And, because leadership levels may change, leadership on any given issue may shift from one unit or group of units to another, as the issue evolves through the policy cycle. Over time, many different units are likely to assume leadership functions as some units reduce and others increase their activity. Thus, the present pattern of state dominance in economic policy innovation may well be followed by other patterns that give more prominence to local, federal, or county agencies. Leadership patterns, from this point of view, reflect the fluid dynamism of the society as a whole. (Anton and Reynolds, 1985)

THE POLITICS OF PROGRAM DEVELOPMENT: CASE STUDIES

Program Contingency

Enactment of a new program is only one step in a process that begins in recognition of some condition as a "problem" and continues through the actual delivery of some benefit to an individual or an organization. To appreciate the activity that takes place after a program has been enacted, however, it is necessary to challenge the widely accepted idea that it is extraordinarily difficult to eliminate or change a program once it has been put in place (Kaufman, 1976). Reports of heavy-handed bureaucrats, blindly following an outdated administrative book rather than coping with current problems, occur with sufficient frequency to lend credibility to the idea of program and organizational immortality, but in fact the idea is quite wrong. Federal programs in particular are likely to be in constant flux precisely because they involve the joint action of several government units, each of which has different constituents, budgets, and procedural norms. It is more realistic and more useful analytically to view all programs as contingent rather than permanent.

The contingent view is based on the extensively documented relationship between politics and program design (Anton, 1980). Recall (Chapter 4) that federal programs often emerge from coalitions that are too weak to achieve their ends within a single jurisdiction. By joining together in search of higher-level support, weak local or state coalitions can gain strength and obtain benefits they desire from higher units. Recall too that the typical price of such political success is program vagueness: To enact a new policy, program objectives must be stated in terms broad enough to attract a majority coalition. Policy purposes are thus defined with deliberate vagueness—to "provide a decent home" or to "fight crime"—and the policy mechanism is often money, which can be used in a variety of ways once it is delivered to a beneficiary. On occasions when policy objectives are given with greater clarity, other mechanisms are used to gather coalition support, such as defining eligibility in the broadest possible terms (Stein, 1984).

In many cases, therefore, the politicians who provide a benefit in the form of a new program quite literally do not know what specific actions will be taken, by which organizations or individuals, in pursuit of what specific definition of public purpose. In these situations, the "program" enacted by some new piece of legislation or new administrative order may be hardly more than a blank page to be filled in by those who actually administer the new activity.

Political Skill and Program Change

Although filling in the blanks is usually done by program managers who have administrative titles in government organizations, the activity itself is supremely political. Because purposes are so often either unclear or contradictory, implementation rules cannot be simply derived from legislative language. Moreover, the coalition that came together to enact the program can gain or lose strength. If strength is lost, the program itself may be threatened and ultimately terminated. How then do bureaucrats responsible for implementation deal with their ambiguous and insecure position?

Clever program managers who understand the fragility of new programs repeatedly have been observed to follow two simple but effective political rules: (1) cultivate the original coalition, and (2) expand the coalition. Administrators cultivate their coalitions by seeing to it that supporters of the program and those in a position to affect its future receive benefits. Legislators who support the program with votes or executives who support it through testimonials are consulted frequently and, whenever possible, allocated benefits. Administrators expand their support coalitions by expanding the number of beneficiaries as much as they can. Restrictive statements of purpose are loosened; narrow definitions of eligibility are broadened; focused benefit distributions become more inclusive. In time, legislative support expands well beyond a simple majority to include all the lawmakers whose districts gain from the program. As benefits spread to include more and different jurisdictions, conceptions of program purposes change. This phenomenon of spreading is often associated with the phenomenon of program instability, as new beneficiaries are justified. As I have suggested elsewhere: "In the beginning the purpose of the coalition may be the program, but, over time, the purpose of the program is the coalition" (Anton et al., 1980, p. 122).

The process of cultivating and expanding a program coalition carries within it the seeds of its own demise. As a program becomes broader in eligibility and looser in purpose, groups of beneficiaries find their interests more and more difficult to reconcile with those of other groups of beneficiaries. One or more such groups may seek to redefine the program to better fit its interests, thus threatening the interests of other coalition members. In either case, the support coalition is weakened. Similarly, legislators whose votes are necessary for continuation gradually discover that programs of ambiguous purpose but broad eligibility severely restrict their abilities to control or claim credit for program benefits. Under those conditions, incentives for continued support are weakened, and legislators terminate the program or seek to reassert control (as well as their ability to claim credit) by imposing more restrictive purposes and eligibility criteria (Stein, 1984). These constraints define a new program, with a different support coalition, and the process of cultivation and expansion begins once again.

Recent studies by a number of scholars have given us new and helpful insights into these policy cycles. In his careful examination of the hypothesis that political factors (such as membership on authorizing or appropriating committees) affect benefit distributions, for example, Michael Rich discovered that political factors were indeed important, but their importance varied with the political context. As he writes:

> The political variables were found to be statistically significant more frequently during the initial years of a program and during those times when program continuation was being seriously challenged by either the president or the Congress, periods in which the nurturing of legislative coalitions are most important. (Rich, 1985, p. 292)

These findings are very much like Robert Stein's report of his study of federal benefits over a 35-year period. According to Stein, most federal aid programs begin as narrow, conditional grants, but

> . . . with time, narrow purpose project grants with high application costs evolve
> into broad based, non-conditional entitlements and block grants. Moreover,
> participation and legislative support for these programs similarly grows from
> small sized minimum winning coalitions to oversized and eventually universal
> coalitions. (Stein, 1984)

In other words, the political imperative to spread benefits is important
during the early years of a program, when majority coalitions must be built
and sustained, and during periods when criticism leads to a search for
even larger coalitions to support program continuation. During less
threatened periods, as Anagnoson and others have suggested, benefit
allocations are more likely to reflect bureaucratic desires to achieve
designated agency purposes (Anagnoson, 1980; Rundquist, 1980). Interacting across time, these perspectives appear to produce patterns of
expansion followed by stability or decline in program benefits.

Oppenheim has proposed a useful conceptualization of these cycles in
his analysis of FMHA and SBA disaster assistance programs. Arguing that
federal disaster assistance ". . . emerges from a series of policy cycles that
have identifiable characteristics," Oppenheim proceeds to identify those
characteristics:

> First, triggered by a natural disaster, there is a policy surge at the federal level:
> wide-spread expressions of concern are quickly responded to with the liberali-
> zation of program procedures. Next, there is a period of spreading, as aid for
> specific disaster situations is generalized on the grounds that equal benefits
> should be distributed to all disaster events. Third there is a period of reform,
> often following reports of inappropriate uses of program funds, in which
> program rules are adjusted to prevent continued high rates of spending. The
> length of the cycle period ranges from a matter of months to years, depending
> on disaster activity, organizational influence, and user demand. (Oppenheim,
> 1983, p. 173)

Oppenheim based his conceptualization on observations of disaster
assistance programs, but his model of "surge, spread, and reform" seems
to fit a large number of federal programs. It is a particularly fitting
complement to the work of scholars such as Rich or Stein, both of whom
examined program development for decades and thus were able to observe
cycles very similar to the Oppenheim model. To further illustrate these
policy cycles, let us observe three different federal activities in somewhat
more detail. The first is the planning assistance program authorization by
Section 701 of the 1954 Housing Act, which was an effort by the national
government to encourage local and state governments to improve their
planning capacities. The second is the Law Enforcement and Assistance
Administration, which supported a series of programs to help local and
state government fight crime. Finally, we examine the Community Development Block Grant program, enacted in 1974 to help local governments
improve and preserve their communities. These activities are all "federal"

in the sense of involving joint actions by national, state, and local governments, but they are aimed at different issues, they have been funded at very different levels, and they have had different political histories— indeed, two of them no longer exist. They offer instructive insights into the contingent quality of federal programs.

701: The Rise and Fall of Technical Assistance

The 1954 Housing Act was a major statement of national goals that introduced the concept of urban renewal to American urban policy. To qualify for support from the urban renewal program, communities had to indicate that they met seven conditions of a nationally defined "workable program," including a requirement that the community have a master plan to guide development. National officials, of course, knew that few local governments had developed master plans. To encourage them to do so, Section 701 of the Act created a program of local planning assistance through which the national government agreed to pay 50 percent of the cost of preparing a local plan.

Since a plan was required for an acceptable "workable program," communities that wanted urban renewal funds could not avoid the effort. But the 50 percent local share was not required to be made in hard cash. Many communities were thus able to generate a plan at little or no cost to themselves. The national desire for local planning reflected judgments about what was required for best use of federal dollars as well as the capacities of most local governments. In this sense, 701 rightfully may be regarded as a technical assistance program, designed to encourage and support lower-level capabilities rather than to distribute political rewards through the classic pork barrel.

What pattern of development might be anticipated for a technical assistance program? One might anticipate that program growth would be related to technical achievements, monitored through careful estimates of expenditure and performance over time, with spurts resulting from technical breakthroughs or new problem discoveries. Figure 5.1 charts the growth in national appropriations for the 701 program from 1954 through 1972 and in doing so casts considerable doubt on the "technical" model of program growth.

For the entire period, the familiar ratchet of public expenditure increase is apparent: A period of slow or moderate growth is followed by a large increase, which in turn is followed by another relatively stable period, and so on. Note, however, the timing of the major increases. Appropriations more than doubled in 1960 and again in 1962; a very large increment was achieved in 1968; appropriations were again doubled in 1972, when funds appropriated exceeded $100 million for the first time. This is hardly a large federal program—total accumulated appropriations through 1974 amounted to barely $500 million—and it is nominally a purely technical assistance program. But three of the years in which a major appropriations increase occurs were presidential election years, and the fourth happened to be a congressional election year. The pattern hardly seems coincidental.

Closer examination of the program changes associated with appropriations increases offers some insight into the character of this pattern. As originally enacted, 701 provided planning assistance funds for communities of 25,000 or fewer persons and for state, metropolitan, or regional agencies engaged in urban planning. In 1959 eligible recipients were broadened to include cities of less than 50,000 population, groups of adjacent municipalities with less than 50,000 persons, and state planning agencies "for state and interstate comprehensive planning." Other amendments increased the national share from one-half to two-thirds (1961) and authorized grants for all counties (regardless of size); agencies established by interstate contract; Indian tribes; regional agencies; the Appalachian Regional Commission; areas affected by growing federal installations; areas affected by declining federal installations; and even for areas affected by international treaties. By 1970 it was difficult to find an agency that was not eligible for 701 assistance. Like other experienced federal bureaucrats, 701 program managers clearly were eager to expand the constituency of the program in order to insure continued political support. As one clientele group was satisfied, another was added or earlier constituencies were redefined to expand the base of support. More than 6,000 of the nation's general purpose local governments had received 701 support by 1970, along with a myriad of other county, state, regional, and interstate organizations.

Bureaucratic cultivation of clientele groups, of course, is typically associated with equally solicitous cultivation of relevant members of Congress. A review of 701 grants by state reveals that the average accumulated grants to states represented on the relevant congressional appropriations committees was considerably higher than the cumulative average for the fifty states (Table 5.1). Average accumulated grants to states whose representatives were actually present at appropriations hearings, moreover, were considerably higher than grants to states whose representatives were absent and far exceeded the all-state average. Since these are cumulative figures and since the number of states represented changed somewhat over time, it seems apparent that program managers gave very careful consideration to the concerns of committee members. Of the 1972 appropriation of some $102 million, for example, more than $56 million went to the eleven states represented on the HUD, Space, Science, and Veterans Subcommittee—including substantial grants to such "urban" states as Mississippi, Indiana, Maine, and Nebraska, each of which had long-term and powerful representation on the Appropriations Committee.

Careful cultivation of the "right" legislators coupled with broad distribution of 701 funds discouraged serious review of the program until the late 1960s, when some officials began to wonder what distinguished this planning program from the dozens of others supported by the national

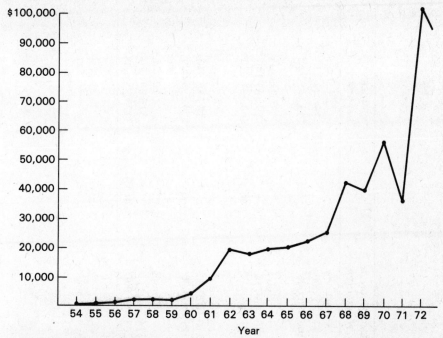

Figure 5.1 *Comprehensive Planning Assistance Grant Program, 1954–1974* **(Dollars in thousands)**

SOURCE: Appropriations based on figures from: *The Budget of the United States* 1954–74 (Washington, D.C.: Government Printing Office, 1956–1974) for fiscal year ending June 30 (actual expenditure).

government. This was a difficult question to answer, because the concept of "planning" itself resisted easy definition. It was even more difficult to establish that the varied activities conducted with "urban planning" grants had accomplished very much, other than providing a technical justification for obtaining still other federal grants. When a major new program for cities was enacted in 1974 (see below), one major justification for a separate "urban" planning program was undermined and a concerted drive began to eliminate the program. Led by successive presidents, the drive was resisted by Congress, which agreed to reduce appropriations but not to terminate the program. By 1981, however, a new president with a determination to reduce domestic expenditures overcame the severely weakened congressional coalition: 701 was terminated in October 1981.

LEAA: Design for a Money Shovel

In many respects the Law Enforcement Assistance Administration (LEAA) program, created in 1968, contrasts sharply with 701. Whereas 701 began as a small appendage to a larger and broader program (urban renewal),

Table 5.1 701 Grants to All States and "Represented" States

YEAR	ALL STATES AND TERRITORIES[a]	U.S. ONLY[a]	MEMBERS ON APPROPRIATIONS[a]	MEMBERS AT HEARINGS[a]
1968	54 states and terrs. $3,614,203 $191,271,000[b]	50 states and D.C. $3,778,627	25 states $4,335,800 $108,395,000[b] (55%)	11 states $3,942,720 $43,369,920[b] (22%)
1970	54 states and terrs. $5,292,629 $285,802,000[b]	50 states and D.C. $5,522,294	21 states $6,268,714 $131,642,944[b] (46%)	7 states $9,483,140 $66,381,980[b] (23%)
1972	55 states and terrs. $7,718,018 $424,491,000[b]	50 states and D.C. $8,196,784	18 states $10,102,500 $181,845,000[b] (43%)	7 states $13,556,570 $94,895,900[b] (22%)
1974	55 states and terrs. $10,726,200 $589,941,000[b]	50 states and D.C. $11,398,607	18 states $14,944,111 $268,944,000[b] (46%)	10 states $15,981,200 $159,981,200[b] (27%)

[a] Average federal grant.
[b] Cumulative total.

SOURCE: Thomas J. Anton. "Federal Assistance Programs: The Politics of System Transformation." From *National Resources and Urban Policy*, ed. Douglas E. Ashford. New York: Methuen, 1980, p. 30. Reprinted by permission of Methuen & Co.

LEAA was itself the larger and broader program. Whereas 701 was introduced without fanfare or much public notice, LEAA emerged from the currents of presidential politics in which one attorney general was charged with "softness" and promises were made to bring in a tougher man to deal with the wave of urban riots that had become an election year issue. Whereas 701 appeared to be a narrowly defined grant program, requiring formal application, extended negotiations with national bureaucrats, and extensive reporting after receipt of the grant, LEAA was basically a block grant that left considerable discretion in the hands of state and local officials.

Some 65 percent of LEAA Action Grant funds were to be made available to state and local governments according to population, with the remainder to be allocated at the discretion of national officials. Within each state, funds were to be disbursed by state planning agencies after receipt of applications from local governments. The only control available to national officials was a statewide comprehensive plan, prepared annually, that required federal approval before grants could be disbursed. Finally, whereas 701 was a small program, LEAA appropriations began at just over $60 million and increased dramatically to more than $850 million in just five years. Later increases confirmed that both Congress and the Justice Department were serious about spending money to "fight crime."

These differences aside, LEAA seemed in other respects similar to 701. Lacking an operational definition of what it meant to "fight crime," apart from a vague list of eligible activities that seemed all-inclusive, the statute placed heavy emphasis on a "planning" strategy. The national policy was to

> . . . assist state and local governments in strengthening and improving law enforcement on every level by national assistance, it is the purpose of this title to (1) encourage states and units of general local government to prepare and adopt comprehensive plans based upon their evaluations of state and local problems of law enforcement; (2) authorize grants to states and units of local government in order to improve and strengthen law enforcement; and (3) encourage research and development directed toward the improvement of law enforcement. (U.S. Congress, 1968)

Since most states did not have the planning agencies required by the act, the first LEAA appropriation provided $19 million to get them started. Not surprisingly, all states rushed to obtain their share of the planning funds, which were quickly consumed as the states began to develop plans for improving law enforcement. Within six months of the time when all states were reported to have created planning agencies, all state plans had been approved, including one in excess of 6,000 pages submitted by California. Within another six months nearly 250 million grant dollars were on their way to state and local governments to fund the activities proposed by the states. Within five years, appropriations had grown to nearly $900 million.

Although spawned in the drama of a presidential campaign and designed to bring every state into a supportive coalition, LEAA suffered from two major political defects that became apparent as expenditures reached high levels. The first was the design of the program itself. By distributing most of the money by formula and establishing universal eligibility for all states, the program virtually eliminated any role for Congress. Representatives could neither claim credit for the dollars flowing into their jurisdictions nor exert control over decisions that were made by state and local agencies according to plans approved by the Department of Justice. Members of Congress had to vote to supply funds, however, and it was clear that they were troubled over their lack of control.

From the beginning, individuals such as Senator John McClennan (D-Arkansas) expressed concern over the capacity of states to use such large sums effectively. Questioning Attorney General Mitchell, McClennan wondered whether the states had "sufficient" experience: ". . . in other words, are they prepared to utilize more money . . . or had we better watch it and make them demonstrate the effectiveness of their plans before we give them more money" (U.S. Senate, 1969). Mitchell and later program managers insisted that grants would be used "for the requisite purposes," but how could LEAA administrators know? LEAA approval of state plans came before rather than after expenditures were made, leaving national officials little effective leverage once the dollars had left Washington. In a knowledgeable exchange with the third LEAA administrator, Jerris Leonard, Democratic Congressman Neal Smith clarified the problem:

> What I am really getting at is this—and other members tell me that they hear the same thing—it's not a matter of illegal expenditure of funds. In fact, the act itself is very vague. The guidelines are rather loose. If you are too strict in enforcing guidelines, they complain about red tape. If you are not strict enough, anybody who wants some money comes in under the name of law enforcement and makes application. This is what has been happening. . . . What goes on is that they find out the big money now is coming from LEAA. So if they need some money, they figure out an application which can be put under that program. (U.S. Congress, 1972)

If formula funding and universal eligibility weakened support in Congress, vague program purposes similarly weakened support among other members of the original LEAA coalition. The state agencies that distributed LEAA funds were themselves coalitions of the more prominent components of each state's criminal justice system. Inevitably, therefore, the more powerful elements in these state coalitions wound up with disproportionate shares of the state's allocation. In time, support for LEAA among these less powerful components gave way to efforts to form coalitions that could guarantee funding for "their own" interests.

Members of Congress seeking greater control over the LEAA program were natural coalition partners in such efforts. Between 1970 and 1976

Congress added new programs or earmarked portions of LEAA funds for prisons, juvenile justice, and neighborhood crime prevention, none of which had been given high priority by the police and court organizations that tend to dominate state systems of law enforcement. Thus by 1976 LEAA had become a general grant program in which separate allocations were set aside for various beneficiaries, rather than a block grant, through a process that the ACIR has labeled "creeping categorization." Congressional interest in reasserting control was combined with beneficiary interest in narrower definitions of program purpose to undermine the original LEAA coalition.

Having lost support among beneficiary and congressional supporters, LEAA proceeded to lose its most important supporter when Jimmy Carter used the 1976 presidential campaign to attack the program. Unable to offer persuasive evidence that its grants had been effective in attacking crime, and burdened by charges of wasteful spending for "Dick Tracy" gadgets, LEAA proved unable to survive the Carter presidency. Funds for the major grant programs were eliminated in the 1980 budget, and no funds at all were requested in the 1981 budget. An effort was made to revive the coalition, led by state attorneys general, the National Governors Association, and the American Bar Association, but the effort was unsuccessful (Cohodos, 1980). On March 20, 1982, all remaining LEAA personnel were either transferred to related law enforcement agencies or laid off ("LEAA: The End Is Here," 1982). After an effective life of little more than a decade, from fiscal 1969 through fiscal 1979, LEAA had ceased to exist.

The Community Development Block Grant

One product of President Nixon's effort to create a New Federalism through program consolidation and decentralization was the Community Development Block Grant, created in 1974. Although technically a new program, CDBG was a consolidation of eight older programs that had been enacted at various times to deal with the problems of poverty and deterioration that plagued large cities. Stein's recent analysis of the development of those programs reveals familiar patterns. In each case

> Program spending increased dramatically, as did the scope of eligible recipients for each program. Similarly, program requirements declined with time, culminating in the adoption of the 1974 block grant. Interestingly, a number of grants expanded eligibility by establishing special provisions and funds for targeted recipients. Amendments to the Open-Space program established funding for both urban and low-income communities without reducing outlays for other eligible recipients. Similar amendments in 1966 to the 1949 Housing Act extended the Urban Renewal Act to "smaller cities." Program use was extended in the case of the Model Cities program by limiting the amount of aid money any one state could receive. These cases suggest that a shift towards less restrictive broad based aid programs can also be achieved in a less direct fashion through administrative regulation. (Stein, 1984, p. 23)

Despite these patterns of decreasing constraints, broadened eligibility and expanded funding, the eight programs retained features the Nixon administration regarded as undesirable. Application, reporting, and auditing requirements were extensive enough to discourage many communities from participating in the programs, and national bureaucrats were unnecessarily involved in decisions the administration believed to belong properly to local officials. The consolidated CDBG program, accordingly, reduced application requirements drastically, essentially eliminated national review of these minimal applications, and offered guidelines that, according to Dommel

> . . . were defined so generally in terms of broad national objectives and a long list of eligible activities that at the outset of the program recipient communities enjoyed considerable latitude in deciding on the specific kinds and mix of activities they would fund. With the exception of model cities, the grants consolidated into the CDBG had been more specific about what activities would be federally funded. In addition, the two major consolidated programs, urban renewal/neighborhood development and model cities, implied that some parts of the city were to be excluded from the programs. Such geographic constraints were initially absent from the block grant program. Thus in two important areas, what to do and where to do it, local governments had considerably more discretion under the block grant. A community could carry out housing rehabilitation if it wished; it could give rehabilitation assistance in the form it chose—loans, grants, interest subsidies, loan guarantees or combinations of these; it could set the income eligibility standards for assistance. Alternatively, it could put all its entitlement into a flood control project if that were an urgent community need, and the project could be planned and engineered without step-by-step federal control. . . . In short, in the important areas of project choices, project location, and organizational arrangements, local governments enjoyed considerable freedom of choice. (Dommel, 1982, pp. 45–46)

This initial freedom from national constraint, coupled with a threefold increase in the number of communities receiving CDBG funds in the first year of the program, created a political problem that will now also seem familiar. On the one hand, congressional concern over program control became very visible, as evidenced in a remark made by Senator William Proxmire (D-Wisconsin) to a CDBG official in 1976: "What isn't clear is whether the program that you have been administering is the program Congress passed" (quoted in Dommel, 1982, p. 45). On the other hand, important beneficiary groups became disaffected and sought to alter the benefit distribution. Many of the communities designated as "entitlement" communities in the CDBG program were suburbs and smaller cities, particularly in the South and West, which had never before received federal assistance. At the same time, many older cities in the North and East received less from the CDBG formula than they had been receiving from the eight consolidated programs. Although good politics from the point of view of the Nixon and Ford administrations, many of whose supporters were found in suburbs and smaller cities, the CDBG program also created losers who would be certain to express concern over their losses.

The opportunity to express that concern came very quickly. In 1976 Jimmy Carter was elected president with substantial support from the big cities that were big losers under CDBG. Carter's receptivity to big city interests, coupled with congressional interest in asserting greater control over program spending, led to formula changes in 1977 that allocated a greater share of CDBG funds to the older cities that had been the major targets of previous urban assistance efforts. Tighter constraints and reporting requirements were also enacted in order to assure local compliance with federal goals of providing assistance to low-income groups, thus substantially reducing local spending discretion.

As Stein has pointed out, however, these changes were accomplished without reducing the level of participation in CDBG by the suburban and small city jurisdictions that had become new recipients of federal aid (Stein, 1984). Thus, both older and newer beneficiaries had reason to continue their support of the modified program. Later efforts by the Reagan administration to reduce application and reporting requirements —which would have reinstated the 1974 program design—have been consistently rebuffed by Congress, although funding for the program has been reduced somewhat. In the mid-1980s, CDBG continues to be a major component of federal urban policy.

REVISITING THE DYNAMICS OF PROGRAM IMPLEMENTATION

Beneficiaries vs. Purpose

Earlier I drew on studies by Rich, Oppenheim, and Stein to offer an initial model of federal policy dynamics built on the concepts of "surge, spread, and reform." The preceding review of the three programs gives us a closer look at the forces that drive events which occur after a policy has been enacted. Federal program managers typically are handed policy assignments that allow them considerable discretion, either because statements of purpose are imprecise and thus have to be developed in practice, or because more precise objectives have to be applied to very different environments.

In considering how to exercise discretion, program managers typically follow the politically wise course of concerning themselves as much with the supporters as with the purposes of a program. To satisfy the coalition, program benefits are allocated to supporters as much as possible; to sustain the coalition, benefits are "spread" to additional beneficiaries who can then provide additional increments of support that will allow the benefits to continue. These coalition maintenance and expansion activities are not automatic; they must be carefully attended to by persons familiar with both the vertical and horizontal dimensions of the coalition. If they are not paid sufficient attention, or if they are not dealt with skillfully, the coalition may fall apart and benefits may cease. Successful programs, in short, generate their own constituencies.

Several important consequences follow from this focus on the "who" as well as the "what" of program development. One is that federal program purposes are inherently unstable across time. As new allies are brought into the supporting coalition by spreading benefits more broadly, eligibility criteria are redefined and program constraints—where they exist—are loosened. In time, original intentions fade and new definitions are developed to justify the current distribution of benefits. Programs thus define themselves as they go along, often changing dramatically in the process. A second consequence is that all programs are vulnerable to invasion by temporarily "hot" issues, which in turn causes considerable duplication. If the currently hot issue is energy, many programs will focus on the environment; if it is discrimination, many programs will embrace affirmative action; and so on. At any given time, therefore, there will be many programs devoted to the same set of objectives, rather than a single one.

Ultimately, of course, tension between purpose and beneficiary becomes unavoidable. Larger and larger coalitions necessarily include more diverse groups, whose common interest is increasingly difficult to discern. At the same time, fuzzy constraints make it increasingly difficult for officials to control or benefit from program activities. Under these conditions, some coalition members will strike out on their own to improve their benefits, while other members will assert greater control over the flow of benefits. The common ground for both groups of members is reform, in which stricter eligibility standards and clearer definitions of purpose are used to reshape the coalition.

What is really at stake in reform, typically, is a shift of control from bureaucratic to legislative actors at the horizontal level, accompanied by a restriction of benefit flows to more clearly demarcated groups at the vertical level. Clarification reduces the size of the coalition, restricts benefits, and thus sets the stage for the development cycle to repeat itself. Although cycles of surge, spread, and reform vary a great deal in length and by program, and are frequently interrupted entirely by program termination, the underlying mechanism driving these processes is the same: the search for support for some desired benefit.

Reform vs. Change

Changes in program design in the wake of coalition change occur constantly in American federal politics. Vast differences in socioeconomic conditions from one part of the nation to another cause different problems to appear on political agendas, producing a never-ending supply of solutions to be copied or modified in other jurisdictions. Implementing those solutions, however, usually requires cooperation from some other government in the form of funding, administrative help, or both. The search for cooperation—or the pursuit of conflict—is guaranteed by irregular budget cycles that force some units to respond to the actions of other units, whether or not there is initial agreement on the desirability of action. Unending supplies of problems and solutions combine with repeated cycles of action and response to produce a system whose major characteristic is constant change.

Coalitions are always in motion, some growing stronger while others grow weaker, which means that the programs they support also are always in motion. Tending to the changing needs of coalition partners is a constant preoccupation of public officials, who can be successful only if they possess high levels of intellectual flexibility and the communication skills necessary to maintain relationships with all the coalition partners. Whether or not they believe in reform ideologically, all American public officials are forced by the circumstances of their work to be reformers.

It seems fair to ask, however, whether in fact any of this frenetic activity constitutes reform. Real reform, one might argue, requires something more than annual or biennial tinkering with programs, in an ad hoc way, to reflect some change in coalition composition. From a "rational analysis" point of view, certainly, the processes described here might better be called change rather than reform, since there is little evidence of precise program goals, careful evaluation of the extent to which goals are achieved, or analyses of alternative mechanisms that might be utilized to pursue identified goals. Even if all these ad hoc changes were added together, furthermore, they would still not constitute reform because they reflect piecemeal adjustments rather than efforts to restructure the federal system as a whole. The system is fluid enough, but a rationalist might well suggest that directionless and uncoordinated fluidity should not be given the label *reform*.

There are a number of appropriate responses to this rationalist critique. One is that it overlooks the extent to which a series of small changes, extended far enough in time, often produce major results—in recent political history, we can look at the growth of the Food Stamp program. Another response is that the critique also overlooks the extent to which major segments of the system have in fact been "reformed" through careful analyses—surely the radical reduction in school districts from 67,000 to 15,000 that took place during the 1950s and 1960s is a good example. But let us put aside these kinds of responses for the moment and grant that the rationalist critique makes an important point about American federal politics: In a system whose design leads to constant change, comprehensive reform is nevertheless very difficult to achieve. Why should this be so?

To see why, we need only ask whether the benefits of comprehensive reform are enough to mobilize a majority coalition in its support. Raising this political question leads immediately to a major problem—identifying the benefits of "reform." Some advocates of reform propose greater constraints on state and local governments and greater authority for the national government to devise and coordinate national policies (Thurow, 1980). Such proposals would drastically alter the system, but it is difficult to imagine why state or local officials would support them. Other reform advocates propose some form of decentralization; current national programs might be "devolved" to state and local governments. The difficulty here is that such proposals often take away benefits from so many current beneficiaries that no substantial coalition is possible. More recently, proposals have been made to "sort out" functions among governmental levels in order to clarify responsibilities and thus increase effectiveness (OMB, 1983). These proposals combine elements of centralizing and decentralizing plans and thus suffer from the political liabilities of both. State and local jurisdictions whose authority would be diminished in programs that are centralized would object, as would jurisdictions whose benefits would be diminished if national programs were devolved to state or local governments.

It might be possible to overcome the objections if there were an overwhelming national consensus on the need for reform, but achieving such a consensus is bound to be difficult. As we have seen (Chapter 1), the legal doctrine of "dual federalism" that posited clearly separate spheres of national and state action has little current impact, and nothing has replaced it as a prescription for the division of federal authority. Although a form of functional specialization among levels appears to have emerged (Anton, 1985), pragmatism rather than a theory of reform has been the driving force. Efforts to develop a theory of "system overload" as a justification for reform have been made by scholars and others (Beer, 1977; Beam, 1979), but little has come of that effort, perhaps because the theory itself is more powerful as a critique than as a prescription.

President Reagan's so-called new federalism initiative, which proposed that the national government and the states swap responsibilities for health care and welfare, and that forty or so national programs be "turned back" to the states, appears to have been based on this overload or "mess" theory, but no substantial support for the proposals could be generated (a more detailed treatment of the Reagan plan will be provided in Chapter 9). Indeed, the proposals may have produced more opposition to than support for reform. Having noticed that the swap and turnback plan was accompanied by a $30 billion reduction in federal grants, many state and local officials concluded that the proposals were very little different from other federal "shift and shaft" initiatives—that is, efforts to shift programs to state and local jurisdictions and then "shaft" those units by withdrawing financial support. Not surprisingly, these officials have become wary of "reform" plans emanating from Washington.

If an extremely popular president with strong convictions has been unable to mobilize a coalition in support of comprehensive reform, it seems highly unlikely that reform will occur through normal political processes. The benefits of major reform seem so ambiguous and the costs so high that widespread interest, let alone support, is virtually impossible to generate. This should not necessarily be taken to be a criticism of American federalism, since changes that are more limited in scope occur every day as federal officials respond to the problems they confront. Over time, these limited and piecemeal adjustments do lead to major changes in the system of intergovernmental relationships, allowing the system to cope with new issues without facing the task of redesigning the system itself. Although uncoordinated and certainly not comprehensive, the American approach has at least this virtue: Serious blunders can be made in hundreds of places without threatening the system itself. That is no small advantage in a system designed to produce continuous change, but without a theory to guide reform.

REFERENCES

ACIR, 1981. Advisory Commission on Intergovernmental Relations. *Protecting the Environment: Politics, Pollution, and Federal Policy.* Washington, D.C.: Government Printing Office.

Anagnoson, 1980. J. Theodore Anagnoson. "Politics in the Distribution of Federal Grants: The Case of the Economic Development Administration." In *Political Benefits: Empirical Studies of American Public Programs.* Lexington, Mass.: D.C. Heath.

Anton, 1980. Thomas J. Anton. "Federal Assistance Programs: The Politics of System Transformation." In *National Resources and Urban Policy,* ed. Douglas E. Ashford. New York: Methuen.

Anton, 1985. Thomas J. Anton. "Decay and Reconstruction in the Study of American Intergovernmental Relations." *Publius* 15: 65–97.

Anton et al., 1980. Thomas J. Anton, Jerry P. Cawley, and Kevin L. Kramer. *Moving Money.* Cambridge Mass.: Oelgeschlager, Gunn and Hain.

Anton and Reynolds, 1985. Thomas J. Anton and Rebecca Reynolds. "Old Federalism and New Policies for State Economic Development." Providence, R.I.: Taubman Center, Brown University, unpublished manuscript.

Beam, 1979. David R. Beam. "The Accidental Leviathan: Was the Growth of Government a Mistake?" *Intergovernmental Perspective* 5(Fall): 12–19.

Beer, 1977. Samuel Beer. "Political Overload and Federalism." *Polity* 10(Fall): 5–17.

Berry, 1982. Jeffrey M. Berry. "Consumers and the Hunger Lobby." In *Food Policy and Farm Programs,* ed. Don F. Hadwiger and Ross B. Talbot. Montpelier, Vt.: Capital City Press.

Cohodos, 1980. Nadine Cohodas. "Local and State Officials Organize to Save LEAA Grants Slated for Cuts." *Congressional Quarterly,* Vol. 38, No. 15 (April 12), p. 955.

Dommel, 1982. Paul R. Dommel and Associates. *Decentralizing Urban Policy: Case Studies in Community Development.* Washington, D.C.: The Brookings Institution.

Franklin and Ripley, 1984. Grace A. Franklin and Randall B. Ripley. *CETA Politics and Policy, 1973–1982.* Knoxville: University of Tennessee Press.

Gray, 1973. Virginia Gray. "Innovation in the States: A Diffusion Study." *American*

Political Science Review 67 (December): 1174–1185.

Hansen, 1983. Susan B. Hansen. *The Politics of Taxation: Revenue Without Represen-tation.* New York: Praeger.

Herbers, 1985. John Herbers. "The States Learn to Rely on Their Own Devices." *New York Times,* October 13.

Hershey, 1985. Robert D. Hershey, Jr. "Congressional Conferees End Financing of Synthetic Fuels Program." *New York Times,* December 17.

Jones, 1975. Charles O. Jones. *Clean Air: The Policies on Pollution Control.* Pitts-burgh: University of Pittsburgh Press.

Kaufman, 1976. Herbert Kaufman. *Are Government Organizations Immortal?* Wash-ington, D.C.: The Brookings Institution.

"LEAA: The End Is Here," 1982. *Congressional Quarterly,* Vol. 40, No. 15, (April 10), p. 807.

Light, 1982. Paul Light. *The President's Agenda.* Baltimore: The Johns Hopkins University Press.

Liroff, 1976. Richard A. Liroff. *A National Policy for the Environment: NEPA and Its Aftermath.* Bloomington: Indiana University Press.

Malcolm, 1986. Andrew H. Malcolm. "Human-Organ Transplants Gain With New State Laws." *New York Times,* June 1.

OMB, 1983. Executive Office of the President. Office of Management and Budget. *Budget of the United States Government FY 1983.* Washington, D.C.: Government Printing Office.

Oppenheim, 1983. John E. Oppenheim. "Federal Response to Natural Disasters: A Spatial Political Analysis." Ph.D. dissertation, University of Michigan.

Pious, 1975. R. M. Pious. "Sources of Domestic Policy Initiatives." *Proceedings of the Academy of Political Science* 32(1): 448–449.

Rich, 1985. Michael Rich. "Congress, the Bureaucracy and the Cities: Distributive Politics in the Allocation of Federal Grants-in-Aid for Community and Econom-ic Development." Ph.D. dissertation, Northwestern University.

Roberts, 1986. Steven V. Roberts. "Phil Gramm's Crusade Against the Deficit." *New York Times Magazine,* March 30.

Roche, 1986. John P. Roche. "A Constitution Short on Intent." *New York Times,* May 18.

Rockman, 1984. Bert A. Rockman. *The Leadership Question: The Presidency and the American System.* New York: Praeger.

Rundquist, 1980. Barry Spencer Rundquist. *Political Benefits: Studies of American Public Programs.* Lexington, Mass.: D.C. Heath.

Savage, 1985. R. L. Savage. "When A Policy's Time Has Come: Cases of Rapid Policy Diffusion, 1983–1984." *Publius* 15: 111–125.

Schon, 1971. Donald A. Schon. *Beyond the Stable State.* New York: Norton.

Stein, 1984. Robert M. Stein. "Growth and Change in the U.S. Federal Aid System." Paper presented at the Southern Political Science Meeting, Savannah, Ga., November.

Stockman, 1986. David A. Stockman. *The Triumph of Politics: How the Reagan Revolution Failed.* New York: Harper & Row.

Sundquist, with Davis, 1969. James L. Sundquist, with David W. Davis. *Making Federalism Work.* Washington, D.C.: The Brookings Institution.

Thurow, 1980. Lester C. Thurow. *The Zero-Sum Society: Distribution and the Possibilities for Economic Change.* New York: Basic Books.

U.S. Congress, 1968. *U.S. Code Congressional and Administrative News,* 90th Congress, 2nd Session, 1968–1975, Vol. 1, p. 237. St. Paul, Minn.: West.

U.S. Congress, 1972. Hearings before the House Subcommittee of the Committee on Appropriations, Departments of State, Justice, Commerce, the Judiciary, and Related Agencies FY 1973, 92nd Congress, 2nd Session, Part 1, p. 1126. Washington: Government Printing Office.

U.S. Senate, 1969. Hearings before the Senate Subcommittee of the Committee on Appropriations Departments of State, Justice, Commerce, the Judiciary, and Related Agencies FY 1970, p. 140. Washington, D.C.: Government Printing Office.

Walker, 1969. Jack L. Walker. "Diffusion of Innovations Among American States." *American Political Science Review* 63 (September): 880–899.

West, 1984. Darrell West. *Making Campaigns Count.* Westport, Conn.: Greenwood Press.

CHAPTER 6

FINANCING THE INTERGOVERNMENTAL SYSTEM

Any service or good provided by government costs something. As economists tirelessly and rightfully remind us, there is no free lunch. To provide a good or service, government agencies must raise funds, either by taxation or by the imposition of fees or other charges. Increases in government activity that have occurred during the past two centuries have been accompanied by repeated tax increases that have raised taxes to the present level of nearly one-third of our gross national product. This is a substantially lower level of taxation than in most other advanced industrial nations, but the funds raised to support public sector programs are nevertheless enormous. In this chapter we consider the sources of tax and other revenue for American national, state, and local governments, paying particular attention to recent changes in patterns of revenue extraction. For those who have followed the argument this far, it will come as no surprise to learn that financing patterns are easily as complex as service delivery patterns.

TAX COALITIONS

Taxing, Spending, and Public Opinion

If every government action requires funding, it follows that funding increases are necessarily tied to government expansion. The tie may not always be close—inflation, inefficiencies, and occasional corruption are bound to create slack—but in general spending and taxing are two sides of the same coin. Despite the apparent simplicity of this observation, many observers treat spending and taxing as separate activities. Taxpayer organizations, in particular, focus so exclusively on taxation that the driving forces behind higher taxes are obscured or ignored altogether. In the United States as in other democratic systems, for example, virtually no one admits to being in favor of higher taxes, yet taxes continue to rise. These facts are difficult to reconcile if taxes are viewed in isolation from the expenditures they support. Viewed as the price of the public services we receive, however, rising tax levels can easily be understood as a reflection of societal preferences for more and better public benefits. Where do such preferences come from?

In the long run, of course, societal preferences in democratic states reflect citizen desires. But revenue decisions are not made in the long run; they are made in the present by politicians responding to the pressures and incentives of the moment. Citizen desires are often among the operative pressures and incentives, especially at election time, but citizen views generally have little to do with decisions to levy a particular tax or impose a particular fee. Fiscal relationships among American governments are so incredibly complex that few citizens—indeed, very few officials— understand enough to exert influence over funding decisions. Some years ago I attempted to portray this complexity by outlining the difficulties a governor might have in attempting to control a state budget. Although focused on a single official at the state level, the discussion remains a valid portrait of difficulties any federal official might face in comprehending his or her agency's sources of support:

> The first—and probably most important—obstacle is the truly staggering complexity of the state's system of financial bookkeeping. Constitutional limitations, marvelously incoherent divisions of financial accountability, in- comprehensible budget documents and, worst of all, an intricate maze of general funds, revolving funds, loan funds, trust funds, federal funds, local funds, all conspire to shroud the state's financial situation in mystery. Illinois, with only forty or so (the number changes from biennium to biennium) special funds to worry about in addition to the general purpose fund, is perhaps more fortunate than most states in this respect. But consider Connecticut, which finances expenditures from roughly 100 funds (only 5 of which are included in the budget), or Wyoming, where no less than 168 special funds are used to support state spending. The governor who hopes to fight for financial righteous- ness in these circumstances will surely be hard-put to locate the battlefield, let alone lead his forces to victory. (Anton, 1967)

If these kinds of difficulties confront virtually everyone in public office, it is not surprising that citizens who lack daily access to official documents should be largely unaware of their public finances. Indeed, citizens appear sufficiently uninformed regarding their taxes that Susan B. Hansen recent- ly has challenged "the underlying assumption of much public opinion research . . . that there is some more or less well-defined 'public opinion' out there somewhere that can be described if we can ask the right questions or devise the right measures." On the contrary, Hansen's exhaustive review of public opinion on taxation led her to conclude that "public attitudes are confused, multidimensional, and fluctuate considera- bly over time." Such confusion and instability, she writes:

> . . . flow directly from . . . the monumental ignorance of the U.S. public concerning not only the basic structure and economics of taxes, but the

amounts they themselves pay and the government services they receive. There is little understanding not only of abstractions such as redistribution, horizontal equity, or elasticity, but of quite basic issues such as whether one would gain or lose from a specific reform proposal. . . . They are thus hesitant to express opinions about such unfamiliar concepts. And many who do offer opinions do not know what they are talking about, or cannot link their own tax preferences to those of parties and candidates.

It is tempting to conclude, therefore, that in many instances we are dealing with what Philip Converse has termed "nonattitudes." Our efforts to model opinions may simply represent attempts to impose structure where there is none. (Hansen, 1983, pp. 256, 257, 259)

Hansen's point is not that citizens are wholly without influence. She makes clear that major changes in tax policies often result from "realigning" elections in which electoral coalitions are fundamentally altered— although taxes are seldom the central issues in such elections. Her point, rather, is that most citizens are neither much interested in or informed about taxes, that their policy options are severely constrained by officials even when they are given opportunities to vote directly on tax matters, and that to understand tax policies, it is essential to understand the actions of the politicians in control of our public institutions. A system as complicated as American federalism, in short, imposes high costs on anyone seeking to learn enough to exert influence on the tax system. Most Americans, reluctant to pay these costs, are content to leave tax policy to political insiders, even as they grumble about their increasing tax bills.

The Major Contenders

Under conditions of "profound ignorance," to borrow Hansen's phrase (Hansen, 1983; p. 258), the coalitions that determine tax policy are likely to be small, narrowly focused, and often quite invisible to the general public. Among both supporters and opponents of taxation, however, some are quite visible. Having been established to deliver some benefit, and having been funded through taxes to support the salaries and other organizational costs associated with the delivery of that benefit, every public agency has a strong and continuing interest in maintaining a level of taxation sufficient to sustain or expand its program. Public officials themselves are thus important participants in coalitions that form to support continued or increased taxation. The larger the size of government, the larger the number of employees and the greater the pressure that can be brought to bear in support of taxes and other public revenues. In this sense, the spenders are also the taxers. An important cause of growth in public expenditures, therefore, is the real interest of government agencies in their own life. For public agencies and their employees, taxes are indeed a benefit to be savored.

On the other side, wealthy individuals and corporate taxpayers are organized to oppose tax increases. Wealthy individuals are usually subject to high levels of taxation, which encourages their interest in the kinds and amounts of taxes they pay, as well as a desire to pay less—or at least not pay more. Since real estate constitutes much of the wealth of individuals, homeowner and neighborhood associations together with real estate business interests often provide the organizational structure for these individual interests. Corporate and other business taxpayers regard taxes as a business expense; lower taxes imply higher profits. While all business firms thus seek to restrain taxes, larger firms are more successful at avoiding national and state taxes than are smaller firms, presumably because their size gives them political clout and their resources allow them to retain expensive lawyers and lobbyists (Salamon and Siegfried, 1977).

Despite these differences, larger and smaller firms typically join together to form organizations that monitor trends in public spending and taxing, produce studies designed to improve public sector efficiency, and participate in the shaping of tax legislation. These Taxpayer Federations, Civic Leagues, or Expenditure Councils are found in all states and most larger cities and are usually among the most influential "few" participants in the development of tax policy. Although the interests of larger and smaller firms are not always the same on specific proposals, there is a shared presumption in favor of tax restraint that provides the unifying spirit for such organizations.

In general, then, federal tax politics is largely uninfluenced by public opinion, which is too uninformed and unorganized to do much except in the rare "tax revolt" cases to be discussed below. Within this context, most taxing coalitions can be small and largely invisible, confined to the few technicians who understand intergovernmental finance and use their expertise to shape tax policies out of public view. Clearly within public view, however, are two large and very visible opposing coalitions that predictably take positions for and against tax increases. One, led by politicians seeking some reform or improvement and including large numbers of public employees, consistently supports tax increases to fund desired programs. The other, led by organizations representing wealthy individuals and corporations, consistently opposes tax increases and, when possible (which is not often), seeks tax reductions.

These statements are generally valid, but it is important not to treat them as stereotypes. While it is true that public employees generally understand that taxes are necessary to maintain their positions and act accordingly (Courant, Gramlich, and Rubinfeld, 1979), their actions more often take the form of voting support than active issue leadership. Municipal employees, particularly teachers, are often involved in active agitation, but state and national employees are far less likely to be. Similarly, while business organizations generally oppose tax increases, there are occasions when they support or do not oppose higher taxes. A tax that produces revenues earmarked for some purpose beneficial to some business is tantamount to having taxpayers foot the bill for something that otherwise would have to be paid for by the business itself. A tax on a profitable activity may not be opposed if the political consequences of opposition could be damaging: "For example, firms earning higher than average profits may shy away from political action if they fear that such action would attract public attention to the monopoly position that yields them these large profits" (Salamon and Siegfried, 1977; p. 1033). As always, then, it remains important to appreciate that both issue and context can lead individuals and organizations to actions different from their normal preferences.

THE MAJOR TRENDS

The Rise of the Nation-State

Until this century, most American government was state and local government. The bulk of public services offered by governments were the traditional health, public safety, and education programs for which state and local governments were primarily responsible. National government obligations were conceived to be limited to defense, foreign affairs, postal service, and pension programs that required relatively little money and few employees. Until World War I, therefore, the national government was able to finance its limited activities from limited sources of revenue: customs duties, the sale of public lands, and excise taxes. The more extensive education and housekeeping services provided by state and local governments were funded largely from property taxes, occasionally supplemented by public land sales. Neither national nor state and local tax levels were particularly burdensome, amounting to 5 percent or less of the gross national product well into the second decade of the twentieth century (Break, 1982; Hansen, 1983).

A fundamental change occurred when first a world war, then a major economic depression, then another world war brought massive new expenditures and extensive use of new taxing authority. The little-used income tax was substantially increased to fund World War I and quickly became the major source of national government revenue. Faced with a depression that neither the private sector nor state and local programs seemed able to combat, the national government substantially increased the income tax during the 1930s—initiating major new spending programs to guarantee the security of individual incomes—and along the way quadrupled the national government's share of the gross national product.

Reacting to the same intractable economic pressures, state governments drastically reduced their reliance on property taxes, replacing them with general sales and excise taxes. Local governments remained bound to the property tax which, by the end of the decade, had become an almost exclusively local tax. As Figure 6.1 reveals, these changes radically altered the fiscal significance of each level of government. In the mid-1930s the national government share of total government revenues exceeded the

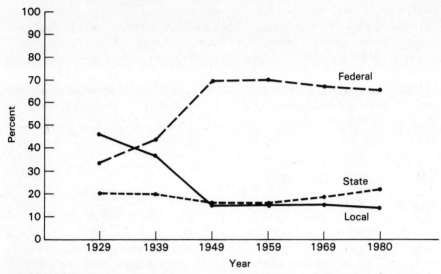

Figure 6.1   Percentage Distribution of Government Revenues by Level of Government, 1929–1980

SOURCE: ACIR, Significant Features of Fiscal Federalism, 1985–1986, p. 11.

local government share for the first time, reflecting the profound revolution in American public finance that was under way.

Although the new welfare and economic stimulation obligations assumed by the national government in the mid-1930s were an important source of national tax expansion, a far more important source was World War II, which simultaneously enlarged the income tax to pay for the war while restraining state and local spending for less essential goods and services. One result, clearly evident in Figure 6.1, was that national government taxes quickly became dominant, accounting for nearly 70 percent of all government revenue by the late 1940s. A second result, deriving in part from a new attitude on the part of national politicians, and in part from pent-up demand that could not be met during the war, was that national revenues retained their dominance rather than falling back to prewar levels. The new attitude, summarized by Break, was apparent in 1946:

> Like a trumpet call announcing the advent of a new era, the Full Employment Act of 1946 proclaimed the formal departure of U.S. government policy from the concept that Washington's job was to balance its budget and let business run the economy. For better or worse, the federal government was now to become a full partner in the management of the economy, gearing tax and expenditure decisions to needs determined by the business cycle. Stabilizing the economy so as to "promote maximum employment, production, and purchasing power" ("a dollar of stable value" was added to this list in 1953) was declared the new national goal. This pronouncement far transcended the

Monroe Doctrine as a momentous statement of U.S. government policy. (Break, 1982, p. 48)

National politicians now played a much more active role, working closely with business to rebuild war-torn economies around the globe and to expand markets for American enterprise. More important from a federal point of view, national politicians began to work much more intensively with state and local officials in searching for solutions to what had previously been regarded as "their" problems. By the early 1950s, national officials were deeply involved in new relationships with both private sector and state and local organizations. Indeed, the national involvement appeared so pervasive that President Eisenhower determined to reduce and clarify this new partnership. But as George Break has noted:

> Ironically, it succeeded only in entangling itself even further in partnership arrangements. Prodded by the post-war boom in babies and automobiles, Washington poured out capital to finance construction of housing, schools, and highways. Shocked by Sputnik, the government showered money upon schools to enrich their instructional programs. Even its sustained attempt to make a clear separation between state and federal functions and revenue sources made little progress. (Break, 1982, p. 49)

It was during the Eisenhower administration that national activism became entrenched in the form of new programs of construction, social assistance, and education, to say nothing of the largest public works project of the twentieth century: the 1956 Interstate Highway Program. Later administrations, both Democrat and Republican, built on these foundations by adding social service programs and expanding social security benefits, paving the way for the very large increases in federal spending and taxing that took place during the 1970s.

New Patterns of Intergovernmental Finance

The postwar activism of national politicians led to other adjustments in the intergovernmental financial system. Having largely abandoned the property tax in favor of sales taxes during the 1930s, state and local officials found it necessary to tap other revenue sources, particularly after 1950, when new construction and service programs began to require new funding. One result was a gradual increase in revenues raised from state personal and corporate income taxes. The most remarkable result, however, was the very rapid escalation in federal aid to state and local governments, portrayed in Table 6.1. Less than $3 billion in 1954, only $7 billion in 1960, federal aid more than tripled in the 1960s, to $22 billion, and nearly quadrupled in the explosive 1970s, to some $84 billion by 1980 (ACIR, 1986, 59). Federal funds became the largest single source of state and local revenue during the 1970s, surpassing sales, property, and income taxes in amounts raised (Anton, 1980). By 1979, federal aid as a proportion of source revenues amounted to more than 36 percent for state governments and 17.6 percent for local governments, although federal aid to hard-pressed big cities often amounted to upward of one-fifth of source revenues.

Increases in national assistance to states and localities obviously allowed those jurisdictions to increase their services without proportionate increases in state and local taxes. Although this had the positive effect of shifting much of the state-local tax burden to the generally more progressive national income tax base, there were other consequences that seemed less positive. One was greater financial centralization, both national and state. As the national government increasingly assumed the role of banker for state and local programs, more and more influence over those programs was exercised in Washington. Within the states, several forces were at work to increase state influence over spending and taxing. Many national assistance programs, for example, allocated funds to state governments for reallocation to local governments, making states brokers for the national government bankers.

In response to demands from local officials, moreover, states increasingly supplanted the property tax with increases in income and sales taxes that grew rapidly with inflation and could better meet demands for education and social services. So great were these pressures that by 1986, "state funding of local schools surpassed 50% of their revenues for the first time in history" (*State Budget and Tax News*, 1986, p. 12). Finally and

Table 6.1 Federal Aid to State and Local Governments

INTERGOVERNMENTAL REVENUE FROM FEDERAL GOVERNMENT AS A PERCENTAGE OF GENERAL REVENUE FROM OWN SOURCES		
Fiscal Year	*State*	*Local*
1955	20.9%	2.5%
1960	31.0	2.6
1965	32.3	3.6
1970	33.5	5.1
1972	37.9	7.1
1974	35.5	13.3
1975	37.3	12.9
1976	39.1	14.6
1977	37.9	16.3
1978	37.0	17.5
1979	36.1	17.6
1980	36.6	16.3
1981	36.2	15.4
1982	32.1	12.8
1983	31.7	11.7
1984	30.5	10.6

SOURCE: Advisory Commission on Intergovernmental Relations. *Significant Features of Fiscal Federalism, 1985–1986.* Washington, D.C.: Government Printing Office, 1986, p. 59

somewhat ironically, the so-called tax revolt of the late 1970s added a further thrust toward state centralization by removing discretion from the local officials who controlled the property tax in favor of the state politicians who controlled the larger and more elastic sources of revenue.

Growing fiscal centralization meant that local governments in particular became more dependent on external funds. The Local Government Dependency Index computed by the Advisory Commission on Intergovernmental Relations, for example, rose from $0.44 in 1962 to $0.73 in 1975 and $0.79 in 1980. For every dollar of revenue raised by local governments themselves, state and national aid contributed 79 cents in 1980 (ACIR, 1985–86, p. 62). While still the major local source of local revenue, the property tax clearly has been a casualty of the recent trend toward fiscal centralization.

The expansion of federal aid to state and local governments was brought to a halt by President Carter in 1978. When Reagan succeeded Carter in 1981, he immediately began to implement his very strong belief that the federal system had become "a confused mess" (OMB, 1983 Budget Message). Large reductions were made in 1981 in many of the social assistance programs that provide state and local governments with much of their national revenue. In addition, some fifty-seven previously separate programs were combined into just nine block grants, giving the states much more discretion in the use of the reduced funds.

Unfortunately for state and local governments, these national government reductions took place at a time when the severe recession of 1981–83 had already reduced state and local revenues from their own sources. To sustain programs, therefore, the states—which had enacted 54 separate tax reductions during the tax revolt period of 1978–80—turned around and enacted 28 income tax increases and 30 sales tax increases during the 1981–83 recession (ACIR, 1985–86, p. 76). As the economy improved in 1984 and 1985, many states rescinded the increases, and some even reduced their rates below 1982 levels. "In contrast, most of the sales tax increases of 1982 and 1983 were retained, and several more states raised the sales tax in 1984" (Gold, 1986, pp. 22–23). By the mid-1980s, state and local revenue systems had recovered from the recession, but greater reliance on sales than on income taxation, coupled with continuing reductions in federal aid from the progressive federal income tax base, had made state revenue systems more regressive (Gold, 1986, p. iii).

State and Regional Differences

These observations about the nation as a whole are subject to many qualifications when regions or individual states are considered. As we have noted (Chapter 2), states differ in the extent to which state or local governments are the dominant service providers, and these differences typically structure what Gold has called a "trade-off . . . between state and local taxes—if one is particularly high, the other tends to be relatively low, and vice versa" (Gold, 1986, p. 4). Referring to the data shown in Table 6.2, for example, Bahl has noted that "Southern and western states are more heavily reliant on sales taxes, northern states are more dependent on property and income taxes, southern states make relatively little use of income taxation, and western states have the most diversified tax structures."

Bahl goes on to point out that these differences reflect differences in service responsibilities: "Where local government involvement in the delivery of services is strong, there tends to be much heavier use of the property tax. Since the southern states tend to be more state government dominated, there is less reliance on property taxation" (Bahl, 1984, p. 140). It should also be noted that taxes represent a higher fraction of total revenue in the property tax states than in southern and western states, which obtain more revenue from user charges, particularly for universities and hospitals, or rents and royalties from the sale of minerals (Gold, 1986, p. 38).

Another very important source of variation in state-local revenues is the distribution of federal grants. National assistance dollars are allocated according to a formula (usually including population among its terms) or on a project-by-project basis. Because the coalitions that support these programs are dynamic, changes in both distribution formulas and project preferences occur with some frequency, altering the state-to-state distribution of federal grant funds. Table 6.3 shows the changes that occurred during the 1970s, when total federal grants exploded from $173 per person in 1971 to $463 per person in 1980.

By comparing the per capita amount for the nation as a whole with the per capita sums for each of the nine Census Divisions or the four Census

Table 6.2   Regional Variations in State and Local Government Finances

	NORTHERN TIER STATES	SOUTHERN TIER STATES	WESTERN TIER STATES
Per capita debt outstanding	$1,578	$1,358	$1,538
Debt outstanding as percent of personal income	14.4	14.2	14.0
Percent of revenues derived from			
Property tax	27.8	17.8	19.6
Sales tax	14.4	18.5	18.3
Income tax	22.0	12.3	18.2
Per capita federal grants	$ 396	$ 352	$ 427
Federal grants as a percent of own-source revenues	26.0	28.7	26.4

SOURCE: Roy Bahl. *Financing State and Local Government in the 1980s*. New York: Oxford University Press, 1984, p. 139. Copyright © 1984 by Oxford University Press, Inc. Reprinted by permission.

Table 6.3 **Per Capita Formula, Project and Total Grants, by Division and Region, 1971 and 1980**

	FORMULA GRANTS				PROJECT GRANTS				TOTAL GRANTS			
	1971	Rank	1980	Rank	1971	Rank	1980	Rank	1971	Rank	1980	Rank
New England	110	6	364	4	66	1	146	1	176	5	510	2
Mid-Atlantic	120	5	406	1	51	3	113	5	171	6	519	1
E.N. Central	89	9	306	8	58	9	94	9	127	9	400	9
W.N. Central	105	8	293	9	43	8	116	4	148	8	409	8
South Atlantic	110	6	324	6	51	3	99	7	161	7	423	6
E.S. Central	148	3	373	2	51	3	118	3	199	3	491	3
W.S. Central	132	4	318	7	45	7	94	9	177	4	412	7
Mountain	153	2	349	5	62	2	131	2	215	1	480	4
Pacific	163	1	369	3	51	3	108	6	214	2	477	5
Northeast	117	3	396	1	55	1	122	1	172	3	518	1
N. Central	94	4	302	4	40	4	100	4	134	4	402	4
South	125	2	332	3	49	3	101	3	174	2	433	3
West	160	1	364	2	54	2	114	2	214	1	478	2
Nation	122		353		51		110		173		463	

SOURCE: Thomas J. Anton. "The Regional Distribution of Federal Expenditures, 1971–1980." *National Tax Journal* 36 (December, 1983): 429–442, p. 438. Reprinted by permission of the publisher.

Regions, we can see the substantial differences from the national average that exist across the country—differences that would be even more striking if the states were listed individually rather than by division or region. Comparing 1971 and 1980 figures, especially for total grants, shows the significant changes that took place during the decade. All areas of the country benefited from large increases in federal aid, but as I have pointed out elsewhere:

> . . . the largest sums and the most rapid growth rates were recorded by the states east of the Great Lakes and north of the Mason-Dixon line. Except for the upper Mid-West, all the states west of the Mississippi fell in divisional ranking between 1971 and 1980, despite their per capita dollar increments. The large increases in grants to state and local governments during the past decade, therefore, were unusually beneficial for the states of the northeast. (Anton, 1983, p. 438)

It is perhaps worth adding that the states of the upper Midwest did not fall in rank because there was nowhere to fall—they began the decade in the bottom two ranks and remained there, despite considerable improvement in receipts from project grants. If, as some commentators had suggested, there was another "war between the states" for federal funds during the 1970s, then the Northeast clearly won the war while the Great Lakes states remained the "poor relations of American federalism" (Anton, 1983, p. 431).

The extraordinary volatility of the federal tax system as a whole during the 1970s and 1980s was capped in 1986 by passage of the first comprehensive reform of the federal income tax since 1954. While the consequences of that reform have yet to be played out, at a minimum they will include substantial changes in state tax laws in states that link their income taxes to the national tax, as well as a continuing shift away from the principle of progressivity—or ability to pay—in our tax systems.

Other significant changes are likely, but it is not possible to specify them, particularly since changes in major expenditure programs such as Medicare or social security could easily contradict any forecast. Whatever changes occur, however, will alter a revenue system defined by the following twentieth-century trends:

1. The sudden emergence and later growth of the income tax as the dominant source of national government revenue
2. State government reliance on sales and, more recently, on income taxes as major revenue sources, after abandonment of the property tax in the 1930s
3. Continued reliance on property taxes by local governments, but a decline in the share of local revenue produced by property taxes
4. Massive increases in federal aid to state and local governments in the 1960s and 1970s, leading to greater fiscal centralization and greater financial interdependence among all American governments

5. A recent period of extreme tax volatility, during which increases in federal aid to state and local governments were halted and then reduced, state taxes were reduced, increased, then reduced again, and the first comprehensive national income tax reform in more than three decades was passed

INTERDEPENDENCE IN FEDERAL TAXATION

Legally Separate But Financially Linked

The increasingly interdependent character of federal revenue is clear from the vast expenditures now being transferred from the national government to state and local governments, as well as from states to their localities. Less obvious, but equally significant, is the extent to which national and state tax systems are themselves intertwined. Many states with income taxes tie their rates directly to the federal tax code, so any change in federal rates automatically changes state income taxes, which in turn often requires adjustments by state officials.

The federal tax code subsidizes state and local governments by allowing interest earned on state and local bonds to be exempt from federal taxation, thus reducing the price and improving the marketability of such obligations. State and local governments, in turn, subsidize the federal government by permitting interest earned on federal securities to be exempt from state income tax, by exempting purchases made on military bases from sales tax, and by exempting federal buildings from local property taxes. The federal tax code also subsidizes state and local taxpayers by permitting them to deduct state and local taxes in calculating their federal tax obligations. In turn, 16 of the 41 states with income taxes allow federal taxes to be deducted in calculating state tax obligations (U.S. Treasury, 1985). American tax systems may be legally separate, but in practice their operations are both interrelated and interdependent.

The interdependence of public revenue sources often leads to actions that produce unintended or perverse consequences. California voters may have discovered perversity after giving overwhelming approval in 1978 to Proposition 13, which reduced property taxes to no more than 1 percent of market value. Reducing property taxes, however, also reduced the amount taxpayers could deduct from federal tax returns. As a result, Californians who voted so strongly for property tax relief were voting as well to increase their federal income taxes—according to one estimate, by as much as $30 billion (Hansen, 1983).

Even more ironically, federal grants to California municipalities were reduced as a result of the interaction between property taxes and certain provisions of federal grant programs. General Revenue Sharing, for example, distributed funds according to formulas that included a "tax effort" provision, with "effort" defined as total taxes divided by total personal income in a given jurisdiction. By lowering property taxes,

California voters were decreasing their level of local tax effort and thus reducing the number of federal dollars they could legitimately claim. Other national programs include provisions that require local or state governments to match federal funds with local revenues in varying proportions. Since reductions in property taxes ultimately reduced the revenue available for local matching requirements, the flow of federal funds was necessarily less. Californians wanted property tax relief, and Proposition 13 gave it to them. They almost certainly did not want either federal tax increases or reductions in federal assistance, but Proposition 13 gave them those "benefits" as well.

Unraveling Complexity: A Case Study

Whether Californians or citizens of other states could have designed a proposition that avoided these unintended consequences seems doubtful, in view of the enormous complexities of interdependent taxation. Consider a proposition voters in Michigan were asked to approve in 1978. The proposal was similar to Proposition 13 in that, if passed, it would have required a 50 percent reduction in local property tax assessments. In an effort to aid public debate, researchers at the University of Michigan who had been studying federal grant programs decided to develop estimates of the impact the proposition would have on the flow of federal grant funds into the state. Their effort offers a revealing insight into the complexities of tax interdependence.

One of their first discoveries was that federal assistance was not only large in amount—nearly $4 billion in 1978 alone—but delivered through some 400 separate assistance programs, each with its own regulations and matching rates. To understand the impact of property tax reduction on this flow of funds, therefore, it was necessary to list each program, the amount of money delivered in 1978, and provisions such as matching rates that would affect the availability of funds. This was done through a laborious review of the *Catalog of Federal Domestic Assistance*, a publication of the U.S. Office of Management and Budget. Not all of Michigan's 83 counties (the local units chosen by the researchers for analysis) received funds from these programs, however. Indeed, the number of programs operating in a given county ranged from a low of only 4 in Keweenaw County in the upper peninsula to a high of 135 separate programs in Wayne County, which includes Detroit.

To estimate the impact of a 50 percent assessment reduction in the state, therefore, it was necessary to tally the number of programs operating in each county, along with their amounts and matching rates. But some counties relied more heavily on the property tax than others; obviously, the more revenue generated from sources other than property taxes, the less affected local governments would be by a loss in property tax revenue. To deal with this problem, the researchers had to develop a property tax dependency ratio for each of 83 counties, defined as total property tax divided by total local revenue for all units of government within a county. Across the state, this meant additional calculations for some 2,800 cities, villages, and towns.

There was yet another complication, however. Faced with a 50 percent assessment reduction, local decision-makers might react in ways that were unknown and impossible to predict. It seemed unlikely that a 50 percent assessment reduction would translate directly into a 50 percent revenue reduction, for several reasons. Tax base growth might occur; local officials might choose to reduce expenditures or find other sources of revenue; or, as in California, state aid might increase. Rather than guess what the outcomes would be, three alternatives were calculated. The first and largely theoretical alternative was that an assessment reduction would produce an equivalent revenue reduction and thus the loss of half of all funds available for matching. At the other extreme, the possibility that efficient and fortunate communities might be able to replace as much as 40 percent of lost revenues led to projections based on no more than a 10 percent loss in local revenues. The most plausible outcome was thought to fall somewhere between these extremes—30 percent loss in local revenues available for matching.

Table 6.4 summarizes the results of all these calculations by showing dollar losses per person, by level of property tax dependency, under conditions of maximum, moderate, or minimum impact. These calculations were based on matching rates by individual program and the

Table 6.4 Impact of a 50 Percent Assessment Reduction in the Flow of Federal Funds to Michigan, under Net Reduction Assumptions of 10, 30, and 50 Percent

	PER CAPITA REDUCTION		
	Maximum Impact (50%)	Moderate Impact (30%)	Minimum Impact (10%)
80% property tax dependent or less			
Total dollars lost	39.75	23.85	7.95
Federal dollars	26.39	15.84	5.29
80–90% property tax dependent			
Total dollars lost	59.20	35.52	11.84
Federal dollars lost	39.13	23.48	7.83
90% or more property tax dependent			
Total dollars lost	64.15	38.49	12.83
Federal dollars lost	43.32	25.99	8.66

SOURCE: Thomas J. Anton. "Outlays Data and the Analysis of Federal Policy Impact." In *The Urban Impacts of Federal Policies*, ed. Norman Glickman. Baltimore: The Johns Hopkins University Press, 1980, p. 148. Reprinted by permission of The Johns Hopkins University Press, Baltimore/London.

estimates were conservative: More than $73 million in program dollars for which no specific matching rates could be identified were excluded from the analysis. Excluding these "variable match" programs, of course, significantly understated the potential losses in federal funds. Even with these conservative procedures, the analysis revealed that as little as $76 million or as much as $378 million in federal dollars might be lost to Michigan if property taxes were reduced by half.

Were these calculations accurate? Probably not, given other complications too arcane to be reported here, although they certainly can be regarded as informed guesses. Could citizens have developed such information to help them decide whether to support or oppose the proposition? The answer, I think, is almost certainly not, unless they had the time and resources similar to those available to university researchers. The average citizen has no such resources and thus cannot be expected to grasp the excruciating convoluted details of American tax interdependence.

The Power of Interdependence

However complex it may be, tax interdependence remained intact in the recent reform of the federal income tax, despite a determined effort by the Treasury Department and the president to do away with its major base, the deductibility of state and local taxes from federal tax returns. Since this deduction has been estimated to cost the federal treasury some $30 billion in lost revenue each year, it is worth asking why it should have been retained—particularly in light of the $200 billion annual federal budget deficits of the mid-1980s. The answer, as always, lies in the coalitions that formed to protect the interests of state and local citizens and officials.

Those who sought to eliminate deductibility included many economists and a few political technicians who offered arguments based primarily on considerations of equity. Since deductibility is available only to taxpayers who itemize their returns, and since only a third of the 95 million taxpayers itemize, deductibility was attacked as a benefit available only to a minority of taxpayers and thus not justifiable. Furthermore, it was argued, the minority who benefitted from deductibility were largely upper-income people who did not need the tax savings it conferred. Finally, because the value of deductibility was higher for individuals in states with higher levels of taxation than for residents of low-tax states, deductibility amounted to a subsidy for expensive government programs paid for by states that had chosen not to have such programs.

These arguments were not entirely without merit, but the powerful coalition that formed to preserve deductibility quickly formulated a position that had far more political influence. Perhaps the leading figure in the deductibility coalition was Governor Mario Cuomo of New York. New York is a state with very high taxes and thus has a great deal to lose from the elimination of deductibility. In speeches, articles, and interviews,

Cuomo defended deductibility as a central principle of American federalism, reflecting a spirit of cooperation without domination. Eliminating deductibility, he suggested, would force taxpayers to pay a federal tax on state and local taxes they had already paid. This would certainly increase national revenue, but it would also make it more difficult for state and local governments to support their programs. The probable effect, he thought, would be to cause taxpayers to seek reductions in state and local taxes to offset federal tax increases. If so, the ability of the states to meet their growing obligations would be seriously undermined and the federal system made weaker. Surely it made little sense, he argued, to weaken state and local revenue systems at a moment when both the president and Congress were reducing federal aid and asking states and localities to assume larger responsibilities (Schmalz, 1986; Smothers, 1986).

These arguments too had considerable merit. Indeed, official studies conducted by the U.S. Treasury Department and the Advisory Commission on Intergovernmental Relations in 1985 confirmed Governor Cuomo's assertion that elimination of deductibility would be extremely costly for state and local governments. But the merits of the argument were far less significant than its politics. Simply put, deductibility conferred substantial benefits on too large and too influential a constituency to be eliminated.

Taxpayers from every state except South Dakota benefit from deductibility, on average, although the benefit is worth much more in states such as New York ($67.57 per person) or Maryland ($51.92 per person) than in states such as Louisiana ($1.64 per person) or Wyoming ($2.68 per person) (U.S. Treasury, 1985, p. IX.26). Some officials from states with smaller benefits who had less reason to support deductibility chose not to follow the lead of Governor Cuomo and other officials from high tax states. Most state and local officials, however, were committed to maintaining the benefit, particularly when it became clear that its beneficiaries were both more numerous and more influential than critics seemed to recognize.

The claim that deductibility benefits only a third of all taxpayers, for example, overlooks joint returns; when they are taken into account, 41 percent of all tax returns include itemized deductions, most of which are deductions for state and local taxes. In states such as Colorado, Utah, New York, or Maryland, more than half of all returns include itemized deductions (U.S. Treasury, 1985, p. ix.24). Nearly 70 percent of all those who deduct state and local taxes, furthermore, earn between $20,000 and $50,000, and this group receives some 57 percent of total deductibility benefits (Dye, 1985, p. 551). Far from being primarily a benefit for the rich, deductibility turns out to deliver most of its benefits to middle-income taxpayers. Since politicians know that such people are likely to own their own homes, to vote, to exert influence in their communities, and to be very conscious of increases in their taxes, it is easy enough to understand the reluctance to take away this broad-based benefit. Whatever merits the arguments on both sides may have had, elimination of deductibility was simply not a politically viable idea.

STRATEGIES FOR RAISING REVENUES

The Accountability Dilemma

The haste with which politicians retreated from the tax increase implicit in the proposal to eliminate deductibility reflects an enduring pattern in federal tax politics—namely, caution in raising taxes of any kind. This may seem paradoxical, given the enormous tax increases enacted during the past several decades, but both reluctance to raise taxes and decisions to raise taxes reflect valid political judgments. Taxes are always a potentially explosive issue in democratic systems, and federal politicians are fully aware that most citizens would prefer that their taxes not increase. There is enough evidence of elected officials losing their jobs after voting to increase taxes, moreover, to lend credence to the belief that tax increases are politically dangerous (Hansen, 1983).

Politicians also know, however, that citizens not only demand high levels of public service, but believe that government is morally obligated to deal with a variety of common problems (McClosky and Zaller, 1984). Lack of resources, for example, will not be an acceptable excuse for the governor or mayor who fails to deal with an unexpected disaster. Elected officials are thus liable to be both damned if they do (raise taxes) and damned if they don't (provide essential services). It is a difficult dilemma, made even worse by the difficulty of predicting when and how either kind of damnation will occur.

Political Strategies

In trying to cope with this dilemma, politicians have some important resources at their disposal. One is the "profound ignorance" noted by Hansen: Very few people understand either their taxes or the relationship between taxes and expenditures (Hansen, 1983). Citizens can be mobilized for or against taxes in general, usually around election time, but they are normally too uninformed to have much day-to-day influence. A second resource is tax interdependence itself, which is a further source of confusion for citizens, but which can provide clever officials with useful revenue options. Finally, officials who control the government institutions often can use the processes built into those institutions—budget cycles, the timing of elections, the fund structure, legal and constitutional constraints—to protect themselves against criticism while providing a satisfactory level of public services. What strategies are used to exploit these resources?

Strategy 1: Misrepresentation Given the complexity of public budgets and accounting systems, it is always difficult to know the "real" condition of government finances. Thus it is always possible to offer very different interpretations of a government's financial position, each of which can seem plausible to a public that has no ability to evaluate competing interpretations. Particularly during elections, Americans are repeatedly offered sharp criticisms by the "outs," who charge that the "ins" have mishandled the public purse; the "ins" defend themselves by offering evidence of "responsible and prudent" fiscal actions. With equal regularity, newly elected presidents, governors, and mayors attack the "mess" they have inherited from their predecessors in order to justify proposals for actions that can clean up the mess. Although dramatic and obvious, electoral incentives to distort the "true" condition of government finances in favor of one or another candidate are only a portion of a much larger phenomenon. "Strategic misrepresentation," in fact, is an option chosen by officials in a wide variety of circumstances (Larkey and Smith, 1981).

Perhaps the most common form of strategic misrepresentation, well documented in the public finance literature, is the tendency of budget officials to underestimate revenues and overestimate expenditures, particularly in jurisdictions that require an annual "balance" between revenues and expenditures. Conservative income forecasts and expansive expenditure projections suggest that the budget problem is worse than it really is, thus providing justification for coalitions in favor of revenue increases or expenditure cuts. Why should the chief executive typically responsible for budget preparation systematically misrepresent the annual budget problem? In their imaginative analysis, Larkey and Smith suggest the major incentives:

> Misrepresentation is an important means to increase the probability that the government will not run a deficit, but instead a small to moderate surplus. For chief executives, deficits are bad and surpluses within limits are good for two major reasons. First, deficits, particularly recurrent deficits, suggest nonfeasance and incompetence on the part of those charged with financial management, providing there is no compelling explanation (e.g., severe winters, unexpectedly large mid-year arbitration rewards, or the collapse of major taxpaying industries). Surpluses are almost always attributed to efficient and effective management even when the surplus results from curtailing services or some unforeseen revenue windfall not due to financial management acuity. . . .
>
> Second, surpluses help ease the administrative, financial, and political burdens of chief executives. Surpluses reduce the possibility of conflicts among organizational subunits within the government, especially conflicts that might arise if chief executives were forced to reduce already appropriated funds because of shortfalls in anticipated revenues. . . . Surpluses provide a hedge against uncertainty over the actual revenue and expenditure totals in the upcoming budget year. . . . Experienced chief executives are habitual pessimists, budgeting for unexpected revenue losses . . . or unforeseen expenditure increases. (Larkey and Smith, 1981, pp. 8,9)

To say that strategic misrepresentation is commonly practiced by chief executives, however, is not to say that it is always practiced in the same way. Larkey and Smith go on to point out, for example, that ". . . there is a much stronger bias in the formulation of budget problems in years of proposed tax increases than in years in which tax rates remain the same. Revenues are consistently underestimated more frequently and to a greater degree; expenditure requirements are consistently overestimated more often and to a larger extent; and, as a result, the reported budget gap is consistently overestimated more frequently and to a greater degree" (Larkey and Smith, p. 16).

Strategic misrepresentation, in short, is a common device used by officials to mobilize support for tax increases or to justify retention of larger revenues than are essential for operating their programs. The device can also be used to avoid tax changes, especially in election years. Jones, for example, has shown that city officials have consistently overestimated revenues from federal grant programs in order to achieve a "balance" between projected revenues and expenditures (Jones, 1985). Similarly, Stockman has recently revealed systematic overestimation of projected savings in federal expenditures by OMB to justify tax reductions desired by the president (Stockman, 1986). Whether in the more common pursuit of a usable surplus, or in less common but still frequent pursuit of other policy goals, government officials repeatedly misrepresent financial conditions for strategic reasons.

Strategy 2: Hide the Taxes   Public hostility to tax increases can be avoided by hiding the taxes. If existing taxes are to be increased, small changes are vastly preferable to large increments. If new taxes are to be imposed, the less visible they are, the better. Sales taxes are popular in part because they appear to be part of the price of a product, rather than a tax. Automatic witholding of income tax payments avoids the hostility that might be induced if taxpayers were required to make the payments themselves. Taxes levied on business firms are largely unnoticed by taxpayers, although prices they pay for business products may rise as a result.

As time passes, the repeated search for invisible taxes produces revenue systems of great ingenuity—and even greater complexity. In their painstaking review of the City of Pittsburgh's revenue system during the course of a half century, for example, Kaufman and Larkey reveal a ". . . decreasing reliance on visible sources and increasing reliance on semi-visible and invisible sources," such as mercantile, license, privilege, and utility taxes (Kaufman and Larkey, 1980, p. 12). Increasing reliance on hidden taxes clearly presents taxpayers with an even more difficult "cognitive problem" today than in years past, as Kaufman and Larkey note (p. 74). From an official point of view, however, use of many different and often invisible taxes can improve the stability of total revenue yields while offering some protection against possible taxpayer hostility. Accordingly, hiding taxes is a frequently pursued strategy.

Strategy 3: Shift the Tax Burden   It is often possible to shift the burden of paying taxes away from residents of a given jurisdiction. A tax on income earned within a city or state will generate revenue from persons who live outside of as well as within the jurisdiction. Taxes on "occupancy" or meals can generate substantial revenue from visitors to cities and states that are attractive to tourists. Cities with substantial shopping facilities can generate significant sales tax revenue from nonresident shoppers. In addition to such devices for exporting some portion of the tax burden to residents of other jurisdictions, taxes can be shifted from the general to a more specific base through imposition of user or service fees. Services such as water, sewer, or garbage hauling are commonly funded by such fees, thus relieving some of the pressure on more general sources of taxation. Finally, it is possible to shift some of the tax burden from present to future taxpayers through borrowing. Constitutional and legal constraints typically restrict the amount and type of debt that can be incurred by state and local governments, but bond issues remain a strategic option that can suppress the present need for additional taxes.

Strategy 4: Share the Tax Burden   During the past quarter century, the extraordinary growth of federal aid has produced a system in which the costs of providing public goods and services increasingly have been shared by national, state, and local governments. Although federal aid is often viewed as an imposition by national politicians on unwitting mayors and governors, it is important to remember that mayors and governors wanted most of the programs, lobbied for them, and in many cases helped to design them (Beer, 1976; Dommel, 1974). From this point of view, therefore, the growth of federal aid represents a remarkable achievement by state and local officials, who successfully persuaded the national government to bankroll activities that otherwise would have been supported entirely by state and local taxpayers, or not provided at all.

These patterns of cost sharing have become so established that even the determined effort made by the Reagan administration to reduce their significance has had only marginal impact (Stockman, 1986). Partly because of these efforts, however, state and local governments recently have shown more interest in horizontal as well as vertical cost sharing. In states such as California and Massachusetts, where voters have reduced local revenues by referendum, officials have been particularly active in seeking innovative sharing mechanisms to fund services (Kirlin, 1982; Sears and Citrin, 1985). Sharing the revenue burden is likely to become even more comprehensive and significant in the future than it has been in the recent past.

Strategy 5: Tax Timing   Tax increases that cannot be avoided can nevertheless be timed to minimize political damage. It is especially dangerous to propose higher taxes in election years, and politicians go to considerable lengths to avoid that danger. Fully 80 percent of all state sales and income taxes adopted since 1900, in fact, have been adopted in nonelection years (Hansen, 1983, p. 167). Politicians also go to great lengths to put as much distance as possible between a tax increase and the next election. In observing all tax increases and new taxes adopted by the states between 1960 and 1976, for example, Mikesell discovered that nearly two-thirds of all tax changes occurred in the first year after a governor's election; virtually none were enacted in the fourth year (Mikesell, 1978). Obviously it is not always possible to control the timing of tax increases. To the extent that control can be coordinated with the election cycle, however, politicians can do a great deal to ensure that public wrath over taxes will not be visited on them.

CONCLUSION: CYCLES OF CHANGE

Normal Change

The increasing complexity of a revenue system based on tax interdependence and developed by strategic ingenuity suggests that effective tax coalitions will continue to remain tiny and largely insulated from public visibility. Public officials responsible for the provision of goods and services will continue to seek and find sources of revenue by pursuing strategies designed to avoid creating public hostility. A few technocrats representing taxpayer and corporate organizations that can afford to hire them will participate in many of these decisions. Taxes will continue to increase over the long run to fund increasing expenditures, but tax reductions as well as increases will occur periodically as officials solve their annual budget problems, giving rise to short-run cycles of change. Since the cycles of increase and decrease will occur at different times in different jurisdictions, tax volatility will continue, and will continue to provide opportunities for revenue innovations.

The Tax "Revolt": Was It Real?

I offer these projections of what can be expected if the federal revenue system behaves "normally" in order to provide a framework for considering activities many observers have regarded as quite abnormal. Public approval of California's Proposition 13 in 1978, followed by tax reduction or limitation actions in several other states, led many analysts to conclude that a "tax revolt" was under way. By 1981 and 1982, when many states raised their taxes, analysts flocked to the opposite conclusion: The tax revolt was dead. Fortunately we now know enough about these tax limitation actions and their consequences to suggest a less dramatic but more accurate interpretation. Tax reduction referendums in California, Massachusetts, and a few other states were indeed important events that, along with later efforts to reduce federal taxes, emphasized the interdependence of tax opinions as well as tax policies. But "revolt" is far too strong a term to describe the events of 1978–80, and later state and federal actions to raise taxes do not imply that limitation sentiment somehow has disappeared. What the events of the late 1970s made clear was not that a popular rebellion against taxes was under way, but rather that, under certain conditions, broad-based coalitions can replace the tiny, technocratic coalitions that normally determine tax policies. In the aftermath of the late 1970s, it is also clear that these conditions are unlikely to occur with great frequency.

In order to appreciate popular tax sentiments during the 1970s it is necessary to rely on some indicator that is more meaningful and more comprehensive than those typically used as evidence of tax hostility. Although referendum votes in states such as California and Massachusetts provided clear evidence for citizen preferences that had measurable tax reduction consequences, many of the propositions voted on during the late 1970s did not cut spending at all; they simply limited the future rate of increase in spending. Not all of these proposals were approved, however, and those that passed often were so loosely worded as to constitute no limitation at all. Since fewer than half the states permit tax initiative referendums, furthermore, much of the evidence for tax hostility comes from actions taken by legislative bodies that reflected a wide variety of different state or local impulses. Some referendums passed and some failed; some states acted to limit taxes in various ways and some did not. Interest in taxes clearly was high in the late 1970s, but this record is hardly the stuff of revolution.

An indicator that is both more comprehensive and easier to interpret is popular voting on state and local bond issues. State and local governments issue bonds every year, most of which are subject to public approval. Voting on bond issues is a tangible expression of public fiscal sentiment because bond purposes typically are stated and because annual debt service on the bonds must be paid for through taxes or other general revenues. Figure 6.2 tracks the percentage of all state and local bond issues that were approved by voters across the country between 1956 and 1985, a period long enough to offer some perspective on the brief period some have referred to as the "tax revolt."

The proportion of bonds approved declined in the late 1950s, jumped back up in the mid-1960s, and then fell disastrously, though erratically, in the period 1967–1975. By the late 1970s the proportion of total bonds approved had recovered to levels close to those of the early to mid-1960s. With the economic recovery of 1983–85, bond approvals once again reached levels in excess of 80 percent of all sums requested. Thus at a time when taxpayers were said to be in revolt, they were approving two-thirds of all bonds proposed. It was during the early 1970s rather than later that the greatest public hostility toward new debt was expressed.

No single indicator is decisive, of course, but the bond approval ratio follows a track that seems suggestive when combined with other information. We know, for example, that taxes began to increase more rapidly than

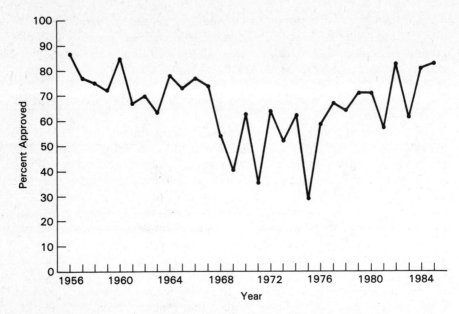

Figure 6.2 State and Municipal Bond Election Results, 1956–1985
SOURCE: The Bond Buyer 1985 Municipal Statbook. New York: The Bond Buyer, Inc., p. 24.

personal income in the early 1970s, that inflationary pressures during this period eroded purchasing power while increasing income taxes through "bracket creep," and that state and local expenditures as a percent of GNP continued to grow through 1975 (Kirlin, 1982, p. 29). Taxpayers were thus faced with raises that were very visible—for income and property taxes in particular—during a period when their own purchasing power was either stable or actually in decline. We know too that confidence in government was shaken by the American involvement in Vietnam, declined dramatically as a result of Watergate, and remained suppressed by our apparent inability to prevent or cope with energy price increases (Traugott, 1984).

In retrospect it is not difficult to understand why taxpayers, unhappy at the decline in their purchasing power and frustrated by repeated tax increases to support governments in which they had less and less confidence, should have been interested in reducing taxes. Bond issues provided an early opportunity to resist because they were routine annual events. Later, where procedures for initiative or recall were available, citizens occasionally were able to join with existing antitax coalitions large enough to use those devices. From this perspective, the events of the entire decade, rather than of its final segment, were in fact a steady flow of efforts to bring taxation down to levels more acceptable to large groups of citizens. The so-called tax revolt was a continuation of these efforts, rather than a new initiative.

While considerably less dramatic, this view is more in keeping with the events themselves. To begin with, action on tax limits was far from universal and very much dependent on the institutional context. Susan B. Hansen suggests, for example, that the most important determinant of whether or not a state acted on tax limitation was the presence of citizen initiative:

> Of the 21 states that permit voter initiatives, 11 or 52 percent passed tax or expenditure limitations between 1976 and 1980; 4 others in this group had them on the ballot although they were defeated. But of the 29 states that do not permit initiatives, only 6 (21 percent) passed tax or expenditure limitations during this period—a pattern highly unlikely to arise by chance. . . . Presence of initiative provisions proved to be the most important predictor of adoption of spending limitations, and the only [statistically] significant one. . . . (Hansen, 1983, pp. 233–234)

Moreover, surveys of voters in both California and Michigan make clear that, in voting for tax reduction or limitation, people were not voting for lower service levels. Indeed, a striking discovery in both states was that citizens were not only generally satisfied with existing services, but tended to want more rather than less government (Courant, Gramlich, and Rubinfeld, 1979; Sears and Citrin, 1985). Why, then, did citizens vote for lower property taxes in California and tax limits in Michigan? One answer was that many citizens in both states believed taxes could be reduced without harming services. Trimming the fat from wasteful government budgets would provide the same services at lower tax levels. Another answer was that lack of understanding of the tax-service relationship led citizens of California to seek "something for nothing" (Citrin, 1979), and encouraged Michigan citizens to pursue what Courant and his colleagues call "the unending search for a free lunch" (Courant, Gramlich, and Rubinfeld, 1979).

John J. Kirlin's rich contextual analysis of tax reform in California suggests yet another answer that may have considerable general relevance. Kirlin notes that rapid tax increases in California during the 1970s were accompanied by numerous efforts to deal with the problem, none of which achieved majority support among citizens or politicians. This dual frustration with tax increases and political deadlock was accompanied by a third problem—inability to find a way to impose some control on California's exceedingly complex revenue system. In Kirlin's view, therefore, popular support for Proposition 13 had three strong foundations:

> First, it cut property taxes, the source of major concern to California voters. Second, it provided opportunity to vent hostility against distrusted politicians, who had been unable to provide property-tax relief. Third, it provided certainty in a turbulent world in which citizens could find no other means to act generally against inflation and specifically against increased property taxes. . . .
> Voters were offered a tax-relief proposal far simpler and easier to comprehend than any of the measures considered by the legislature in the previous decade

and also simpler than the three tax-reform initiatives previously rejected. (Kirlin, 1982, p. 51)

Kirlin's intriguing suggestion that approval of Proposition 13 was due in part to voter frustration over tax complexity may well have more general relevance. Certainly revenue systems across the nation have become much more complicated, and the strategies commonly pursued by tiny tax coalitions can only increase complexity. Under these conditions, lashing out against current tax levels may represent the only choice available to citizens who lack enough information to participate in more focused tax politics.

As long as the real estate and corporate groups that typically resist higher taxation continue to promote tax resistance, the potential exists for this permanent coalition to be enlarged by frustrated citizens seeking tax relief. Tax actions during the early 1980s, however, make clear that mobilization of these potentially large coalitions is strongly influenced by the state of the economy, which affects personal income, as well as the strategies pursued by public officials. The outlook is for greater tax complexity, higher levels of citizen frustration, and continued efforts to reduce taxation as economic and political conditions allow. A widespread revolt is unlikely, but cycles of continuous change seem certain.

REFERENCES

ACIR, 1985–1986. Advisory Commission on Intergovernmental Relations. *Significant Features of Fiscal Federalism, 1985–1986*. Washington, D.C.: Government Printing Office.

Anton, 1967. Thomas J. Anton. "Roles and Symbols in the Determination of State Expenditures." *Midwest Journal of Political Science* 11 (February): 27–43.

Anton, 1980. Thomas J. Anton. "Federal Assistance Programs: The Politics of System Transformation." In *Natural Resources and Urban Policy*, ed. Douglas E. Ashford. New York: Methuen.

Anton, 1983. Thomas J. Anton. "The Regional Distribution of Federal Expenditures, 1971–1980." *National Tax Journal* 36 (December): 429–442.

Bahl, 1984. Roy Bahl. *Financing State and Local Government in the 1980s*. New York: Oxford University Press.

Beer, 1976. Samuel Beer. "The Adoption of General Revenue Sharing: A Case Study in Public Sector Politics." *Public Policy* 24 (Spring): 127–195.

The Bond Buyer, 1986. *The Bond Buyer 1985 Municipal Statbook*. New York: The Bond Buyer Inc.

Break, 1982. George Break. "Government Spending Trends in the Postwar Period." In *The Federal Budget: Economics and Politics*, ed. Michael Boskin and Aaron Wildavsky. San Francisco: Institute for Contemporary Studies.

Citrin, 1979. Jack Citrin. "Do People Want Something for Nothing: Public Opinion on Taxes and Government Spending." *National Tax Journal* 32 (June): 113–129.

Courant, Gramlich, and Rubinfield, 1979. Paul Courant, Edward Gramlich, and Daniel Rubinfield. "Public Employee Market Power and Level of Government Spending." *American Economic Review* 69: 806–816.

Dommel, 1974. Paul R. Dommel. *The Politics of Revenue Sharing*. Bloomington: Indiana University Press.

Dye, 1985. Thomas R. Dye. "Federal Tax Reform: The View from the States." *Policy Studies Journal* 13 (3): 546–562.

Gold, 1986. Steven D. Gold. "State and Local Tax Systems in the mid-1980's." Legislative Finance Paper #52. Denver, CO: National Conference of State Legislatures, Fiscal Affairs Program.

Hansen, 1983. Susan B. Hansen. *The Politics of Taxation: Revenue Without Representation*. New York: Praeger.

Jones, 1985. Bryan D. Jones. "Speculative City Budgeting and Federal Grants." Unpublished paper. Texas A&M University.

Kaufman and Larkey, 1980. Sanda Kaufman and Patrick D. Larkey. "The Composition and Level of Municipal Revenues: An Adaptive, Problem-Solving Explanation." Pittsburgh, Pa.: Carnegie-Mellon University, mimeo.

Kirlin, 1982. John J. Kirlin. *The Political Economy of Fiscal Limits*. Lexington, Mass.: D.C. Heath.

Larkey and Smith, 1981. Patrick D. Larkey and Richard A. Smith. "Strategic Misrepresentation and Justification of Budget Problems." Pittsburgh, Pa.: Carnegie-Mellon University, mimeo.

McCloskey and Zaller, 1984. Herbert McCloskey and John Zaller. *The American Ethos: Public Attitudes Toward Capitalism and Democracy*. Cambridge, Mass.: Harvard University Press.

Mikesell, 1978. John Mikesell. "Election Periods and State Policy Cycles." *Public Choice* 20: 49–58.

OMB, 1983. Executive Office of the President. Office of Management and Budget. *Budget of the United States Government FY 1983*. Washington, D.C.: Government Printing Office.

Salamon and Siegfried, 1977. Lester Salamon and John J. Siegfried. "Economic Power and Political Influence: The Impact of Industry Structure on Public Policy." *American Political Science Review* 71 (September): 1026–1043.

Schmalz, 1986. Jeffrey Schmalz. "Moynihan Says Cuomo Can't Dictate Tax Plan." *New York Times*, May 8.

Sears and Citrin, 1985. David O. Sears, and Jack Citrin. *Tax Revolt. Something for Nothing in California*. Cambridge, Mass.: Harvard University Press.

Smothers, 1986. Ronald Smothers. "Cuomo Pledges Unity on Taxes with Moynihan." *New York Times*, May 9.

State Budget and Tax News, June 30, 1986, vol. 5, no. 12.

Stockman, 1986. David A. Stockman. *The Triumph of Politics: How the Reagan Revolution Failed*. New York: Harper & Row.

Traugott, 1984. Michael W. Traugott. "Recent Trends in Trust in Public Institutions and Leaders." Paper prepared for delivery at the 2nd Public Forum on the Greenhouse Compact. Brown University, February 22.

U.S. Treasury, 1985. United States Treasury Department. Office of State and Local Finance. *Federal-State-Local Fiscal Relations: Report to the President and Congress*. Washington, D.C.: Government Printing Office.

CHAPTER 7

THIRD-PARTY FEDERALISM

In the United States, many public policies are carried out by nongovernmental agencies. Construction of highways, schools, and other public buildings typically is done by private firms for whom government contracts represent just one among several sources of profit. Health care, education, social assistance, and other public services are often provided by nonprofit organizations such as hospitals or day care centers that rely to a considerable extent on the work of volunteers. Government reliance on both profit-making and nonprofit organizations to achieve policy goals reinforces two important American values. One is limited government; the second is organizational pluralism. Enlisting private sector organizations in the work of government keeps government smaller than it might otherwise be without sacrificing desirable public policy goals. Public use of private sector agencies also emphasizes the essential contributions to the public interest that can be made only by nongovernmental institutions.

These are old values in American federalism, reflected in a long tradition of cooperation between public and private institutions. Joint action increases the benefits available to citizens beyond those available from government agencies alone. By implicating many private agencies in the production of public benefits, furthermore, public-private cooperation vastly increases the number of individuals and organizations with direct interest in public policies. Coalitions in support of various public policies thus become larger and more diffuse than they might otherwise be, as interested nongovernmental agencies seek to protect or expand their benefits. This chapter examines some of the major vehicles through which this tradition of "third-party federalism" operates.

PRIVATE WELFARE AS GENERAL WELFARE

Private Gain as Public Policy

At the outset it is important to emphasize something that is often overlooked—namely, that the health and further development of the American economy is a pervasive concern of American governments. The preamble to the U.S. Constitution lists promotion of the "general welfare" as one of the major purposes of the new governing system. American politicians have consistently interpreted that phrase as justification for a wide variety of policies designed to improve the economic well-being of individuals and business firms. American citizens too regard government as an important source of resources that can be used to promote their own financial security (McCloskey and Zaller, 1984). Thus, from the college students who prize summer jobs with the state highway department, to the brokers who earn large fees from insurance contracts with the government agencies, to corporations such as General Dynamics or Litton, which generate much of their income from defense contracts, to the farmers who earn large sums from crop support payments, a great many Americans and American organizations pursue their own economic betterment through relationships with various American governments.

In a society premised on opportunity, the public sector is, has been, and will continue to be a major source of economic gain for all who seek to promote their own interests—and in doing so, promote the "general" welfare. In the United States, the generation of personal and corporate wealth is a major public policy objective. The objective is pursued, in part, through contracts awarded to individuals or corporations to produce goods or services that otherwise might be produced by government workers themselves. As government has grown at all levels, the value of these contracts has increased enormously. Entirely new industries have developed on a foundation of government contracts—defense, space exploration, and computers are prominent examples.

Whether to use public or private agencies to perform some service or produce some good is a recurring issue, since most activities, including police and fire protection, can be performed by both sectors. The issue is often settled in legislation that either creates a governmental body to undertake the desired activity or requires the work to be done under contract or by specific private organizations. An amendment to the General Revenue Sharing program, for example, required all governmental recipients of GRS funds to have an "independent audit" of expenditures from those funds—some promptly began referring to this provision as "the CPA amendment" (Nathan and Adams, 1977). In general, American national politicians have had a bias in favor of using private sector agencies whenever possible, which helps to account for the lack of growth in federal government employment during three decades of rapid financial expansion. On the other hand, state and local politicians have preferred government agencies, as evidenced by the extraordinary growth in state and local government employment during the past three decades (Chapter 2).

The New Privatization

A recent surge of interest in "privatization" (Hatry, 1983, Savas, 1982) suggests that the political bias in favor of using private sector agencies to accomplish public purposes has grown stronger, particularly at the local level. Faced with reductions in federal aid imposed by the Reagan administration, and reluctant as ever to propose new taxes to weary local electorates, municipal and county officials have searched for ways to maintain services at reduced funding levels. During the 1980s, that search has led to more contracts with private firms to perform a variety of public functions.

Table 7.1 reports results from a survey conducted by the International City Management Association in 1984 on city and county uses of private contractors. As is evident from these data, privatization encompasses many different kinds of services, from waste disposal to hospital management. Because private contractors are usually less encumbered by union contracts and civil service regulations than local governments, officials have found that these services often cost less than they would if government employees performed them. Understandably enough, many local officials are pleased at the results of privatization. Contracting out allows officials to emphasize their role as policymakers—they can determine the mix of services they want without the trouble of acting as service providers. Moreover, they can do so without losing control and accountability. As George Lattimer, Mayor of St. Paul, Minnesota, has argued, contracting out ". . . gives local government more flexibility. It gives us options. And remember, we write the specifications. We write the contracts" (Tolchin, 1985).

Despite the recent wave of optimism over privatizing public services, it is not at all clear that the benefits are nearly as great as some officials appear to believe. Research has shown that some services contracted out to private organizations have been provided at less cost and higher quality than similar services provided by public agencies. But, as Bendick and Levinson point out, the private sector advantage

> . . . typically applied in cases where the service at issue was technical in nature, where it was produced with well-known processes, and where it was easily measured and monitored—such as street paving. When the same arrangements have been applied to complex human service needs—whether retraining the hard-to-employ, revitalizing ghetto communities, or transforming the life chances of the disadvantaged—then the record of private firms shows no consistently higher achievement than that of the public sector itself. (Bendick and Levinson, 1984, p. 472)

The same authors remind us, furthermore, that the willingness of profit-making organizations to undertake unprofitable activities is quite limited, ". . . confined primarily to circumstances where public subsidies generate substantial profit incentives. Even then, the deeper the water of social trouble, the less likely they are to participate even when enticed by substantial subsidies" (p. 475). It appears, then, that the use of private sector agencies to provide services in place of public agencies can be an

Table 7.1　City and County Uses of Private Contractors

TYPE OF SERVICE	NATIONAL PERCENT OF PUBLIC SERVICE GIVEN TO PRIVATE CONTRACTORS BY CITIES AND COUNTIES
Public Works and Transportation	
Commercial solid waste collection	41%
Residential solid waste collection	34
Solid waste disposal	26
Street repair	26
Traffic signal installation/maintenance	25
Snowplowing and sanding	14
Public Utilities	
Street light operation	38
Utility billing	12
Utility meter reading	9
Safety and Recreation	
Vehicle towing and storage	78
Ambulance service	23
Emergency medical service	13
Parks maintenance	9
Health Services	
Operation/management of hospitals	25
Insect/rodent control	13
Support Services	
Legal services	48
Fleet management and maintenance	
Heavy equipment	31
Emergency vehicles	30
All other vehicles	28
Labor relations	23
Data processing	22
Building/grounds maintenance	19
Payroll	10
Building security	7
Public relations	7
Tax assessing	6
Personnel services	5
Secretarial services	4

SOURCE: International City Management Association Survey. Reported in the *New York Times*, May 28, 1985, p. 1.

effective strategy, but only for services provided through known and measurable technologies. Where problems are more difficult or technologies uncertain, private sector firms are less likely to be interested, and no more likely to act effectively than are public agencies.

There are other problems as well. Private contracting is an ancient practice of American governments, not a new idea, and the history of government contracting is littered with scandal and corruption. Indeed, the idea of a professionalized municipal civil service is itself a direct outgrowth of widespread corruption in the private provision of local transportation and other services around the turn of the century. Recent contract scandals in New York City, Chicago, and elsewhere make it clear that the danger of corruption in private contracting has not diminished at the local level, any more than it has diminished for the nation's largest source of private contracts, the Department of Defense.

Proponents of privatization, in fact, have taken to publishing advice about how to avoid contract corruption (Marlin and Feiden, 1986, p. 27). Carefully drawn specifications, prebidding conferences, clear contracts, and close monitoring of performance are among the recommendations being offered. But following such recommendations would require additional effort, which normally means additional personnel at additional cost. Privatization may thus increase supervisory costs even if it decreases service delivery costs. Without careful monitoring, of course, private contractors can easily subvert—indeed, profit-making organizations have incentives to subvert—important public values such as affirmative action, minimum wage guarantees, or the delivery of services to disadvantaged populations. Privatization, in short, can be an important service delivery option, but its advantages are clearly limited.

Economic Development Policy

In addition to contracting out much of what they do, American governments pursue a host of policies whose explicit purpose is to subsidize individuals and business firms in order to encourage economic development. Tax breaks, for example, are universally available. At the local level, municipal officials often manipulate the property tax to reduce the costs of doing business for desirable firms, either by favorable assessments or, more recently, by offering tax reductions ("abatements") to such firms (Wolkoff, 1981). State tax systems also favor business by exempting various materials and equipment from state taxation, offering tax incentives for various kinds of investments, allowing firms to carry profits and losses backward and forward across years in order to minimize tax liability, and so on (Anton and Reynolds, 1985). And of course the federal tax code is literally riddled with credits, exemptions, deductions, incentives, and other devices designed to encourage investment by reducing the corporate and individual tax burden. These federal "tax expenditures," in fact, have grown more rapidly than any other form of federal spending in recent years, amounting to nearly $450 billion in 1986 (OMB Special Analysis, 1988).

Table 7.2 lists some of the larger tax breaks available to corporations and individuals in 1986. Even after the 1986 tax reform, many of these advantages remain in place, testimony to the continuing emphasis on economic betterment as a public policy goal. Nor is this all: Enormous public investments are made each year in the infrastructure necessary to support economic development. These investments, averaging just under $80 billion annually for the past decade (CBO, 1985) are largely controlled by state and local officials who are firmly committed to their use as economic stimulants. One recent study quotes an Iowa county supervisor's view that "We're not going to get economic development when you rob the infrastructure of funds. You won't see economic development in Blackhawk County, Iowa, if I can't run a sewer line out to the new industrial site." The same study reports the view of the Speaker of the New York State Assembly that "Public spending for roads, bridges, and mass transit may be even more useful than new tax cuts in attracting business to New York State" (Pagano and Moore, 1985, p. 104).

The popularity of such views among state and local officials across the country often encourages interstate and intermunicipal competition to

Table 7.2 Outlay Equivalent Estimates for Tax Expenditures by Function, 1986 ($ millions)

DESCRIPTION	CORPORATIONS	INDIVIDUALS
National defense	$ 0	$ 2,425
International affairs	2,315	2,405
General science/space/technology	5,995	210
Energy	1,860	1,825
Natural resources/environment	2,125	545
Agriculture	135	1,305
Commerce/housing credit	74,920	114,075
Transportation	115	*
Community/regional development	650	220
Education/training/social service	5,260	28,500
Health	2,090	37,635
Social security/Medicare	0	18,425
Income security	0	114,345
Veterans benefit/services	0	2,290
General government	0	295
General fiscal assistance	4,380	31,700
Interest	0	850
TOTAL	$99,845	$357,050

*$2.5 million or less. All estimates have been rounded to the nearest $5 million.

SOURCE: Office of Management and Budget. *Special Analyses, Budget of the United States Government, FY 86.* Washington, D.C.: Government Printing Office, 1986, pp. G38–G42.

attract new industries, in which officials strive to put together packages of tax and infrastructure benefits that can induce new industries to enter a jurisdiction or old industries to remain. This competitive spirit was made very visible in the efforts of many state and local officials to attract the new Saturn automobile plant of the General Motors Corporation. After General Motors announced it was seeking a site for the new plant, 24 governors personally visited GM headquarters to press the advantages of their states. More than a thousand locations in 38 states ultimately were offered to the corporation (Corrigan, 1985). Although this kind of competition between jurisdictions can be intense, its underlying premise is that cooperation between government and business is both desirable and essential for continued economic progress.

Cooperation between business and government reached new levels during the early 1980s, when state governments became very active not only in assisting business, but in joining business. Nationally, the economic recessions of the 1970s had stimulated much debate over "industrial policy," but little action to implement such a policy (Magaziner and Reich, 1982; Schultz, 1983). Confronted with an even more severe recession in 1983, as well as the reluctance of the Reagan administration to address the industrial policy issue, states began to fashion their own economic development policies. Much state action followed traditional preferences for improving the business climate: tax reductions or incentives, elimination of costly regulations, and so on. But many states also developed innovative programs in which state agencies themselves became sources of venture capital for new enterprises, or shared ownership with corporate partners, accepting the risk of loss as well as the possibility of gain, or provided market assessment and strategy services to firms seeking to test new products (Anton and Reynolds, 1985; Grady, 1986). Interestingly enough, even these "new" programs appear to have been derived from established patterns of public-private cooperation. Thus Anton and Reynolds, referring to recent innovations in state economic development policies, conclude:

> . . . the programs themselves reveal a focused concern for the dominant economic interests in each state; in this sense they are "pluralist" programs, based on economic and political power rather than analytic design. The Ben Franklin Partnership in Pennsylvania, for example, not only involves major state industries with the most important educational institutions in the state, but takes care to locate partnership investments in each of the principal regions of the state. . . . Recent program initiatives in New York, Massachusetts, Michigan and other states are similarly careful to include benefits for important areas as well as important industries, adding further testimony to the political influence of geographic, as well as interest, representation. The rhetoric attached to such policies celebrates the wisdom of "building on what you have" (good) rather than "trying to develop activities that cannot be supported by the present economic infrastructure" (bad). Whether or not such sentiments are "wise," they clearly reflect the power of established state interests. (Anton and Reynolds, 1985, p. 18)

Recent policy innovations, particularly by the states, have added new weapons to an already large arsenal of policies designed to promote private wealth. Governments continue to generate private sector profits through contracts for goods and services; they continue to offer tax breaks worth hundreds of billions of dollars; and they continue to invest heavily in public infrastructure in order to promote economic growth. More and more, however, governments have decided to enter the market through active partnerships with private firms, rather than simply trying to affect the market context. Indeed, "partnership" has become the newest buzzword as American governments energetically extend the tradition of public-private cooperation.

Although the national government has been less innovative than state and local governments in recent years, it continues to promote economic growth through its tax, loan, loan guarantee, and expenditure programs, and it continues to cooperate with local governments in the innovative Urban Development Action Grant program (UDAG), through which small national grants are combined with local government contributions to "leverage" or stimulate private investment in central city renewal (Clarke and Rich, 1982). Private action as a substitute for government action in this area would be unlikely; private action in cooperation with government action is an old tradition whose strength has been reaffirmed by the newest innovations in economic development policy.

The Cost and Value of Private Subsidy

Apart from wars and other periodic national emergencies, then, the promotion of private economic gain has always been the central preoccupation of public policy in the United States, consuming far more resources than any other governmental actions. In fiscal 1986, for example, tax and loan subsidies to private agencies probably amounted to some $370 billion or more, including massive amounts from federal programs and substantial contributions from state and local assistance programs (Table 7.3). If government contracts for goods and services are added to this calculation, a conservative estimate of total government spending to promote private enterprise would easily approach $500 billion. Much of the defense budget—perhaps $100 billion of the $280 billion total in 1986—supports weapons and research industries that would not exist apart from government support. If so, and if only one-fourth of our $80 billion annual expenditure on infrastructure is counted as primarily support for business enterprise, then the total figure is very close to a half-trillion dollars of public resources devoted to private enrichment. These estimates cannot be entirely accurate, but they do offer a useful ballpark estimate and, in doing so, underline a comment made by former U.S. President Calvin Coolidge: The business of American government is business.

An enduring issue surrounding these public subsidies for business is whether or not they "work." The issue is difficult to resolve because the

Table 7.3 Public Subsidies for Profit-Making Organizations, 1986 ($ billions)

Tax expenditures for business	$225
Direct loans (federal)	40
Loan guarantees (federal)	25
GSE loans (federal)	60
Local property tax abatements	10
State tax provisions	10
TOTAL	$370

SOURCE: Estimates derived from OMB, Special Analyses, Fiscal Year 1986, analyses F and G. Tax expenditure estimates exclude housing, health, education, and social service categories. Direct, guaranteed, and GSE loans exclude housing and student loan categories.

purposes of many subsidy programs are unclear, and because it is often impossible to determine whether the activities supported by a public subsidy would have occurred without that subsidy. Corporations and individuals make investment decisions for many reasons. Disentangling the effect of a subsidy, compared to factors such as location, labor supply, availability of materials, general economic conditions, and so on, is a complicated task that has produced no certain answers (Gold, 1985).

Local subsidies are particularly difficult to evaluate because so many governments appear to offer subsidies as a matter of routine. Wolkoff discovered, for example, that local officials offered essentially identical abatement plans to all applicants, regardless of the type of business pursued, and that virtually all who applied were granted the abatement. In New York City, 95 percent of the 300 applications filed through 1980 were approved, while none of the first 100 applications for property tax abatement in Detroit was denied. Further, while Michigan local officials are permitted by law to limit their awards, they never did so: "Michigan economic development officials reported that of the two thousand projects abated since 1974, they are unaware of one that received less than the abatement cap" (Wolkoff, 1983, p. 81). Similar patterns were discovered in Ohio cities, suggesting that few local officials have clear objectives in offering subsidies other than tax reductions for corporations that ask for them.

In this sense, most of the subsidy programs do "work," since they achieve the apparent objective of providing financial assistance to business firms. Whether or not local, state, and national subsidies "work" in the sense of stimulating new investment or new jobs that otherwise would not have been created is less clear, but also less significant. The fact is that most governments accept them as legitimate contributions to the public welfare, that business firms expect them, that individuals also expect them, and that all parties have become accustomed to their availability. Former Budget Director David Stockman has likened the beneficiaries of these subsidies to "hogs at the trough" (Stockman, 1986). The public trough has always been available, however, and it is now so large that neither the corporate nor the individual hogs who frequent it would willingly abandon its contribution to their—and therefore the public—welfare.

NONPROFIT FEDERALISM

A Bias toward Voluntarism

Government collaboration with profit-making agencies in the pursuit of desirable social goals is matched by an equally dense network of collaborative relationships between government and nonprofit agencies. Awareness of these relationships was at best fragmentary until very recently, when a major step forward was provided by the work of Lester M. Salamon and Alan J. Abramson. Through careful compilation of Treasury and Census data, these authors have given us the first comprehensive analysis of the nonprofit sector as a whole, as well as the mechanisms through which government and nonprofit agencies interact (Salamon and Abramson, 1982; Salamon, 1984). Their analysis makes clear that the "general welfare" pursued by American public and private institutions is much broader than the search for economic betterment, however prominent that goal may be. In seeking broader goals, American governments have repeatedly turned to nonprofit agencies that reflect American traditions of neighborliness and voluntarism.

These traditions have several mutually reinforcing sources. First, as a frontier society, the United States offered no preexisting governmental structures to the successive generations of immigrants who came to North America and then spread across the continent. If common action was required, as it often was, it could occur only through voluntary actions of individuals who agreed to work together for some common purpose. Governments eventually came into existence in the many American frontier settlements, but they functioned on a preexisting base of voluntary participation in community betterment. Always perceptive, in the nineteenth century Alexis de Tocqueville made this assessment:

> Americans of all ages, all stations of life, and all types of disposition are forever forming associations . . . to give fetes, found seminaries, build churches, distribute books and send missionaries to the antipodes. . . . In every case, at the head of any new undertaking, where in France you would find the government or in England some territorial magnate, in the United States you are sure to find an association. (cited in Salamon, 1984, p. 263)

Second, as an immigrant society, the United States encouraged community organizations based on ethnic identity. The waves of Europeans and Asians who came to this country in the nineteenth and twentieth centuries were offered jobs but little else. To survive, these new settlers turned to others like themselves, who shared a language and a culture, and who could thus provide the support systems necessary for assimilation.

These ethnic organizations often provided a wide range of services, from social and athletic events, to health care, education, housing, pension plans, and other forms of social assistance—all based primarily on voluntary membership contributions (Glazer and Moynihan, 1970).

Finally, as a society that offered (and continues to offer) religious freedom, the United States has provided a home for many religious groups that stress neighborliness and community participation as a moral duty. The result is a large number of voluntary activities based on religious membership that provide a variety of social services, from job counseling to soup kitchens. Taken together, these ethnic and religious impulses, operating in a frontier environment, have created a long and strong tradition of voluntarism in the pursuit of community welfare, as well as a dense network of nonprofit organizations.

The Size and Structure of Nonprofit Efforts

Well-publicized media events such as Live Aid, Farm Aid, Hands across America, or the various television charity campaigns all suggest that the tradition of caring is alive and well. In a typical recent year, for example, ". . . some 84 million Americans, or 37 percent of the total population, have provided at least some volunteer effort" (Bendick and Levinson, p. 463). Americans also provide very large financial contributions to support community improvement. Bendick and Levinson have tracked total per person charitable contributions in the United States back to 1955, and the result reveals a pattern that is cyclical to some extent—contributions decrease during recessionary periods and increase in periods of economic strength—but that is marked by substantial long-term growth. In 1983 Americans contributed some $93 per person, an amount that was 85.8 percent higher than it had been in 1955, even with inflation taken into account. Bendick and Levinson point out that "This rate of increase outstripped that of total income per capita (measured by gross national product), which grew only 58.7 percent in the same period" (Bendick and Levinson, 1984, p. 468). During the past three decades, therefore, Americans appear to have become more generous with their time and money, increasing their charitable contributions more than their own incomes have increased.

This increasing generosity has helped to support a network of charitable nonprofit organizations that rivals the government sector in size and complexity, if not in expenditures. Using IRS data on organizations that had filed for tax-exempt status, Salamon and Abramson developed the information displayed in Table 7.4. Some 103,026 nonprofit organizations existed in 1977, employing 4.4 million people and spending more than $116 billion in 1980. Salamon and Abramson argue:

> These organizations clearly constitute an important part of the nation's service delivery system. They account, collectively, for almost 5 percent of the Gross National Product. They employ five times as many workers as the automobile

industry and account for one-third of the employment in the nation's rapidly growing service sector. In many fields of activity, in fact, they are the principal service providers. Thus nonprofit organizations deliver most of the hospital care, much of the postsecondary education, and a considerable portion of the social services (such as foster care and family counseling) provided in this country. They are also a major presence in the fields of art, music, culture, and research, and are the principal channel for a host of civic-action and community-organization activities. (Salamon and Abramson, 1982, p. 222)

While individual generosity has been an important source of support for this huge nonprofit sector, governments have also provided extensive support. Until this century, state and local governments were largely responsible for the health, education, and social service activities that have become the main interests of nonprofit organizations. As demands for these services increased, state and local jurisdictions increasingly looked to nonprofit agencies to complement the institutional care available in state and local facilities. By the turn of the century, city and state agencies had already established extensive patterns of cooperation with nonprofit agencies, including substantial public funding for their activities.

The Great Depression of the 1930s led to a dramatic expansion of social service programs by the federal government, primarily through grants to state governments to support their cash assistance programs for the needy. Later, from the 1950s through the 1970s, the national government became more active in other areas as well, including health, education, and community development. Grants to state and local governments remained the major instrument through which a more active national government expanded its role, but the federal bias in favor of private rather than governmental service providers became increasingly prominent. In the social services area, for example, the national government:

. . . made specific provision, through the 1962 amendments to the Social Security Act and even more so in the 1967 amendments, for state agencies to enlist nonprofit organizations in the actual delivery of the services. By 1971, in fact, purchases from non-profit providers constituted about 25 percent of the expenditures under the various social service programs that in 1972 were folded into the federal social services block grant program (Title XX). This pattern of contracting out has, moreover, increased even further in recent years. (Salamon and Abramson, 1982, p. 39)

And just as federal contracts with profit-making organizations have stimulated development of wholly new industries, federal support for the nonprofit sector has led to the development of new types of nonprofit organizations, such as community health clinics or regional planning agencies (Yin, 1980). Indeed, one recent survey of some 3,400 nonprofit organizations, excluding hospitals and institutions of higher education,

Table 7.4   The Charitable Nonprofit Sector in the United States

TYPE OF ORGANIZATION	NUMBER	PERCENT OF TOTAL	EXPENDITURES ($ BILLIONS)	EMPLOYEES (000)
Social/legal services	42,084	40.8%	$13.2(11%)	688.9
Civic, social, fraternal	34,121	33.2	5.4(5%)	255.9
Education/research	11,034	10.7	25.2(22%)	980.1
Health care	12,307	11.9	70.0(60%)	2431.0
Arts/cultural	3,480	3.4	2.6(2%)	59.8
TOTALS	103,026	100%	$116.4(100%)	4415.7

SOURCE: Lester M. Salamon and Alan J. Abramson, *The Federal Budget and the Nonprofit Sector* (The Urban Institute, 1982), Tables 1 and 2; Salamon and Abramson, "The Nonprofit Sector," in Palmer and Sawhill, eds., *The Reagan Experiment* (The Urban Institute, 1982), Table 7–1, p. 222. Organization and employee figures are for 1977; expenditure estimates are for 1980. Reprinted with permission of The Urban Institute Press.

discovered that more than 60 percent of these organizations had been created since 1960 alone (Salamon, 1984). During the past several decades, in short, the national government has joined state and local governments in providing substantial support for nonprofit agencies; it provided more than $40 billion in 1980, compared to some $22 billion in private donations.

Table 7.5 shows the distribution of federal contributions to the major categories of nonprofit organizations in 1980. Health care organizations received by far the largest contribution, accounting for nearly $25 billion of the $40 billion total, and supporting some 36 percent of total health care spending by nonprofit organizations. Federal contributions were smaller for social service and civic organizations, but such agencies depended on the national government for well over half of their total revenues. Education and research organizations were not as dependent on federal contributions, but their receipts of $5.6 billion nevertheless represented a substantial level of support.

Table 7.5   Nonprofit Revenues from Federal Programs, 1980

	FEDERAL SUPPORT ($ BILLIONS)	TOTAL SPENDING	FEDERAL AS SHARE OF TOTAL SPENDING
Social service	$7.3	$13.2	58%
Civic	2.3	3.2	72
Education and research	5.6	25.2	22
Health care	24.9	70.0	36
Arts and culture	0.3	2.6	12
TOTAL	$40.4	$114.2	35%

SOURCE: Lester M. Salamon, "Nonprofit Organizations: The Lost Opportunity," in Palmer and Sawhill, eds., *The Reagan Record* (The Urban Institute, 1984), p. 267. Copyright 1984 by the Urban Institute. Reprinted by permission of Ballinger Publishing Company.

These data understate the significance of government support for private nonprofit organizations because they do not include contributions made by state and local governments, which amount to roughly 10 percent of nonprofit revenues. Taking those contributions into account makes clear that the nonprofit sector is even more dependent on government funding than the data suggest, with more than 40 percent of revenues derived from government sources. In choosing to support nonprofit organizations so extensively, American governments clearly have expressed their preference for partnership relationships with this sector, as well as with the profit-making sector. Such relationships are as varied as the sector itself, but they are also comprehensive, underlining the extent to which an extensive network of private agencies pursues public goals in the American federal system.

THE STRENGTH OF THIRD-PARTY FEDERALISM

Coping with Budget Cuts

The existence of a dense and differentiated nonprofit sector increases the complexity of an already complex service delivery system. But the variety that adds complexity is also a source of strength. Shortly after assuming office, for example, President Reagan was able to achieve significant reductions in many federal domestic programs, apparently without realizing that these reductions would also reduce funding for the many nonprofit agencies that received support from those programs (I use the word "apparently," because the president was simultaneously advocating a reinvigoration of voluntary associations). Since the level of federal support across agencies was varied rather than uniform, however, the impact of federal budget cuts also varied considerably. Many universities and hospitals were able to raise fees enough to replace lost federal funds, thus suffering minimal losses. Social service agencies, on the other hand, could hardly recover federal funding losses from clients already in poverty, particularly since federal funds were so large a fraction of their total resources. Many social service agencies, accordingly, were forced to reduce services, or to eliminate some services altogether. In many other cases, these agencies were able to secure replacement funding from state or local governments, thus blunting the overall impact of President Reagan's funding reductions.

In general, the members of the public-private partnerships that characterize third-party federalism in the United States reacted to President Reagan's budget reductions with considerable ingenuity. Nathan and Doolittle, in their revealing study, *The Consequences of Cuts*, report numerous examples of "coping" behavior on the part of state and local officials that allowed them to maintain services despite reductions in federal aid: Costs were shifted from one budget year to another; clients were shifted from one program to another, or from government to the private sector, and so on (Nathan and Doolittle, 1983).

Imaginative administrative action by state and local officials, combined with congressional action in 1982 and 1983 to restore some of the earlier reductions, took much of the political steam out of Reagan's program to reduce domestic expenditures (Palmer and Sawhill, 1984). Program growth was slowed in some areas, to be sure, but the services available when the president assumed office remain largely available today, a result attributable in no small measure to the extraordinary coping capacity built into the system.

An excellent example of ingenuity in the nonprofit sector is the response to the attempt to do away with the Legal Services Corporation. Legal Services was established in 1974 as a private nonprofit corporation, funded by the national government, to provide civil legal services to the poor. Although never a major program, funding had grown to $320 million in 1980 and was expected to continue to increase (OMB Budget Appendix, 1982, p. I-V89). In typical fashion, federal funds were used to provide grants to some 360 local programs across the country, employing 7,000 attorneys and 3,000 paralegals who actually delivered the services.

This level of support met only a fraction of the need, but federal policy explicitly acknowledged the obligation of members of the legal profession to contribute their time to an "overall legal services effort" composed of public and private contributions. The Carter administration, in fact, sought to have the corporation ". . . take the lead in encouraging and coordinating pro bono services, including use of Corporation staff, research projects, and technical assistance to demonstrate ways to fulfill attorney commitments. Expansion of legal services for the poor," the Carter administration suggested, "must rely primarily on this approach, rather than on Federal compensation for private attorney services" (OMB Budget Appendix, 1982, p. I-V89). Here, then, was yet another effort to promote a public good through a federal-local-nonprofit partnership.

President Reagan, however, had a different idea. Unhappy with the activities of Legal Services in California during his term as governor, Reagan entered the presidency determined to curtail its influence. In its first budget, therefore, the Reagan administration offered ". . . a different approach: providing States with flexibility and discretion to use block grant funds, and relying on private attorneys to fulfill their ethical obligations to provide services to the poor." The "flexibility" was to flow from existing Social Services Block Grants which, according to the administration, ". . . include adequate authority to fund legal services activities States may wish to provide for their citizens."

As for relying on the "ethical obligations" of attorneys, this was to be accomplished by eliminating the Legal Services Corporation altogether, ending all federal funding for its activities. "The Administration believes the private bar can and should do more to fulfill their obligations through pro bono public services. In addition," it announced, "the Federal

Government should no longer subsidize the private bar in the fulfillment of its ethical responsibilities to the poor" (OMB Major Themes, 1983, p. 33). Instead of working with state, local, and nonprofit agencies to "encourage" and "coordinate" legal services for the poor, the Reagan approach was simply to abandon any national responsibility for such services.

This all-out assault on the Legal Services Corporation was resisted strenuously by Congress, which has continued both the corporation and its federal funding despite repeated proposals to discontinue the agency in every succeeding Reagan budget. However, the president did succeed in reducing federal appropriations to the corporation by 25 percent, forcing a substantial reduction in grants and thus a substantial reduction in free legal services for poor people. In this program, as in others, Reagan policies placed a traditional public-private partnership arrangement under considerable strain.

Although skeptics surely had cause to wonder about the wisdom of any policy that relies on "ethical obligations" for its effectiveness, state governments and bar associations across the country have in fact fashioned an innovative response to the challenge. Borrowing a concept used successfully in Canada and Australia for some years, most states have established programs commonly referred to as IOLTA: Interest on Lawyers Trust Accounts. The idea is simple. As described by David Richert, "The small amounts of money that lawyers hold for short terms on behalf of numerous clients are combined in interest-bearing accounts. That interest is then used for legal services to the poor, as well as for student aid and 'to improve the administration of justice'" (Richert, 1982).

Lawyers historically had placed such funds in non-interest-bearing accounts that could be withdrawn on demand, so any interest earned on such funds would be new money. And since trust or escrow funds held for any individual are often small in size and short in duration, paying interest to clients would be impractical. "It doesn't make sense," according to an Illinois State Bar Association official, "to put a 14-cent interest check in an envelope and send it to a client by using a 20-cent stamp" (quoted by Richert, 1982, p. 449). In the aggregate, however, these small individual amounts can add up to very large sums, particularly in states with large numbers of attorneys, such as California (50,000) or Ohio (30,000).

Florida established the first IOLTA program in September 1981, followed by California in 1982, and other states in succeeding years. By April 1986, 41 states and the District of Columbia had adopted IOLTA programs, either through legislation or by action of state supreme courts. More than $50 million in cumulative income had been collected by mid-1986, and annual receipts were climbing beyond $30 million ("Income Tops $50 Million, 1986"). These annual receipts are not yet sufficient to replace lost federal funds, but they are quite significant in allowing states to develop their own approaches to providing legal services to the poor.

As always, states operate IOLTA programs in very different ways. Most programs are administered by foundations affiliated with state bar associations, but wholly separate foundations have been established in some states, supreme courts administer the program in others, and one state (Massachusetts) has authorized three separate agencies to collect and dispense IOLTA monies ("IOLTA Info," 1985). Perhaps most intriguing of all, all these programs are operating with funds that one lawyer has called "found money"—that is, money that did not exist prior to its discovery in response to national funding reductions (Richert, 1982). In its energy, diversity, and imagination, the IOLTA program is an excellent example of the resourcefulness built into a system that relies so much on the contributions of volunteers.

The ability of many nonprofit organizations to adjust to federal funding losses suggests an important point about nonprofit organizations, which is that they are often able to exert considerable influence over public policy. As heirs to a long tradition of voluntarism, they have a historically sanctioned legitimacy. And as providers of services funded with public money, nonprofit agencies have an important stake in the continuation of those funds and services. Like their governmental counterparts, therefore, nonprofit organizations often act as advocates for both their own and their clients' interests.

Nathan and Doolittle, for example, found that one of the most important factors accounting for state and local decisions to replace lost federal funding was the extent to which social service organizations were organized and active in seeking replacement funds (Nathan and Doolittle, 1983). Advocacy by such organizations often had the effect of mobilizing real, but latent, interests. Thus it was not only hospital administrators and trustees, but doctors, nurses, and social workers who mobilized to protest cuts in Medicare and Medicaid that threatened hospital revenues across the country. As providers of public services, in short, tens of thousands of nonprofit organizations have powerful incentives to participate in the political coalitions that shape those services. This is not to say that "ethical obligations" should be discounted as sources of political action. It is merely to point out that, in the nonprofit sector, ethical obligations often join with organizational incentives to motivate political action.

Changing the Health Care Partnership

It is obvious that adding 103,000 nonprofit organizations to the 82,000 governments and the tens of thousands of profit-making firms that are involved in producing public goods and services creates a system of forbidding complexity. Having already noted that the complexity of relationships among governments leads to inherent instability, we can now add that the additional complexity introduced by the involvement of profit and nonprofit organizations with American governments is yet another major source of instability. Virtually every governmental action produces extensive ripple effects in other public and private organizations.

American federal governance—including private as well as public actors—is thus always changing, never at rest. Because dynamic impulses are so numerous, furthermore, changes observed at any given time may appear to be contradictory. Earlier, for example, we noted recent efforts by the national government to withdraw from social assistance programs in favor of greater state and local responsibility, and greater use of private sector contractors. Even as these actions were under way, there was a thrust toward the assumption of greater responsibility by the national government and a diminution of the private sector role. Since this thrust took place in health care delivery, which has been dominated by the nonprofit sector but which relies heavily on public support, it is important to examine the sources and consequences of this movement.

The story, which has been told with great skill by James A. Morone and Andrew Dunham (Morone and Dunham, 1984; Dunham and Morone, 1983), focuses initially on New Jersey. New Jersey state officials had become involved in health care policy in the 1930s, when enabling legislation for a Blue Cross health insurance program was enacted. Although the New Jersey commissioner of insurance was assigned responsibility for both premiums and payments to hospitals, for several decades this authority was largely exercised by the hospitals themselves. As Morone and Dunham write: "It was the hospital association, not the state, that concerned itself with the details of per diems and rising costs. In effect, the hospital industry reviewed itself, then received the stamp of state approval on its decisions" (Morone and Dunham, 1984, p. 74). With hospitals setting their own rates and an insurance commissioner increasingly reluctant to take the political heat associated with raising insurance premiums, the system gradually became unbalanced. By 1969, New Jersey Blue Cross was paying $13 million more to hospitals than it was receiving in premiums.

Under pressure from both Blue Cross, which wanted an improved rate review system, and the hospitals, which wanted protection against newly forming private hospital chains if their rates were to be more tightly controlled, the legislature passed the Health Care Facilities and Planning Act in 1971. A new review process, now involving the health commissioner and a new thirteen-member board, was created, along with a more elaborate planning process. In addition, however, the new law authorized the New Jersey Department of Health to examine hospital budgets to evaluate the efficiency of health care delivery. Although this authority was not immediately used, it represented a significant departure from past policy, which was to encourage and assist but not to become involved in either the practice of medicine or the administration of health care. Potentially, at least, the new legislation was a powerful tool for the expansion of state influence.

The opportunity to use this tool came in 1974, when a public interest group study revealed that the state had not used its authority to deal with hospital costs and a newly elected governor adopted the study as a guide to his own policy. A complex new rate review system was quickly established, but it applied only to Blue Cross and Medicaid payments. As costs continued to soar, hospitals were forced to shift the burden to private payers and commercial insurance companies that were not as closely regulated as Blue Cross and Medicaid. Commercial payers were forced to raise their premiums, producing loud complaints from individual and corporate clients. In 1976 the Health Department proposed to extend its authority to all payers, to gain further control over hospitals by placing all hospital endowments in a state fund, and to develop new reimbursement methods based on case rather than per diem payments. Neither Blue Cross nor the hospitals were willing to tolerate this extension of state power, however, and the bill containing the proposal died in a legislative committee.

Two years later, the Health Department was back with a new proposal that dropped the controversial plan to grab hospital endowments but also proposed to set rates for all payers that included the costs of providing indigent care. This was especially critical for the large urban hospitals in the state because, with few private payers or commercially insured patients to absorb cost increases, they were close to bankruptcy. The new proposal thus represented salvation for the urban hospitals, which made clear that they would have no part of any effort by the hospital association to oppose the plan. Commercial insurers, weary of the additional costs imposed on them by a system that regulated only some payers, added their strong support to the coalition. The Health Care and Financing Administration of the U.S. Department of Health and Human Services also joined in, offering a Medicare waiver that would be worth up to $60 million for New Jersey. Against a background of soaring medical costs and impending hospital bankruptcies, the legislature easily passed the plan offered by this coalition of government, nonprofit, and profit-making organizations. In 1980, the state would set hospital rates for all payers, taking into account the cost of uncompensated care. As Morone and Dunham conclude: "The era of traditional, hospital-dominated politics was over in New Jersey. The state had assumed a role at the center of the hospital system" (p. 80).

The "state" in this case, however, is a federal state, as later events made clear. New Jersey Health Department officials proceeded to implement a new form of hospital reimbursement known as DRGs, or diagnosis-related-groups, under which hospitals receive a fixed price for each of 467 different types of illness, regardless of the treatment given to a patient suffering that type of illness. Hospitals that provide services at less than the fixed price can pocket the difference, a feature designed to encourage greater efficiency. As implementation of this plan began, the hospital association complained that there had been no agreement on the use of DRGs and persuaded the legislature to hold hearings to listen to its complaints. Even before the hearings were completed, however, HCFA notified New Jersey officials that there would be no $60 million Medicare waiver if the DRG system were not put into place. Without the waiver, federal funds that might be used to cover the costs of uncompensated care would be lost, and urban hospitals would again be in trouble. Facing this kind of pressure, but without alternative solutions, the legislature did nothing, apart from passing a resolution complaining about DRG implementation. In New Jersey the state had not only assumed greater control but, in alliance with the national government, was using that control to experiment with an unusually innovative cost-setting plan.

The national significance of the New Jersey experiment became clear in the fall of 1982, when HCFA was asked by Congress to develop a solution to rising costs of Medicare. With very few available options, HCFA proposed the DRG system already in place in New Jersey. In October, 1983, the Medicare program began setting nationwide rates using the DRG system. Medicare is only one component of a very complicated medical care system, however, and the New Jersey experience suggests that control of that one component cannot solve the problems of the system as a whole. Cost shifts to unregulated payers followed by unpopular increases in insurance premiums already have occurred, with no noticeable reduction in overall medical costs. If the national government follows a pattern similar to the New Jersey experience, we may shortly see an expansion of rate setting to all payers and a larger bureaucratic effort to monitor and control hospitals. If so, a national system of health care may be closer to realization than many analysts assumed.

Quite apart from the substantive issue, the New Jersey experience with DRGs is interesting because it offers such a nice illustration of "federal" politics in the broadest sense. Although nonprofit organizations dominated the action, a variety of other actors played important roles, including local governments, various public and private hospitals, state bureaucrats, the state legislature, large commercial insurance companies, Blue Cross, and an agency of the federal government, among others. Although the list of actors would be different for a different public policy problem, the range and variety is not atypical of many federal policy processes affecting programs whose benefits are broadly distributed. Operating to solve their own problem, these actors interacted in a system that had its own momentum.

In other policy arenas, concerted efforts were under way to reduce the influence of government; in this arena, the problem could only be dealt with effectively by increasing the influence of government. Actors in this system moved in that direction as a pragmatic response to problems, regardless of other trends in other issue arenas. They did not "solve" the problem in any final sense because there is no final solution, but they did provide a blueprint for national action that has significantly altered the shape of the problem. These same actors, perhaps joined by others as a result of the altered problem configuration, will undoubtedly be back at the problem again as soon as another coalition forms that is powerful enough to encourage further action.

CONCLUSION: GOVERNANCE BY PARTNERSHIP

American federalism draws no hard and fast lines between government and other social institutions in the development and implementation of public policies. Instead, government organizations work closely with profit-making and nonprofit organizations of all kinds to achieve common purposes. This pattern, as old as the republic itself, reflects several widely shared values. One is limited government, the preference for government organizations whose authority is narrow and whose power is constrained. A second value is voluntarism, a preference for common action derived from individual contribution rather than coercion. A third is pluralism, a belief in both the legitimacy and necessity of agencies outside of government to promote common interests.

Because private agencies work so closely with government in so many arenas, the policies of American governments often reflect the preferences of private agencies. To stimulate economic growth, for example, American governments distribute hundreds of billions of dollars each year to enrich corporations and individuals. Yet because governments work so closely with private agencies in so many arenas, the practices of private sector agencies often reflect the policies of governments. Tens of thousands of private agencies, for example, follow employment, civil rights, or investment policies that would not be followed in the absence of government participation. Public agencies promote private interests and private interests promote public policies in a system of blurred boundaries in which there is no monopoly on public policymaking. Federal "governance" is a much broader and more significant concept than federal government.

A system with so many thousands of organizations and individuals involved in the formation and delivery of public services is inherently complicated, difficult to understand, and perhaps impossible to coordinate —as contrasting policy thrusts in recent years have made clear. From another point of view, however, the system has some impressive advantages. Opportunities for participation in social problem-solving are increased. The involvement of private sector actors in public issues expands the range of ideas expressed and options considered. The availability of many options and many settings in which they can be tested allows for experiments that do not do nationwide damage if they fail, and can be adopted nationally if they succeed. Finally, the vitality of private participation in public policy is a constant reminder that, in a diverse society, the determination of the public's interest is too important to be left to government alone.

REFERENCES

Anton and Reynolds, 1985. Thomas J. Anton and Rebecca Reynolds. "Old Federalism and New Policies for State Economic Development." Providence, R.I.: Taubman Center, Brown University, unpublished manuscript.

Bendick and Levinson, 1984. Marc Bendick, Jr. and Phyllis M. Levinson. "Private Sector Initiatives or Public-Private Partnerships?" In *The Reagan Presidency and the Governing of America*, ed. Lester Salamon and Michael Lund. Washington, D.C.: Urban Institute Press.

CBO, 1985. Congress of the United States. Congressional Budget Office. *The Federal Budget for Public Works Infrastructure*. Washington, D.C.: Government Printing Office.

Clarke and Rich, 1982. Susan E. Clarke and Michael J. Rich. "Partnerships for Economic Development: The UDAG Experience." *Community Action* 1 (no. 4).

Corrigan, 1985. Richard Corrigan. "Kalamazoo May Be Home to GM's Saturn Plant." *National Journal*, July 20.

Dunham and Morone, 1983. Andrew Dunham and James A. Morone. *The Politics of Innovation: The Evolution of Hospital Regulation in New Jersey*. Princeton, N.J.: Health Research and Education Trust.

Glazer and Moynihan, 1970. Nathan Glazer and Daniel P. Moynihan. *Beyond the Melting Pot*, 2d ed. Cambridge, Mass.: The Massachusetts Institute of Technology Press.

Gold, 1985. Steven D. Gold. "State Budget Actions in 1985." Legislative Finance Paper #49. Denver, Colo.: National Conference of State Legislators Fiscal Affairs Program.

Grady, 1986. Dennis Grady. "The Evolution of State Economic Development Policy: A Comparative Analysis of Economic Incentives Offered by States, 1966–1984." Chicago, Ill.: Paper prepared for the Midwest Political Science Association Annual Convention, April 9.

Hatry, 1983. Harry P. Hatry. *A Review of Private Approaches for Delivery of Public Services*. Washington, D.C.: Urban Institute Press.

"IOLTA Info," 1985. *IOLTA Update*. Miami, Fla.: Florida Justices Institute, Summer.

"Income Tops $50 million," 1986. *IOLTA Update*. Miami, Fla.: Florida Justice Institute, Spring.

Magaziner and Reich, 1982. Ira C. Magaziner and Robert B. Reich. *Minding America's Business: The Decline and Rise of the American Economy*. New York: Vintage Books.

Marlin and Feiden, 1986. John Tepper Marlin and Karyn Feiden. "To Avoid Private Firms' Public Scandals." *New York Times*, February 15.

McCloskey and Zaller, 1984. Herbert McCloskey and John Zaller. *The American Ethos: Public Attitudes Toward Capitalism and Democracy*. Cambridge, Mass.: Harvard University Press.

Morone and Dunham, 1984. James A. Morone and Andrew Dunham. "The Waning of Professional Dominance: DRGs and the Hospitals." *Health Affairs* 3 (Spring): 73–87.

Nathan and Adams, 1977. Richard P. Nathan and Charles F. Adams, Jr. *Revenue Sharing: The Second Round*. Washington, D.C.: The Brookings Institution.

Nathan and Doolittle, 1983. Richard P. Nathan and Fred C. Doolittle. *The Consequences of Cuts: The Effects of the Reagan Domestic Program on State and Local Governments*. Princeton, N.J.: Princeton University Press.

OMB Budget Appendix, 1982. Executive Office of the President. Office of Management and Budget. *Major Themes and Additional Budget Details FY 1982: Appendix*. Washington, D.C.: Government Printing Office.

OMB Major Themes, 1983. Executive Office of the President. Office of Management and Budget. *Major Themes and Additional Budget Details FY 1983*. Washington, D.C.: Government Printing Office.

OMB Special Analyses, 1988. Executive Office of the President. Office of Management and Budget. *Special Analysis: Budget of the United States Government FY 1988*. Washington, D.C.: Government Printing Office.

Pagano and Moore, 1985. Michael A. Pagano and Richard J. T. Moore. *Cities and Fiscal Choices: A New Model of Urban Public Investment*. Durham N.C.: Duke University Press.

Palmer and Sawhill, 1984. John L. Palmer and Isabel V. Sawhill, eds. *The Reagan Record*. Cambridge, Mass.: Ballinger.

Richert, 1982. David Richert. "Interest on Clients' Accounts Held in Trust May Help Legal Services for Poor." *Judicature* 65 (8): 448–449.

Salamon, 1984. Lester Salamon. "Nonprofit Organizations: The Lost Opportunity." In *The Reagan Record*, ed. John L. Palmer and Isabel V. Sawhill. Cambridge, Mass.: Ballinger.

Salamon and Abramson, 1982. Lester M. Salamon and Alan J. Abramson. *The Federal Budget and the Nonprofit Sector*. Washington, D.C.: Urban Institute Press.

Savas, 1982. Emanuel S. Savas. *Privatizing the Public Sector*. Washington, D.C.: Urban Institute Press.

Schultz, 1983. Charles L. Schultz. "Industrial Policy: A Dissent." *The Brookings Review* 2 (Fall): 3–12.

Stanfield, 1986. Rochelle L. Stanfield. "Just Saying No." *National Journal*. November 15.

Stockman, 1986. David A. Stockman. *The Triumph of Politics: How the Reagan Revolution Failed*. New York: Harper & Row.

Tolchin, 1985. Martin Tolchin. "More Cities Paying Industry to Provide Public Services." *New York Times*. May 28.

Wolkoff, 1981. Michael Jay Wolkoff. "An Analysis of the Use of Tax Abatement Policy to Stimulate Urban Economic Development." Ph.D. dissertation, University of Michigan.

Wolkoff, 1983. Michael Jay Wolkoff. "The Nature of Property Tax Abatement Awards." *Journal of the American Planning Association* 49 (1): 77–84.

Yin, 1980. Robert K. Yin. "Creeping Federalism: The Federal Impact on the Structure and Function of Local Government." In *The Urban Impacts of Federal Policies*, ed. Norman J. Glickman. Baltimore: The Johns Hopkins University Press.

CHAPTER 8

REGULATING THE SYSTEM

When a government decides to undertake some action, it can take the action itself through an existing or newly created agency, or it can have the action performed by some other public or private organization. If the action is to be taken by another agency, some mechanism is required to ensure that the agency does take the action. Quite often the mechanism is a financial inducement: Government A will pay organization X a sum of money to perform activities desired by government A. Alternatively, where the government agency has appropriate legal authority, it may establish standards to be met by other public and private organizations. Or a legally superior government may issue a direct order to another organization to perform some act or to prohibit some act or class of actions. These kinds of actions by governments to affect the behavior of other governments or private organizations through legally enforceable standards are called *regulation,* and they are the subject of this chapter.

REGULATION AS POLICY

Why Regulation Is Popular

Regulation is an appealing policy instrument because it frequently allows governments to exercise authority at little or no cost to themselves. This is not to say that no costs are incurred—regulation creates no free lunches —but rather that the costs of policy are transferred from the regulating government to the regulated organization. Whenever funds are scarce, therefore, politicians who feel the need to act may find regulation an attractive method for pursuing goals that might otherwise be neglected. On the other hand, regulation is not easy. Programs that mandate actions, prohibit actions, offer financial support, or impose financial penalties all require detailed specification of precisely which actions are affected, as well as the specific conditions under which various rewards or sanctions come into effect.

Inevitably, then, effective regulation intrudes into the day-to-day operations of regulated agencies, causing frequent and energetic complaints about bureaucratic red tape or heavy-handedness, many of which result in legal action. State and federal courts become active participants in defining what can and cannot be done through regulation.

Indeed, we will see that courts increasingly have used their authority to interpret regulatory provisions to not only issue directives to program administrators, but to assume administrative responsibility for the conduct of various public programs such as schools, mental hospitals, or prisons.

Because established legal doctrine makes clear that local governments are creatures of the states and thus subject to comprehensive state control, state regulation of local governments is an old pattern in American public policy. During this century, however, the national government has become an increasingly active regulator, giving rise to new regulatory patterns. These patterns have occurred in three major surges. The first took place during the so-called Progressive Era, roughly the first two decades of this century, when politicians enacted a number of measures to curb the excesses of the trusts, railroads, public utilities, and food manufacturers. A second wave of regulation accompanied the New Deal in the 1930s, with legislation to regulate agriculture, labor relations, trucking, air transportation, the Stock Exchange, and other forms of economic activity. The third and most encompassing regulatory surge began in the 1960s and intensified in the 1970s, vastly expanding the reach of national authority. Largely in response to this most recent surge, regulation has become a major political issue.

Each of the three surges shares some common political characteristics. Mass media were significant forces in each period: newspapers and books during the Progressive Era, the radio during the 1930s, and television during the 1960s and 1970s. Individuals outside government played important mobilizing roles in each period: Lincoln Steffens and other "muckrakers" at the turn of the century, Clifford Odets and other chroniclers of poverty during the New Deal period, Rachel Carson and Ralph Nader, among others, in recent years. In addition, governmental "champions" of regulation emerged to lead the development of regulatory policy in each period: Presidents Theodore Roosevelt and Woodrow Wilson in the Progressive Era, President Franklin D. Roosevelt in the thirties, Senator Edmund Muskie of Maine and Congresswoman Edith Green of Oregon, among others, in the recent past. Despite these similarities, differences between the first two surges of national regulation and the more recent period of growth are sufficiently great to warrant a distinction between the "old" and the "new" regulation.

The Old Regulation

The old regulation represented an effort to use public authority to impose standards and controls on private sector economic interests. It was stimulated largely by the executive branch, and its typical form was the independent regulatory commission. States established public utility commissions to regulate providers of power and transportation, insurance commissions to regulate providers of health and life insurance, and licensing boards to regulate professions such as medicine and law, as well as occupations such as beautician or plumber.

A host of regulatory bodies also was established by the national government, including the Interstate Commerce Commission to regulate railroads, trucking, and other forms of commercial traffic among the states; the Federal Communications Commission to control the telephone and communications industries; the Food and Drug Administration to monitor the safety of food and drug products; and many others. Some of these agencies operate by setting rates that can be charged for the goods or services provided; others operate by controlling entry into an industry or an occupation.

Whatever the mode of operation, the numerous regulatory agencies are in principle invested with enormous power to control private industries. In practice, however, the ability of these agencies to develop and impose their own standards on regulated industries has seemed ambiguous at best. Indeed, a large literature on the old regulation has argued that, as regulatory agencies have aged, they have lost their initial commitment to the public interest and have gradually been taken over—or "captured"— by the very interests they were established to regulate.

Existence of the agencies provides symbolic reassurance to citizens that the public interest is being pursued, but behind the symbols, industries control agendas, set criteria, and determine outcomes (Edelman, 1964, 1971). Barriers to entry such as licenses or certificates limit competition and thus protect the market position of existing firms or individuals. Rates are set to protect corporate earnings rather than consumers. Far from constituting unwelcome constraints on industry behavior, government regulation is actively sought by various industries precisely because it can be used to promote and protect industry interests (Stigler, 1971).

The New Regulation

The new regulation, which differs markedly from the old, poses a substantial challenge to the theory of capture. Although business regulation continues to be important, it has been overshadowed by a host of new efforts to regulate social relationships between individuals and between individuals and governments. Many of these efforts, furthermore, have emerged from congressional rather than executive initiatives, and are conducted less by independent agencies than by units responsive to congressional preferences. As the ACIR concluded in its recent examination of regulatory federalism, the scope of the new regulation has been

> . . . extended into new program areas like civil rights, consumer protection, the environment, occupational safety and energy conservation. . . . More importantly . . . other new requirements extended their reach beyond the private sector through an array of new and intrusive mechanisms of intergov-

ernmental regulation, ranging from partial preemptions like clean air to crossover sanctions in health planning. (ACIR, 1984, p. 65)

Expansion of national regulation to embrace social as well as economic purposes and public as well as private agencies are thus qualities that, along with sheer increase in volume, characterize the "new" regulation. The theory of capture that seemed so persuasive in accounting for the old regulation is far less relevant to the new pattern. Instead of focusing on industries and their interests, modern regulation focuses on problems, such as polluted air and water, or racial and sexual discrimination, and seeks to define a public interest in solving those problems. Instead of protecting market position, the new regulation seeks to expand competition and protect consumers. Instead of delivering subsidies to protected interests, the new regulation authorizes the imposition of substantial costs on industries to clean up chemical emissions. Above all, the new regulation exerts its authority intergovernmentally, imposing rules and requirements as much on public as on private agencies.

From this point of view, the extraordinary growth of federal aid during the past two decades has had a significance far beyond the dollars themselves. By incorporating a wide variety of conditions in federal grant programs, the national government has vastly expanded its authority to intervene in the affairs of state and local governments or private sector organizations. Although this expanded authority is used selectively rather than comprehensively, the potential for national regulatory intervention is now broader in scope and coverage than ever before.

INSTRUMENTS OF REGULATION

Mandates

Table 8.1, taken from the recent ACIR study of regulatory federalism (1984) provides a convenient summary of the major tools of governmental regulation. The most simple tool, of course, is a direct order, or mandate, issued by one government to another public or private organization, backed by civil or criminal legal penalties. Prohibitions against discrimination in education or employment or against emission of environmental pollutants fall into this category. Direct orders can be issued by administrative agencies enforcing statutes or courts enforcing both statutory and constitutional provisions. Because this technique is coercive, the national government has often exempted state and local governments from regulatory provisions that apply to private agencies—as in the case of the Occupational Safety and Health Act. On the other hand, state governments frequently exercise their legal superiority over local governments by imposing mandates on them. Nearly 96 percent of state regulations examined in a recent study took the form of direct orders, while only 18 percent of all national regulations took the same form (Lovell, 1979).

Table 8.1 A Typology of Intergovernmental Regulatory Programs

PROGRAM TYPE	DESCRIPTION	POLICY AREAS
Direct orders	Mandate state or local actions under threat of criminal or civil penalties	Public employment, environmental protection
Crosscutting requirements	Apply to all or many federal assistance programs	Nondiscrimination, environmental protection, public employment, assistance management
Crossover sanctions	Threaten the termination or reduction of aid provided under one or more specified programs unless the requirements of another program are satisfied	Highway safety and beautification, environmental protection, health planning, handicapped education
Partial preemptions	Establish federal standards, but delegate administration to states if they adopt standards equivalent to the national ones	Environmental protection, natural resources, occupational safety and health, meat and poultry inspection

SOURCE: Advisory Commission on Intergovernmental Relations. *Regulatory Federalism: Policy, Process, Impact, and Reform.* Washington, D.C.: Government Printing Office, 1984. p. 8.

Crosscutting Requirements

The national government makes much more extensive use of so-called *crosscutting requirements*—that is, general policy provisions that are applied to all grant programs regardless of program purposes. A national policy of nondiscrimination, for example, is applied to all grants through Title VI of the Civil Rights Act of 1964, which states:

> No person in the United States shall, on the ground of race, color, or national origin be excluded from participation in, be denied the benefits of, or be subjected to discrimination under any program receiving Federal financial assistance. (PL 88-352, Title VI, Section 601, July 2, 1964)

Later national legislation added prohibitions against discrimination based on religion, sex, or age, complementing other crosscutting requirements enforcing national policies in fields such as environmental protection, health, housing, and labor standards. A total of 59 crosscutting requirements was identified by the Office of Management and Budget in a 1980 inventory, of which 23 reflected fiscal or administrative policies and the remainder social and environmental policies (OMB, 1980).

Crossover Sanctions

A third mechanism available to the national government is the so-called *crossover sanction*, which imposes a financial penalty on one program based on defects in another. As the ACIR study suggests: "The distinguishing feature here is that a failure to comply with the requirements of one program can result in a reduction or termination of funds from another, separately authorized and separately entered into, program. The penalty thus 'crosses over'" (ACIR, 1984, p. 9). Although used in areas such as education or health, perhaps the most noted use of the crossover sanction has been in highway policies. During the 1950s and 1960s, the national government used the threat of reductions in highway construction funds to force states to comply with national billboard control policies. In the 1970s the same threat was used to force states to lower highway speed limits to 55 miles per hour. Now, in the 1980s, the threat is again being used to require states to enforce those speed limits as well as to raise the minimum drinking age to 21 (Peterson, 1986; Weisman, 1984). Crossover sanctions, in short, remain popular as a device to ensure state compliance with national policy preferences.

Partial Preemption

A fourth instrument identified by the ACIR study is the partial preemption, through which the national government acts to assume responsibilities from states or localities that fail satisfactorily to implement national policies. National legislation sets the policies, but state and local governments are empowered to implement them so long as they are effective in doing so. If they are not, the national government is authorized to intervene on behalf of its own priorities. An early example of the partial preemption was the Water Quality Act of 1965. It enacted national water quality standards but gave states one year to set their own standards for in-state waters. The secretary of health, education, and welfare, however, was authorized to enforce national standards in any state that failed to enact its own standards. Similarly, the Clean Air Act Amendments of 1970 established national air quality standards but also required states to devise plans for implementing and enforcing those standards. If the states failed to do so, the national Environmental Protection Agency was given broad authority to force states to adopt policies that could meet national objectives. The partial preemption preserves the appearance of national-state cooperation, but is also a device that underlines the reality of the supremacy clause in the U.S. Constitution.

A Spirit of Coercion?

Identification of separate national regulatory mechanisms does not mean that such mechanisms always operate independently. On the contrary, national legislation often incorporates two or more of these tools within the same program design. Thus the 1970 Clean Air Act amendments combined a partial preemption with crossover sanctions that prohibited both EPA and the Department of Transportation from awarding grants to states that had failed to achieve designated air quality standards or had failed to devise adequate plans for meeting those standards (ACIR, 1984, p. 10). Direct orders from courts or administrative agencies in discrimination cases are often accompanied by funding reductions, or threats of funding reductions, particularly in housing or education programs.

Whether used alone or in combination, these regulatory tools are relatively new, most having been adopted since 1960, and they are relatively coercive in their authorization of financial and legal sanctions. Indeed, many observers and practitioners believe that the new regulation has brought with it a spirit of coercion markedly different from the cooperative attitudes thought to be more characteristic of American intergovernmental relations.

This new spirit can be seen clearly in two remarkable studies that compare regulation in the United States and Sweden. Steven Kelman, who has analyzed occupational health and safety regulation, and Lennart J. Lundquist, who has analyzed clean air regulation in both countries, together paint a revealing portrait of political and administrative contrasts. In Sweden policymaking is slow, practical, and accommodating, with enforcement left largely to continuous negotiations between government officials and the affected employers and workers. In the United States, regulatory policy is often enacted very quickly and expressed in exaggerated rhetoric that ignores practicality altogether. As Lundquist writes of the 1970 Clean Air Act amendments:

> Between December 1969 and December 1970 . . . the United States air pollution control policy experienced a major shift in policy emphasis, from technical and economic feasibility to protection of public health. From the health criterion were derived not only national ambient air quality goals and standards but also auto emission standards and national emission standards for new sources and for extremely hazardous pollutants. Very strict timetables for achieving the air quality and auto emission standards were explicitly included in the legislation. With some exaggeration, one could characterize the Swedish approach as one of choosing an adequate objective for the available means, while the United States approach was one of going beyond available means to establish a new, and seemingly absolute, policy objective. (Lundquist, 1980, p. 61)

Kelman argues, furthermore, that in the adversary institutions of the United States, enforcement efforts are punitive rather than cooperative, involving lawyers and courts to an extent that is unheard of in Sweden (Kelman, 1981). Compared to Sweden, then, American regulation appears to pursue large and often unrealistic goals through punitive legal and financial sanctions that are intended to coerce compliance.

REALITY: IMPLEMENTING REGULATION

These developments in the spirit and purposes of regulation are real enough, but implementation of regulatory policy is no less difficult and complicated than implementation of other policies that require large-scale intergovernmental cooperation. Like other public programs, regulatory programs confer benefits and impose costs. Understanding regulation, therefore, requires consideration of the coalitions that develop to support the benefits of regulation, the distribution of those benefits, and the processes through which changing benefit distributions shape and reshape the regulatory programs themselves. When these factors are taken into account, the practice of regulation appears far less coercive than its promise.

Symbolic Ambiguity

A first important clue is the broad and often ambiguous scope of regulatory goals. We have already seen that statements of purpose in many federal aid programs are intentionally vague in order to attract the broadest possible support—reflecting Herbert Kaufman's suggestion that "ambiguity is a solvent of difference and a catalyst of consensus" (Kaufman, 1985, p. 52). In many regulatory programs, however, ambiguities of purpose are accompanied by exaggerated rhetoric and explicit rejection of cost or feasibility considerations, all of which suggests a politics of symbols rather than purpose.

The radical new approach to air pollution legislation embodied in the 1970 Clean Air Act amendments, for example, explicitly ruled out economic and technological factors as criteria for evaluating new air quality standards; only health considerations mattered. Lundquist quotes Senator Edmund Muskie (D-Maine), the Senate leader in environmental policy, on precisely this point:

> Predictions of technological impossibility or feasibility are not sufficient to avoid tough standards and deadlines, and thus compromise the public health. The urgency of the problems requires that the industry consider, not only the improvement of existing technology, but also alternatives to the internal combustion engine and new forms of transportation. . . . Detroit has told the nation that Americans cannot live without the automobile. The legislation would tell Detroit that if this is the case, they must make an automobile with which the Americans can live. (p. 59)

The symbolic posturing implicit in these sentiments was confirmed when, during Senate debate on the measure, Senator Muskie admitted that no discussions had taken place with the auto industry on the deadlines imposed by the bill. As Lundquist notes: "This meant the deadlines were totally unrealistic. The industry would not even have the three and one-half years normally needed to produce a new car model . . . the time available for inventing the totally new technology required for emission control [was limited] to eighteen to thirty months. And that for a technology that had withstood breakthrough efforts for more than fifteen years" (p. 60). Notwithstanding the lack of communication with affected interests or the feasibility of the legislation, both houses of Congress passed it overwhelmingly. Early in January 1971, President Nixon signed it into law. Predictably enough, the history of these amendments since their passage has been filled with deadline postponements and continued controversy over standards.

The Nature of Regulatory Policy Coalitions

The symbolism of "clean air," along with overtones of a "public" interest being served through decisive governmental action, suggest qualities that are often found in regulatory politics. To begin with, the focus of concern is an issue rather than an interest or group of interests. Because the focus is on an issue, action is driven largely by ideas rather than events, and information plays an important role in shaping the ideas. Because information is important, the transmission of information through the media becomes an important fuel for action. Finally, because information and ideas are important, the purveyors of ideas and information become important actors. These "issue mongers" need not be numerous to be effective. They can, in fact, operate essentially as loners, as in the case of a Ralph Nader or Senator Phil Gramm. More frequently, however, issue mongers operate in what Heclo has dubbed "issue networks" in which relatively few people, each motivated by a strong concern for some particular policy problem, exchange ideas and policy proposals that ultimately are put into effect (Heclo, 1978).

Regulatory policy coalitions, accordingly, are often composed of a fairly tight and cohesive issue network whose members develop policy proposals, linked to a much broader attentive public through information supplied by the mass media. Such coalitions can be mobilized very quickly because the media can disseminate information and mobilize support very quickly. Yet they are also inherently fragile, precisely because the mass support motivated by the symbolic idea is satisfied once the idea is enacted as policy. As the symbol is translated into details that specify the prohibitions or mandates to be applied to various organizations, however, those who pay the costs of the prohibitions or mandates are themselves mobilized into coalitions that can subvert implementation of the policy symbol.

If the regulatory symbol is broad enough, implementation efforts almost surely will cause many symbolic supporters to become implementation opponents. Citizens who support nondiscrimination in the abstract, for example, will oppose integration of schools attended by their children or affirmative action plans that may cost them a job. Similarly, many who strongly support clean air in the abstract will oppose efforts to close manufacturing plants whose pollutants cannot be controlled, or increases in automobile costs to pay for emmission-control devices. What Monypenny had suggested about federal grants thus turns out to apply equally well to federal regulatory policy: Specification of purpose and cost inevitably hinders the process of coalition building. Since specificity is inherent in the implementation of both grants and regulations, coalition maintenance is inherently a problem.

There is an important difference between grants and regulation, however. Grants distribute financial benefits, and coalitions can be maintained or expanded simply by expanding the number of specific beneficiaries, or classes of beneficiaries. Regulation distributes symbolic benefits by imposing constraints on legitimate action available to individuals and organizations. Greater specificity, therefore, can only increase the constraints on individuals and organizations, broadening the distribution of costs and narrowing the distribution of benefits. Under these conditions, it should be no surprise that regulatory policies are so very difficult to implement.

Obstacles to Implementation

The first obstacle to implementation, of course, is the abstract symbolism of many statements of regulatory purpose—a difficulty compounded by the fact that many regulatory policies have been enacted with little or no discussion. Title VI of the 1964 Civil Rights Act, for example, was given relatively little consideration in congressional debate, most of which centered on the public accommodations section of the proposed legislation. To the extent that Title VI was discussed, both the Kennedy administration and Senator Hubert Humphrey, the bill's floor manager, took the position that the provision was both relatively insignificant, since it would rarely be used, and noncontroversial, since there was little disagreement over the desirability of ending racial and ethnic discrimination. "If anyone can be against that [Title VI], he can be against Mother's Day," Senator Humphrey argued. "How can one justify discrimination in the use of federal funds? . . . President after president," he said, "has announced that national policy is to end discrimination in federal programs" (ACIR, 1984, p. 73). On these assurances, the major provisions of Title VI against racial and ethnic discrimination were passed overwhelmingly, despite the absence of any clear definition of the meaning of "discrimination."

Brief as it was, the consideration given to Title VI was lengthy compared to congressional review of several subsequent crosscutting requirements. Title IX of the 1972 Education amendments, prohibiting discrimination against women in educational institutions receiving federal aid, was enacted without the benefit of hearings on its fund witholding provisions, nor was Title IX mentioned at all when President Nixon signed the legislation (ACIR, 1984, p. 75). No hearings were held on the Age Discrimination Act of 1975, which, like Title IX, simply adopted language identical to the language of Title VI (but without the qualifications included in Title VI) for new classes of beneficiaries.

Even more striking was the total absence of public discussion of Section 504 of the 1973 Rehabilitation Act, which prohibits discrimination against handicapped persons in federally assisted programs. A memorandum from a House Education and Labor Committee staff member paints a stark portrait of inattention:

> Section 504 did not have one day of Congressional Hearings, not one word was mentioned in the Senate Committee Report, not one word was spoken about it on the floor when the original bill passed, and there was no explanation in the Statement of Managers following the House-Senate Conference. (ACIR, 1984, p. 75)

Legislative intent regarding Section 504 was so unclear, in fact, that a retroactive legislative history had to be included in a Senate report on the rehabilitation amendments of the following year in order to make clear that the executive branch was required to write regulations and enforce the law! As the ACIR has concluded, after reviewing these and other examples of regulatory legislation: "The legislative histories show that Congress, by focusing on widely accepted abstract goals, consistently failed to define its specific policy objectives or attend to the administrative implications of these regulations" (ACIR, 1984, p. 77)

With little more than vague symbols to guide them, the bureaucrats responsible for writing rules to implement regulatory policies have a problem. Rules should reflect congressional intent—but what if intent is not clear? One option is to do nothing. For example, in the absence of any indication at all of who should enforce what in preventing discrimination against the handicapped (Section 504), bureaucrats did nothing. This had the effect of forcing Congress to develop a retrospective legislative history in the following year. Another option for bureaucratic rule writers is to do something, but do it slowly enough to allow all points of view to be taken into account.

This is perhaps the most common option chosen by bureaucrats, and the equally common result is that rules often take years to develop. To be sure, the nine years required to develop rules for Section 504 may have been excessive, but excess in regulation writing is hardly unusual. According to an OMB study: "It took five years for the EPA to issue guidelines (April 16, 1975) implementing Section 508 of the Federal Water Pollution Control Act of 1970. Revision of the Advisory Council on Historic Preservations' 1974 guidelines began in 1977 and was not completed until January 1979." Similar delays have characterized the process of writing regulations in a host of other programs, from Title IX to handicapped education.

Regulatory delays are not caused solely by the absence of clear legislative language, of course. In many cases the problems addressed are so complex that time-consuming scientific investigations are necessary to define appropriate standards—air and water pollution criteria clearly fall into this category. In other cases, the administrative agencies responsible for writing regulations may be understaffed, or administrative difficulties ranging from unfilled positions to poor leadership may create delays.

In still other cases, political disagreement over the purposes of regulation may undermine progress. The rules governing the uses of Community Block Grant funds were interpreted quite differently by the Ford, Carter, and Reagan administrations, causing substantial shifts in the way local governments used those funds (Dommel et al., 1982). Similarly, programs administered by the Small Business Administration changed focus and purpose quite dramatically over a ten-year period, depending on the priorities of different administrations (Rozoff, 1985). Given such differences in political values pursued by successive administrations, administrative caution in implementing regulatory provisions seems quite understandable.

For a number of reasons, then, a great deal of time passes between enactment of a regulatory policy and final publication of the rules that specify what the policy means and how it will be applied. Since all federal agencies are required to publish any proposed regulations and to seek reactions from all interested parties before promulgating final rules, the rule-making period is often characterized by intense activity on the part of coalitions likely to be affected by the new rules. In contrast to the period preceding policy enactment, however, both the settings and the coalitions change. The media events, public hearings, or congressional debates that provide the vehicles through which regulatory symbols are fashioned are replaced by the private offices or conference rooms of administrative agencies charged with writing the regulations. The loose collection of individuals and organizations who publicly pursue the legislative policy symbol is largely supplanted by organizations likely to bear the costs of regulation, whose major interest is minimizing those costs by limiting the scope of regulatory power. It is at this point, in these more private settings, that well-organized interests can undermine legislative intentions by attending to the cost and feasibility considerations that may have been ignored or specifically rejected in the policy enactment process.

TITLE IX AND INTERCOLLEGIATE ATHLETICS: A CASE STUDY

The Development of National Policy

Many of the characteristic qualities of regulatory politics can be observed in the effort to apply the Title IX prohibition against sex discrimination to college and university athletic programs across the country. Enacted in large measure because of the persistent efforts of Congresswoman Edith

Green of Oregon, Title IX amended the Education Act by providing a one-sentence mandate prohibiting sex discrimination "under any education program or activity receiving Federal financial assistance." Enacted in June 1972, this regulatory symbol was not made specific until July 1975, when seventeen pages of Title IX regulations went into effect.

The 1975 regulations provided for a three-year period, ending July 21, 1978, during which colleges and universities were to come into compliance with rules promoting "equal opportunity" in matters such as facilities, opportunities to participate in varsity sports, and athletic scholarships. Unhappily, the rules were not specific regarding the meaning of "compliance"—an ambiguity that confused some universities and discouraged others from taking action until the meaning of the regulations could be clarified. In the meantime, HEW was receiving a constant stream of complaints: As of July 1978 ". . . the Department had received over 63 complaints alleging that 43 institutions were not providing equal athletic opportunities for men and women" (U.S. Department of Health, Education and Welfare, 1978).

An effort to resolve this regulatory ambiguity began in the summer of 1978 when the Office of Civil Rights (Department of Health, Education and Welfare) created a special Work Group on Title IX and Intercollegiate Athletics. The Work Group, which included university representatives among its members, began meeting in August. By the first week of October, a draft memorandum was ready for circulation among government agencies and colleges and universities across the country. As the contents of the draft memorandum became known, athletic directors and other university officials reacted strongly. Letters and telephone calls protesting the proposals were sent to OCR and members of Congress; visits were made to Washington to lobby against the draft. Within a month, representatives from twelve institutions, led by the universities of Notre Dame, Georgia, and New Mexico, met in Chicago to organize a coalition to try to defeat or substantially modify the proposals. DeHart Associates, a Washington, D.C., public relations firm, was retained by these institutions to mobilize a broader coalition and coordinate its efforts.

The reason for this frenetic activity became clear on December 6, 1978, when HEW Secretary Joseph A. Califano, Jr., issued a proposed policy interpretation "to clarify how Title IX and its regulations apply to college athletic programs." Califano's statement introducing the proposed interpretation made it very plain that the Carter administration was seriously concerned about sex discrimination. "Historically," he noted, ". . . most colleges and universities have emphasized intercollegiate sports for men," producing a situation in which only 26 percent of intercollegiate athletes in 1976–77 were women, despite the fact that women comprised nearly 48 percent of all college students. Women athletes, furthermore, ". . . often do not receive their fair share of athletic resources, services and benefits," such as financial aid. Despite these institutional prejudices, Califano noted that the participation of women in both intramural and intercollegiate sports had increased by more than 100 percent from 1971 to 1976. The clear implication was that the prohibition against sex discrimination was more important than ever.

To clarify the mechanisms through which the Title IX goal was to be achieved, the policy interpretation proposed by Califano established a two-part approach to compliance and enforcement:

> The first part is aimed at immediately eliminating discrimination in university athletic programs, taking these programs as they are today. It requires that expenditures on men's and women's athletics be proportional to the number of men and women participating in athletics. This standard of "substantially equal per capita expenditures" must be met unless the institution can demonstrate that the differences are based on nondiscriminatory factors such as the costs of a particular sport (for example, the equipment required), or the scope of competition (that is, national rather than regional or local). This proportional standard applies to athletic scholarships, recruitment, and other readily measurable financial benefits such as equipment and supplies, travel, and publicity. For those benefits and services that are not readily financially measurable—opportunity to receive coaching and academic tutoring, provision of locker rooms, medical services and housing facilities—comparability is required.
>
> Part two of the proposed policy is designed to eliminate over a reasonable period of time, the discriminatory effects of the historic emphasis on men's sports, and to facilitate the continued growth of women's athletics. It requires colleges and universities to take specific, active steps to provide additional athletic opportunities for women—opportunities that will fully accommodate the rising interests of women in participating in athletics. (U.S. Department of Health, Education and Welfare, 1976)

The Universities Respond

Since most institutions had begun to develop and implement plans for additional athletic opportunities for women, part two of the policy interpretation presented no serious problem. Equal per capita expenditures for men and women, however, was a proposal that most administrators of major athletic programs viewed as a serious threat to the entire system of intercollegiate athletic competition. Per capita costs for sports such as football, which requires expensive equipment and large sums of money for athletic scholarships in order to be competitive, or basketball, which requires large sums of money for scholarships and travel, were several times higher than per capita costs for virtually any women's sport. Because universities typically sponsored far fewer intercollegiate teams for women, furthermore, there were typically two to three men for every woman participating in varsity teams in universities across the country. Equal per capita spending for women's and men's sports thus would have required a substantial reduction in expenditures for men or a similarly substantial infusion of additional funds to support women. In major athletic programs, however, men's football and basketball teams generated most of the funds used to support all other teams. Athletic administrators feared that reducing expenditures for these revenue-generating sports would not only weaken these sports, but weaken their ability to generate the revenues used to support all teams.

Interestingly, the proposed interpretation appeared to deal directly with these concerns by allowing differences in per capita spending ". . . if the institution can demonstrate that the differences result from non-discriminatory factors . . . such as variations in the costs of equipment and supplies; and/or . . . cost of travel to distant locations for competition, living expenses while in those locations, more extensive publicity, or the cost of other activities that may vary in accordance with the requirements of local, regional or national competition" (pp. 20, 25). Despite the availability of this rather large loophole to justify differences in per capita spending, opposition among athletic administrators continued to grow. The idea that institutions would have to "demonstrate" that spending differences were not the result of discrimination was offensive to many university officials, since it assumed that they were guilty of discrimination unless they could prove they were not.

It was also clear that universities had little trust in the ability of OCR to be either competent or fair. Thus, at a second meeting of the Title IX coalition held in Chicago on December 18, 1978, President Fred Davison of the University of Georgia described an experience other universities had shared—namely, a compliance visit from OCR officials who seemed unaware of the complexities of athletic administration and unwilling to consider all available evidence bearing on compliance with Title IX. Widespread mistrust, in part engendered by the uncompromising language of the policy interpretation, was important precisely because the interpretation gave so much discretion to OCR. Apart from a few vague examples, no comprehensive list of specific "nondiscriminatory factors" existed. Differences in spending that were allowable would thus be determined by OCR personnel, few of whom had had any experience in athletic or university administration. Contemplating this prospect, as well as a report from President Bud Davis of the University of New Mexico that increases in program costs caused by Title IX would range between $125,000 and $450,000 in the first year alone, depending on the institution, the conferees on December 18 agreed to try to enlarge the coalition in order to generate enough pressure to modify the interpretation.

Ten days later DeHart Associates circulated a position statement to be used in trying to recruit other institutions to the coalition. Charging that the proposed interpretation ". . . ignores the basic fact of university economic life" and goes ". . . beyond the law and the intent of Congress," the coalition offered an alternative proposal. The coalition supported the objectives of Title IX, it said, and offered a plan to insure compliance that would "Permit the use of revenues generated by a revenue-producing sport (whether men's or women's) to pay for the direct costs attached to that sport to enable its continuation at a reasonable level of competition. . . . The revenues in excess of costs from each revenue-generating sport would be allocated to other sports, both men's and women's, in proportionately equal amounts for men's and women's programs, based on the number of men and women participating." In place of the equal per capita standard based on the total costs of men's and women's programs, the coalition proposed to exempt revenue-producing sports cost comparisons with other sports. This was a position that had been defeated in Congress twice, in 1974 and again in 1975, but the coalition clearly was prepared to do battle again.

During the next several months, more and more universities across the country allied themselves with the coalition. DeHart Associates had recommended that each institution evaluate the local economic impact of the proposal, file comments on the proposal with HEW, and most important, "Communicate their views and the economic impact to members of Congress, as well as the media, state politicians, and alums." Ultimately nearly 400 institutions joined the coalition and contributed some $300,000 to coordinate the intense lobbying focused on HEW in Washington. With many state and congressional politicians joining hundreds of administrators from many of the nation's best-known and most prestigious institutions, this was clearly an impressive political force.

The results of these activities became apparent on December 4, 1979, one year after the policy interpretation had been offered, when HEW issued its "final" interpretation for Title IX. The final interpretation responded to those who had criticized the practicality of the earlier proposal by offering a far more detailed treatment of such mundane but important matters as defining "participants." Far more significantly, the final interpretation offered major concessions in the area of athletic expenditures. Whereas the 1978 proposal applied the equal per capita standard to recruitment, equipment and supplies, living and travel expenses, publicity, and financial aid, the 1979 document limited the equality standard to financial aid only. Benefits other than financial aid were now to be measured by a standard that did not require identical benefits and that explicitly recognized the unique nature of particular sports such as football, or special costs such as those associated with the management of large events. These adjustments did not exempt revenue-producing sports from coverage, as the coalition had sought, but they went a long way toward alleviating the concerns of athletic administrators. As the president of a large midwestern university later wrote: "Our conclusion . . . is that we accomplished a good deal and that the final regulations issued were much better than those first proposed. We believe we can probably live with the current regulation, while the initial ones were impossible" (private correspondence).

Were it to end at this point, the Title IX story would be familiar but revealing: a three-year delay in writing the regulations, another three-year period of confusion about the meaning of the regulations, still another year of intense lobbying to clarify their meaning, and finally, in 1980, eight years after passage of the law, some general agreement on what the law means and how it should be implemented. But of course the story did not end in 1980. President Reagan was elected in 1980, bringing to the White House a much different view of the federal role in racial or sexual discrimination. Believing that federal efforts had been too aggressive, Mr. Reagan immediately announced that compliance reviews would be limited, and that the national government would adopt a different approach to the problems of sexual or racial discrimination. Thus, when Grove City College challenged the applicability of Title IX to its programs, on grounds that the only federal funds it received were scholarship dollars given to its students, the administration not only supported the college's view, but intervened on behalf of the college before the Supreme Court.

Whereas previous administrations had taken the view that receipt of federal dollars for one program automatically activated Title IX for all programs, Deputy Solicitor General Paul M. Bator told the Supreme Court in November 1983 that Title IX applies only to the program or programs that actually receive federal funds. In the Grove City case, he said, the college's only link to the federal Treasury was student aid; thus only the student aid program, and not the institution as a whole, was bound by Title IX (Greenhouse, 1983, p. 21). Despite a brief filed by 49 senators and representatives arguing that the intent of Congress in enacting Title IX was "to include entire institutions where students receive federally funded tuition assistance," and despite a 414 to 8 vote on a resolution expressing the "sense of the House" that Title IX should not be interpreted narrowly, the Court later (February 1984) ruled in favor of the administration position. This decision, in turn, prompted majorities in both houses of Congress to pass legislation making clear that the congressional intent was and remains to pursue a broad rather than narrow interpretation of the scope of Title IX. Although President Reagan vetoed this legislation—the Civil Rights Restoration Act of 1988—his veto was overridden by large majorities in both houses of Congress (Willen, 1988). Thus sixteen years after its passage, Title IX finally achieved a clear and settled interpretation.

Did Title IX Fail?

It would be easy enough to read this record simply as another example of failure to implement a symbolic goal. In fact, however, a strong case can be made that Title IX has been extraordinarily successful. Senator Bob Packwood (R-Oregon), in urging support for the broad interpretation put forward in the Civil Rights Act of 1984, made the case:

> Title IX has dramatically improved educational opportunities for women. Consider, for example, that in 1970 only 300,000 high school girls participated on athletic teams sponsored by their schools. By 1979, two million girls were participating. At the college level, there were no athletic scholarships given to women before Title IX; today, there are more than 10,000. Before Title IX, there were virtually no women's national collegiate championships; this year,

the National Collegiate Athletic Association sponsored 30 national champion-
ships for women. And sports is but one of many areas in which Title IX has
opened educational opportunities for girls and women that have always existed
for boys and men. (Packwood, 1984)

The validity of Senator Packwood's argument has been confirmed in the
continuing increases in women participants, scholarships, and national
tournament opportunities. Title IX implementation may have failed, in
short, but the policy has succeeded. Understanding this paradoxical result
will tell us a good deal not only about Title IX, but about regulatory
politics in general.

It is clear, to begin with, that many colleges and universities went ahead
with funding increases for women's athletics despite delay, confusion, and
political disagreement over enforcement priorities. One important reason
for their actions was that university decision-makers generally were in
philosophical agreement with the nondiscriminatory goals of Title IX.
However vague its operating strictures may have been, Title IX provided a
symbol of national purpose that gave legitimacy to all efforts to increase
athletic opportunities for women.

Many university administrators, in fact, were among the informed
individuals who were aware of the sex discrimination issue and formed
part of the loose national coalition that had supported enactment of Title
IX. Once enacted, the brief statement of policy provided a political license
for supportive administrators to move as far and as fast as local conditions
allowed. To say that Title IX was primarily a symbol at the outset, therefore,
is not to say that the symbol was without effect. On the contrary, it granted
legitimacy, offered a goal, and motivated actions that many individuals,
including university administrators, believed to be desirable. When there is
widespread public agreement on a regulatory goal, the political impact of
a symbolic statement of that goal can be quite substantial.

A second important reason for policy success in the face of implementation failure was the strength of pro-Title IX coalitions in various states
across the country. Many of the universities most affected by Title IX are
large state-supported institutions with equally large athletic programs. As
state institutions, they are governed by boards of regents or trustees that
often are elected or appointed by the governor or other state official. These
relationships tie governing boards directly to state politics, increasing their
sensitivity to the views and activities of state political actors. Thus in states
with well-organized and active women's groups, university governing
boards could not avoid the views of such groups; nor could they avoid the
political necessity of responding to such groups. Where women's groups
were able to ally themselves with other organizations sharing their views
about sex discrimination, support for the purposes of Title IX was bound
to be effective. In this sense, the fragmentation of the federal system itself
aided Title IX by allowing its political strength to manifest itself wherever it
could, without being subverted by the delay and confusion over national

implementation. And here too, the existence of a national policy symbol provided both legitimacy and motivation for state-level activists.

Finally, it is important to note that Title IX, like many other products of regulatory politics, created new citizen rights enforceable through court action. Federal courts thus became important arenas in which institutions were pushed toward providing greater opportunities for women athletes. One study not only noted the popularity of this tactic, but offered a plausible explanation for its popularity:

> . . . the filing of lawsuits charging school districts and colleges with sex discrimination or charging DHEW with lack of enforcement of sex discrimination laws has become an instrumental part of the overall political strategy of the groups seeking to achieve educational equity for women. . . . The power that women generally lack in Congress and executive departments may be partially compensated for by the courts, where the lack of political influence is not as critical a factor in determining outcomes. (ACIR, 1984, p. 135)

Filing a lawsuit has several advantages over use of normal political channels. One is that it is relatively easy to do. Because the right to be free from sexual discrimination is an individual right, a single individual can file an action that can impose substantial costs on a governmental or educational institution. The existence of numerous public interest law firms or publicly funded legal services agencies, furthermore, often means that a lawyer will be available at little or no cost to the individual filing the suit. Most important of all, benefits can be "won" through a court filing even if the case is ultimately postponed or even withdrawn. The negative publicity generated by a court action, or even a threat of court action, often leads institutions to try to resolve cases out of court.

For a variety of reasons, then, the courts have provided a popular alternative to normal politics in promoting increased athletic opportunities for women. Together with the political power of women's coalitions in the states and the general agreement of university administrators with Title IX goals, court actions have produced substantial movement toward those goals, regardless of the pace or quality of national implementation.

COURTS AND REGULATION

Policy through Litigation

The use of courts to interpret and enforce Title IX is more than matched by expansion of court activity in other regulatory arenas. By creating legal rights enforceable through court action, regulation has drastically reduced the costs of access to the policy process, encouraging thousands of individuals to enter that process. And by increasing the number of grant programs to which various prohibitions and performance standards are attached, national regulation has vastly increased the opportunities available to individuals and organizations to exercise their new legal rights. The result has been a veritable explosion of litigation, in a context that increasingly accepts legal action as a policymaking tool. As the ACIR reports:

- There were nearly 800 cases filed against federal agencies under the National Environmental Policy Act in the statute's first seven years;
- As early as 1976 there were more than 250 cases contesting various provisions of the EPA's effluent guidelines;
- There were over 150 cases involving implementation of the Clean Air Act as of 1981;
- Following passage of the Equal Employment Opportunity Act of 1972 the number of cases charging employment discrimination rose from 1,000 to 6,000 by 1977;
- Hundreds of suits, amounting to 40 percent of all suits against school districts, have been brought involving the Education for All Handicapped Children Act of 1975;
- With a single exception, business organizations have challenged every OSHA health regulation in court. (ACIR, 1984, p. 130)

Clearly, whatever else may have been accomplished by the new regulation, it has been a bonanza for lawyers, as well as an enormous additional burden for the court system.

Judicial Activism

In general terms, courts have dealt with this burden by adopting a broad view of the range of permissible regulation and by assuming an activist stance in enforcing their views of regulatory intent. Vague and sometimes nonexistent statements of purpose that characterize much regulatory legislation give considerable discretion to agencies charged with writing specific rules. Although written regulations sometimes differ considerably from clear statements of congressional intent—as in some job discrimination regulations—courts typically have upheld agency authority to issue and enforce such regulations so long as they are "reasonably related" to the purposes of the legislation (ACIR, 1984, p. 131–32). Whether or not agency rules are actually enforced, of course, depends on a variety of factors, including availability of personnel, resources, and, as the Title IX case suggests, prevailing political interpretations. From a legal point of view, however, the courts have been quite willing to accept any reasonable rules issued by federal agencies.

But administrative agencies, as we have seen, often take years to develop regulations that may or may not be clear. Where rules are imprecise or nonexistent, the courts most often have imposed even tougher requirements than might have been imposed by administrators. In

his careful review of the court role in interpreting the National Environmental Policy Act of 1969, for example, Frederick R. Anderson concludes:

> The courts have been vigorous in reviewing agency compliance with NEPA.
> They have enforced strict standards of procedural compliance, and in instances
> where Congress failed to specify how the act should be implemented, they
> imposed judge-made requirements which give it wider scope. As a result, the
> courts are thought of as the principal enforcers of NEPA. . . . While avoiding
> "unreasonable extremes," the courts have held the agencies to each detailed
> procedural step mandated by the act, have expanded the range of judicially
> enforceable NEPA duties, and have undertaken close scrutiny of agency
> compliance. (Anderson, cited in ACIR, 1984, p. 133)

Judicial activism reaches far beyond NEPA, however, and it often has
moved beyond enforcement to administration. Federal district courts have
appointed court "masters" to supervise school integration plans in cities
such as Detroit, or federal judges have themselves assumed administrative
responsibility for pollution abatement programs in cities such as Boston.
As one analyst has written:

> Federal district judges are increasingly acting as day-to-day managers and
> implementers, reaching into the details of civic life: how prisons are run,
> medication is administered to the mentally ill, custody is arranged for severely
> deranged persons, private and public employers recruit and promote. (Fried,
> cited in ACIR, 1984, p. 130)

The willingness of federal judges to give strict interpretation to vague
federal rules obviously increases their influence over federal policy, as well
as increasing the influence of individuals or organizations who initiate
legal actions. Since judicial interpretations often impose substantial
compliance costs on states, cities, and other agencies ordered to meet
some federal standard, judicial activism offers yet another example of the
practical significance of national policy symbols, however unclear they
may be.

On the other hand, judicial activism is a chancy thing. Whether or not it
occurs depends on the inclinations of particular judges to make firm
determinations or assume obligations beyond the courtroom. Even when
it does occur, it is far from uniformly effective. Like politicians responding
to a widespread demand for regulatory action, judges often assume the
luxury of ignoring the realities of cost and feasibility when they issue
orders. In ordering prison reforms, for example, one court simply brushed
such considerations aside:

> Let there be no mistake in the matter; the obligation of the respondents to
> eliminate existing unconstitutionalities does not depend upon what the legisla-
> ture may do, or upon what the governor may do, or, indeed, upon what
> respondents may actually be able to accomplish. If Arkansas is going to operate

a penitentiary system, it is going to have to be a system that is countenanced by the Constitution of the United States. *(Holt* v. *Sarver,* 309 F. Supp. 362, cited in ACIR, 1984, p. 46)

Such pronouncements are easy for judges to make, but very difficult for politicians and administrators to live with when they lack the resources necessary to implement the required changes. Judges cannot order tax increases. If politicians or citizens (or both) refuse to provide the resources required by a federal court order, there may be no effective legal remedy. Even strong legal pronouncements, in short, are not self-executing. Because they are not, the effectiveness of court intervention is bound to vary from place to place, depending on the issues at stake, the nature of the court mandate, and the ability of the court to fashion remedies that motivate cooperative reactions.

State Judicial Activism

Judicial activism is by no means confined to members of the federal bench. On the contrary, one of the most interesting developments of recent years has been the increased willingness of state judges to expand individual rights beyond requirements set by the U.S. Supreme Court by grounding decisions on state constitutions rather than the U.S. Constitution. In part a reaction against Supreme Court decisions in recent years that have narrowed the scope of individual rights, and in part a resurgence of state court independence, the new spirit of assertiveness has produced some striking results. Since 1970, according to one analyst, "state high courts have handed down some 300 published opinions declaring that the minimums set by the U.S. Supreme Court interpreting the Federal Constitution are insufficient to satisfy the more demanding precepts of state law" (Pear, 1986a, p. 1). Among these are decisions in New York and Mississippi barring the use of evidence obtained through good-faith reliance on defective search warrants, despite a U.S. Supreme Court decision allowing such good-faith exceptions, an Alaska decision declaring that "the state constitutional guarantee against unreasonable searches and seizures is broader in scope than Fourth Amendment guarantees under the United States Constitution," and a California decision permitting petition activity that had been disallowed by the U.S. Supreme Court (Pear, 1986a).

Even more striking, perhaps, is the recent movement of state courts toward the definition and protection of economic rights, such as rights to housing, food, and clothing. In New York, for example, the Appellate Division of the New York State Supreme Court recently determined that homeless families with children had a right to publicly provided shelter, based on a provision in the New York State Constitution that states: "The aid, care and support of the needy are public concerns and shall be provided by the state and by such of its subdivisions" as the legislature may determine. Across the river, the New Jersey Superior Court decided in

1985 that homeless people had "a right to safe and suitable emergency shelter and other immediate assistance such as food and clothing" under the state's public assistance statute (Pear, 1986b, p. E5).

Even Texas, not noted for the generosity of its human assistance programs, recently enacted judicially enforceable regulations stating that emergency care must be provided by hospitals to all patients, regardless of ability to pay, and prohibiting the transfer of patients from one hospital to another solely for economic reasons. State courts and state administrators clearly have become the trendsetters in defining and enforcing individual rights, assuming a role earlier played by the U.S. Supreme Court. In the process they are providing additional settings in which very small but knowledgeable coalitions work to shape and reshape public policies.

CONCLUSION: THE THREE FACES OF REGULATION

Symbols vs. Reality

Observing the characteristics of regulatory policies and policymaking in the United States suggests several important conclusions: One is that the regulatory bark is clearly much worse than the regulatory bite. The tough and often uncompromising statements found in legislation establishing programs of regulation are seldom followed by equally tough and uncompromising enforcement. Instead, years commonly pass before regulations are written to give specific meaning to legislative statements. Once written, the regulations are themselves often subverted by (1) administrative problems ranging from lack of resources and enforcement personnel to indifference; (2) shifting political interpretations of enforcement priorities; or (3) the varying willingness of other governments and courts to implement the rules.

In a real sense, regulation appears to offer the worst of both worlds: There are too many rules (red tape), and there is too little regulatory impact. This is not to argue that regulatory policies are unimportant. On the contrary, even the vague symbols often found in legislative acts provide legitimacy and motivation for actors who are committed to regulatory goals. But such actors are not uniformly spread across the country. Where they exist, regulation may indeed be quick and effective; where they are absent, regulation may have little or no effect.

The Stages of Regulation

Regulatory politics thus appears to proceed in distinct stages. In the initial stage of policy enactment, politicians in pursuit of an issue ally themselves with other "issue mongers," including members of the media, to enact legislation that is perceived to have broad popular appeal. Such coalitions are often broad in appeal but thin in commitment, producing quick symbolic action with little follow-through. In a second stage of rule writing, more narrow coalitions made up of those who expect to bear the costs of regulation become mobilized, often with enough strength to at least delay, and at most subvert, policy implementation. Lundquist, who uses the fable of the hare and the tortoise to frame his analysis of air pollution regulation in Sweden and the United States, provides a perceptive description of these stages:

> The United States style corresponded to that of the hare. Initially, policymaking proceeded very swiftly and dramatically, with many policymakers trying to take the lead by outbidding each other. The total period of policymaking was very short and compressed, and there was no need for compromises to build up a majority to secure the passage of legislation. Later on, policymaking proceeded at a much slower pace, and the total period of policymaking was very long and drawn out. Policymaking involved complicated efforts to build majorities around carefully designed compromises. These efforts included the organized pressure groups who had been very much left out in the open bidding for broad public support in the period preceding the initial policy choice.
>
> Throughout the studied period, the Swedish style closely resembled that of the tortoise. There were no dramatic jumps but, rather, a slow and continuous movement. Not very many policymakers were involved, and they went to great lengths to find compromises that would make all four legs—the cabinet, the bureaucracy, the Riksdag [Parliament], and the regulated interests—move in the same direction and with the same speed. The key words were compromise and consensus rather than competition, continuity rather than popularity. (Lundquist, 1980, p. 183)

In the American style of regulation, then, a great deal of policy is made after legislation is passed, typically by coalitions that differ in many respects from those responsible for enacting legislation. Because regulation so often establishes new rights or standards of performance enforceable through court action, judges, lawyers, and complaining citizens have emerged as important sources of policy. These legal coalitions are seldom large, but they can be extraordinarily significant. Indeed, activist judges have not only extended and stiffened existing regulations, but they have assumed control of school systems, sewage systems, prisons, hospitals, and other institutions in order to implement regulatory goals. Both federal and state courts, along with the lawyers and citizens who trigger their action, must be regarded as an important "third face" of regulation in the American federal system.

REFERENCES

ACIR, 1984. Advisory Commission on Intergovernmental Relations. *Regulatory Federalism: Policy, Process, Impact, and Reform.* Washington, D.C.: Government Printing Office.

Chicago Milwaukee and S. Paul Railway v. *Minnesota,* 134 U.S., 418 1890.

Dommel et al., 1982. Paul R. Dommel and Associates. *Decentralizing Urban Policy: Case Studies in Community Development.* Washington, D.C.: The Brookings Institution.

Edelman, 1964. Murray Edelman. *The Symbolic Uses of Politics.* Urbana, Ill.: University of Illinois Press.

Edelman, 1971. Murray Edelman. *Politics as Symbolic Action.* New York: Academic Press.

Greenhouse, 1983. Linda Greenhouse. "High Court Weighs Case on Sex Bias." *New York Times,* November 30.

Heclo, 1978. Hugh Heclo. "Issue Networks and the Executive Establishment." In *The New American Political System,* ed. Anthony King. Washington, D.C.: American Enterprise Institute for Public Policy Research.

Kaufman, 1985. Herbert Kaufman. *Time, Chance, and Organizations: Natural Selection in a Perilous Environment.* Chatham, N.J.: Chatham House.

Kelman, 1981. Steven Kelman. *Regulating America, Regulating Sweden: A Comparative Study of Occupational Safety and Health Policy.* Cambridge, Mass.: The Massachusetts Institute of Technology Press.

Lovell, 1979. Catherine Lovell. *Federal and State Mandating on Local Governments: An Exploration of Issues and Impacts.* Graduate School of Administration, University of California, Riverside.

Lundquist, 1980. Lennart J. Lundquist. *The Hare and the Tortoise: Clean Air Policies in the United States and Sweden.* Ann Arbor: University of Michigan Press.

Mason and Beaney, 1954. Alpheus T. Mason and William M. Beaney. *American Constitutional Law.* Englewood Cliffs, N.J.: Prentice-Hall.

OMB, 1980. Executive Office of the President. Office of Management and Budget. *Managing Federal Assistance in the 1980s, Working Papers,* Volume 1. Washington, D.C.: Government Printing Office.

Packwood, 1984. Robert Packwood. "Discrimination Aided." *New York Times,* April 20.

Pear, 1986a. Robert Pear. "State Courts Surpass U.S. Bench in Cases of Rights of Individuals." *New York Times,* May 4.

Pear, 1986b. Robert Pear. "The Need of the Nation's Homeless Is Becoming Their Right." *New York Times,* July 20.

Peterson, 1986. Iver Peterson. "Rebellion Gains in West and the Plains Over U.S. Speed Limit." *New York Times,* June 13.

PL 88-352, Title VI, sec. 601, July 2, 1964. 88th Congress, 2nd Session. Public Law, 88-352. "Civil Rights Act of 1964."

Rozoff, 1985. Jonathan M. Rozoff. "The United States Small Business Administration: Reaction and Redundancy." B.A. Thesis, Brown University.

Stigler, 1981. George J. Stigler. "Theory of Regulation." *Bell Journal* (Spring): 3–21.

U.S. Department of Health, Education and Welfare, 1976. *News Release,* December 6.

U.S. Department of Health, Education and Welfare, 1978. *Draft Memo,* October 5.

Weisman, 1984. Steven Weisman. "Reagan Signs Bill Tying Aid to Drinking Age." *New York Times,* July 18.

Willen, 1988. Mark Willen. "Congress Overrides Reagan's Grove City Veto." *Congressional Quarterly Weekly Report,* Vol. 46, No. 13 (March 26), pp. 774–776.

CHAPTER 9

SYSTEM CHANGE AND THE POLITICS OF REFORM

In previous chapters I have offered a "benefits coalition" framework and argued its advantages for teaching a better understanding of the relationship between federalism and public policy in the United States. Unlike other frameworks derived from economic or administrative theory, the benefits coalition approach is explicitly political, treating public policies as benefits and linking those benefits to the actions of individuals who join together in coalitions. By focusing on the benefits produced by public programs and asking how such benefits are distributed, we can identify patterns of behavior that influence benefit distribution. Applying this framework historically has identified interesting patterns of program development across time. Similarly, applying the framework to public finance, third-party federalism, and intergovernmental regulation has produced useful insights into those important activities. In this final chapter I again use the framework to illuminate the most common and most political of all federal actions: system change.

In a system characterized by thousands of separate governments, overlapping responsibilities, shared power, and multiple access routes, opportunities for change arise repeatedly. As suggested in Chapter 5, the system is permanently unstable. Although instability is frequently attributed to the sloth, venality, or incompetence of public officials, the more important sources of change are qualities built into the federal system itself. We may think of these qualities as inherent "tensions that will neither diminish nor disappear unless the system itself is altered.

After a review of the most important of these tensions, we will examine how they are dealt with in the normal politics of change. From time to time efforts are made to eliminate sources of tension by altering the structure of the system itself. We will refer to structural change as "reform," and consider both its origins and the extent to which it has succeeded. As will become apparent, reform is much more difficult than change, but efforts to achieve it provide important insights into the future of federal governance in the United States.

SYSTEMIC TENSIONS

The Weight of Ambiguous Authority

A major source of tension in American federal governance is the ambiguity that typically characterizes assignments of authority and statements of policy objectives. As we noted in Chapter 1, the U.S. Constitution does not state any principle that might be used to determine the powers that are available to national and state governments. With each proposal for a new program to deal with some perceived problem, therefore, an opportunity is created to reopen the debate over whether government should be involved at all and, if so, which level of government should be responsible for the new activity. Changes in society guarantee that proposals for new activities will be unending, which means that the debate itself is unending. Yet the debate is never resolved because it cannot be resolved in the absence of clear principle.

Instead of principled resolution, the issue is pragmatically temporized, over and over again. Depending on the resources and interests of the coalition, assignments of authority are made that may or may not guide future assignments for the same or similar program areas. Over time, the result is that several different levels of government and several different components of the same level of government may wind up occupying the same policy space. That accommodations to avoid conflict are commonly made in such situations is an important indicator of the good sense of most American public officials. That so many opportunities for conflict exist, however, is an even more important consequence of the ambiguity of constitutional language.

Constitutional ambiguity is matched by the haziness of many national and state legislative policy statements, particularly those that define "federal" policies—that is, policies affecting other governments. As Monypenny has made clear (Monypenny, 1960), such policies are often deliberately vague in order to attract enough votes to secure a legislative majority. Vague statements of purpose of course encourage officials in line agencies to operationalize policy purposes in a variety of different ways, depending on their own personal and agency imperatives. Thus, as Martha Derthick has demonstrated, a national program of assistance for "social services" was used by California, Illinois, and other states to support prisons, educational programs, and other activities that bore little or no relationship to "social" services (Derthick, 1975). As Yin and others have shown, local governments consistently have utilized funds from several different national grant programs to support individual projects in which they have an interest (Yin et al., 1979). Vague statements of purpose, in short, breed vague programs, and vague programs are difficult to understand or evaluate. Instead of clarity, there is confusion; instead of constraint, there is discretion; instead of measurable achievement, there are amorphous outcomes. And, not least, there are repeated opportunities to dispute the "real" purposes of federal enactments.

These patterns are often criticized as wasteful and almost always as confusing. Such criticisms are not without merit, but it seems important to recognize that ambiguity of either authority or policy is not wholly unfortunate. Ambiguous authority allows many governments to respond to the same problems, creating experiments that often help to determine the most effective forms of public intervention. Ambiguous objectives allow many problems to be dealt with by individual programs, expanding their impacts and leading ultimately to refinement in program goals.

Indeed, to appreciate the virtues of ambiguity, one need only attempt to imagine how the system would work without it. Newly emerging social problems that fit none of the existing definitions of authority or program would be left unattended. Each decision to attend to new problems would mean a major constitutional battle, as each level of government and all relevant program managers fought to protect or expand established domains. Under such conditions, the system might seem "clear" or even "precise," but the price almost surely would be a less active and less responsive system. For all its faults, ambiguity can be politically valuable.

Accountability vs. Complexity

A second major source of tension in the federal system is its extraordinary complexity, which continuously confounds the ability of citizens to hold their elected officials accountable. With 50 states, more than 3,000 counties, and 80,000 other units of local government, most of which overlap in function and many of which overlap in territory, public confusion over who does what on whose budget is certainly easy enough to understand. Although the elimination of tens of thousands of school districts has simplified the system somewhat, two other developments of the past several decades have tended to increase system complexity. One, as noted in Chapter 6, is the use of more varied revenue systems among American governments, including a number of hidden or invisible taxes. Since it is not unusual for individual citizens to be affected by a dozen or more taxing jurisdictions, the elaboration of revenue sources among such jurisdictions has substantially worsened an already difficult cognitive problem. The other source of added complexity has been the growth of federal assistance programs during the 1960s and 1970s. Hundreds of new programs were enacted during that time, involving national officials in virtually all the responsibilities of state and local governments. A number of these programs were eliminated or consolidated during the Reagan administration, but hundreds more remain, promoting the continued interpenetration of local, state, and national government organizations.

The consequences of these trends are both clear and significant. On the expenditure side, spending and taxing decisions are often made by different officials, representing different governments, confusing responsibility and undermining the ability of citizens to control spending either by changing officials or by refusing to provide revenues. On the taxing side, tax systems have become so interdependent that efforts to exert control often produce perverse and unintended consequences. Reducing national tax rates increases taxes in some states and decreases taxes in others, depending on the form of the relationship between state and national taxes (U.S. Treasury, 1985). Limiting local taxes through public referendums reduces national assistance payments to, and increases state control over, local governments (Hansen, 1983; Kirlin, 1982). It hardly seems surprising, then, that appeals for simplification of both government and tax structures are constant, or that citizens occasionally lash out in frustration in support of proposals that promise to return some modicum of control to their hands.

Coercion or Coordination in Implementation

Federal politics is for the most part amicable politics: Officials are courteous to one another, they respect each other's turf, they avoid confrontation, and they go to some lengths to avoid commands, even when the authority for such commands is clear. Local officials understand full well that they can be ordered to act or not act by state and national officials, and state officials recognize that, under appropriate conditions, their behavior can be controlled by directives from national authorities. To be sure, there are limits to national coercive authority. When the EPA attempted to order the states to adopt a series of antipollution measures under threat of injunctions, fines, and contempt citations, for example, federal courts intervened to prevent such actions (Derthick, 1986). Nevertheless, beneath the surface amicability of American federal politics, there is a legally coercive reality that shapes official expectations.

The recent expansion of national grant programs has increased official sensitivity to this reality by requiring state and local governments to follow a large number of regulations attached to the grants themselves. Failure to follow such regulations can lead to loss of national funds or to national administration of these programs. These sanctions, however, are seldom invoked, either because of congressional resistance to fund withdrawal, or because, as Derthick has noted recently: ". . . federal agencies generally lack the capacity to supersede the states, and everyone knows it." When EPA assumed responsibility for Idaho's air quality program as a consequence of state refusal to appropriate necessary funds, the federal agency wound up spending five times more than the state would have to do the same job. Or, when EPA assumed responsibility for Iowa's municipal water-monitoring program, it ". . . managed to conduct only about 15% of the inspections formerly performed by the state" (Derthick, 1986, pp. 19, 20, 21).

If these ostensibly powerful sanctions are largely ineffective, why should state and local sensitivity to national power have grown? One answer is that the present administration has reduced national funding for various regulatory programs without reducing or softening the regulations themselves—as symbolized in President Reagan's veto of an $18 billion water quality control appropriation that left the regulations intact but withdrew federal funding for enforcement (Stanfield, 1986). An equally important reason is that many of the new regulatory programs grant legal standing to individuals, allowing them to sue state and local agencies for failure to enforce federal regulations. Buffeted by a federal "shift and shaft" posture on one side, and citizen lawsuits on the other, state and local officials clearly have had reasons to perceive an increase in coercion. What had been a rarely used weapon appears to have become a more visible and more common source of tension.

National Uniformity vs. Local Diversity

The exercise of federal coercive authority often underlines the continuing tension between national uniformity and local or regional diversity. Efforts to impose tough national standards on state behavior have a long history, of course, and are reflected in recent national decisions to insist on a national speed limit for automobiles of 55 miles per hour—a decision opposed by many western states—or to insist on a minimum drinking age of 21, despite the opposition of many state and local politicians (Peterson, 1986; Weisman, 1984). But the imposition of national standards can also lead to weaker and less effective regulation. During the Reagan administration, for example, national regulatory agencies have repeatedly preempted state occupational safety or health regulations even when those regulations were more stringent than, but not in conflict with, national rules. Susan Bartlett Foote recently reviewed many of these efforts, including the Hazard Communication Rule passed by OSHA in 1983. She writes:

> This extensive regulation applied to thousands of plants that use chemicals in the workplace, and regulated many issues including labeling of chemicals, posting, or warnings on-site, and the requirement that companies provide hazard information materials to workers. This rule, which was strongly supported by the American chemical industry, claimed to preempt many state "right-to-know" laws in the process. Thus, while the regulation standing alone looks like more regulation, the goal was to reduce state involvement and mandate a uniformly lower standard of disclosure (Foote, 1987, p. 49)

These kinds of actions make clear that the promotion of national uniformity can work either for or against higher regulatory standards. In either case, tensions between state and national preferences are clearly visible.

Overload?

The several problems arising from ambiguity, complexity, coercion, and diversity have been supplemented in recent years by a more general fear that American federal governance suffers from "overload," or the inability to carry out its increasing responsibilities. Speaking to the Northeastern Political Science Association in November, 1976, Professor Samuel H. Beer of Harvard University, then president of the American Political Science Association, offered an eloquent expression of this view in an address titled "Political Overload and Federalism" (Beer, 1976).

Beer set out to explain the rapid growth of public expenditures in the United States and found proximate causes in two recent developments. The first, he argued, was the emergence of a "professional bureaucratic complex"—that is, a core of officials with scientific and professional training who have come to play important roles in policymaking. The second was the development of what Beer referred to as the "intergovernmental lobby"—that is, ". . . the governors, mayors, county supervisors, city managers and other office-holders, usually elective, who exercise general responsibilities in state and local governments. As a lobby they press their case before higher jurisdictions for some administrative or legislative advantage in favor of their constituents" (p. 9). Both groups work to push public expenditures higher and higher, but because the technocrats were a centralizing force while the intergovernmental lobbyists were a decentralizing force, the unhappy result was "growth without purpose" (p. 17). The fundamental question posed by these developments, therefore, was whether the American polity could any longer

> . . . impose upon public expenditure any rationale, any coherent view of government action, any scale of priorities reflecting an overall view of national needs, if its decisionmaking starts from the extreme pluralism of such a model of public sector politics. The fragmentation of the professionals among their many functional fields unfits them for this task. . . . The spatial fragmentation of the inter-governmental lobby renders them no more capable of an overall view. . . . The problem of overload [thus] dissolves into that classic problem of free government, self-defeating pluralism. (pp. 17–18).

Beer was not at all optimistic that the overload problem could be solved, particularly since political parties seemed to him to be in a state of "disarray and decomposition" (p. 17). To the extent that there was hope, however, it was the presidency that provided its source. So far as Beer could see, only the presidency was ". . . likely to elicit and crystallize a new sense of national purpose" (p. 18). Whether or not a given president might undertake to provide such leadership, of course, remained unknown and certainly unpredictable. Added to the already formidable list of tensions designed into federal governance, this vision of a system flying apart at the seams because of "extreme pluralism" offers a summary judgment that can only be regarded as sobering.

THE NORMAL POLITICS OF CHANGE

Responses to Tensions

For the most part, American politicians respond to these tensions by ignoring them. Structural issues of ambiguity or coordination seldom seem very glamorous, after all, and they seldom attract a great deal of political interest. Instead, as problems emerge and coalitions form to address them, policies are enacted to deal with specific issues. These policies often have the effect of changing existing relationships among governments, but such changes usually are the unintended consequences of actions taken for other reasons. Under normal conditions, therefore, changes in federal governance emerge from issue-focused rather than structure-focused politics.

To say that changes in intergovernmental relationships typically are unintended is not to say that they are either infrequent or insignificant. On the contrary, changes occur constantly because governments are constantly "bumping into" one another, thus challenging existing spheres of competence. Particularly in the fifty states, those bumps often cannot be resolved without recourse to new legislation. Every year, therefore, state legislatures pass thousands of laws permitting municipalities to undertake activities not previously authorized, clarifying the division of responsibilities among local units, or creating new structures to work on newly recognized problems. Changes induced by national legislation may be fewer in number, but no less frequent in occurrence. National legislation to address any new problem inevitably causes state and local governments to adjust their behavior to the requirements of the new programs.

Piecemeal Responses, Major Consequences

Such constant piecemeal adjustments often have major consequences. The state-by-state elimination of tens of thousands of local school districts during the 1950s and 1960s was a revolution in American public education. The federal interstate highway system begun in 1956 was more than a massive public works program: it led to the destruction of large segments of many American cities; it made possible an enormous movement of population from old cities to new suburbs; and it thereby altered both the governing structures and the political processes within American states. General Revenue Sharing, conceived as a mechanism to distribute a nonexistent federal surplus, gave thousands of local governments an interest in national policy that has permanently altered the landscape of federal governance. In their numbers and coverage, the programs that poured from the Great Society to combat poverty, hunger, unemployment, and other social problems together created a very different environment for governmental problem-solving. None of these activities was consciously designed to change the existing system. All of them, however, caused major changes, albeit in ways that were largely uncoordinated. In the American context, even major changes in governance can issue from "normal" politics.

CYCLES OF REFORM

Constitutional and Political Constraints

American politicians occasionally attempt to reform the system rather than pursue the normal politics of change. Efforts at reform usually focus on the federal structure itself, not separate problems, and seek to reduce built-in tensions by changing the structure. Such efforts are necessarily constrained by the Constitution, which guarantees the continued existence of the states and thus eliminates one major avenue of potential structural change. During the past half century, efforts have also been informally constrained by the differing interests of the national political parties. In general, national Democrats have been less interested than national Republicans in system reform. To be sure, programs enacted under Democratic administrations have had important structural consequences: President Roosevelt's welfare programs or President Johnson's Economic Opportunity programs readily come to mind. But national efforts to address the structure itself have been made only by Republican presidents: Eisenhower in the mid-1950s, Nixon in his first term, and most recently, by Ronald Reagan. What can we learn from these experiences?

The Eisenhower Initiative

Seen from the 1980s, the Eisenhower period seems an unlikely source of structural concern. Apart from the president's health and the launching of Sputnik by the Soviet Union, there was little political excitement during the decade, federal grants to state and local governments were a tiny fraction of what they later became, and there was far less "complexity" to stimulate concern over efficiency and accountability. Nonetheless, Eisenhower had been elected on a Republican platform that had expressed strong and deeply held views. As James L. Sundquist has noted recently:

> Consistently since the 1930's, the Democrats have stood for a stronger role for the national government, the Republicans for a smaller one. The Democrats have trumpeted the benefits of federal activism and the welfare state, and the Republicans have denounced the costs—high taxes, intrusive bureacracy and, as they were able to argue, inflation. When the Democrats won, they fulfilled their promises and carried out their programs. . . . When the people did not like what the majority party was doing, they expressed themselves in the normal democratic way—by turning that party out of office and putting the other party in. (Sundquist, 1986, pp. 41–42)

Having been elected on a platform full of strong language critical of federal government growth, and having been given Republican majorities in both House and Senate, President Eisenhower understandably placed federal reform high on his priority list. In one of his first major actions, Mr. Eisenhower requested that Congress create a special Commission on Intergovernmental Relations to determine "the right areas of action for Federal and state government" (Eisenhower, 1953, p. 141). Chaired by Meyer Kestenbaum, a Chicago clothing manufacturer, the commission issued a report in 1955 that effectively rejected the premises on which it had been created.

Instead of documenting national usurpation of state powers, the commission found neither usurpation nor any "threat" to freedom; instead of proposing limits to national government actions, the commission argued that "there are few activities of government indeed in which there is not some degree of national interest" (cited in Sundquist, 1986, p. 43); instead of proposing a clear demarcation of national and state powers, the commission argued that national and state responsibilities were complementary and cooperative rather than separate (Commission on Intergovernmental Relations, 1955). Eisenhower may have hoped for well-documented proposals that would enable him to reallocate governmental functions, but the commission gave him little more than reasons why such hope could only be regarded as unrealistic.

Unpersuaded by his own commission, Eisenhower won reelection in 1956 and moved in the following year to seek similar goals through a somewhat different vehicle. In an address to the nation's governors in June, 1957, the president proposed that they join with him to combat the evils of centralized government by finding national programs that could be turned back to the states (Eisenhower, 1957, p. 496). The joint Federal-State Action Committee was duly organized and proceeded to work for two years under the chairmanship of Vice-President Richard M. Nixon. This effort too proved entirely unproductive:

> Despite strong presidential support, the inclusion of nine state governors on this committee, and "two years of effort in an atmosphere characterized by an absence of partisan disagreement or of conflict along governmental lines, there was . . . still no significant accomplishment." The two programs recommended for transfer to the states amounted to less than $80 million in 1957, only 2 percent of federal grants in that year, but even this modest proposal was never implemented. (Anton, 1984, p. 19)

Observing the same events, Sundquist notes: ". . . there was little support for these limited measures outside the joint committee, and even less in the Democratic Congress, and much opposition from the affected groups. The proposals died unmourned. A decade afterward, an Eisenhower appointee to the joint committee, Robert E. Merriam, suggested that the experiment perhaps put to rest for all time the notion that some neat sorting out of governmental functions could be made." And Sundquist adds: "During the Eisenhower period, more than a dozen new grant-in-aid programs were enacted, including one of the largest of all—the interstate highway system" (Sundquist, 1986, p. 44).

Nixon's New Federalism

John F. Kennedy's successful call for a more activist national government replaced the Republican politics of structure with a Democratic politics of purpose during the period 1960-1968. Determined to solve a myriad of social problems, Kennedy and his successor, Lyndon B. Johnson, initiated hundreds of new federal programs that paid far more attention to problems than to the structures through which they might be addressed. The election of Richard M. Nixon to the presidency in 1968, however, returned to the White House a politician who not only shared the traditional Republican distaste for big government, but who, as chair of President Eisenhower's Federal-State Action Committee, had spent considerable time seeking ways to reduce national influence. After nearly a decade of rapid federal program growth, moreover, a substantial body of professional and political opinion had emerged that was highly critical of federal operations. Drawing on this developing body of criticism as well as his own experiences, President Nixon was able to offer the nation both a diagnosis and a cure.

His diagnosis was that professionally trained specialists in various policy areas had come to dominate government through their control over specialized policy functions. As federal grant programs proliferated, these professionals interacted more and more with others like themselves along vertical lines of communication, paying less and less attention to the elected politicians who were responsible to horizontal local and state electorates. Over time, these patterns of vertical integration enabled local and state specialists to develop close relationships with national specialists in similar functional areas such as education, highways, or health. By controlling information about programs that had become increasingly complex, these specialists were increasingly able to control policy. And by controlling policy, they were able to increase spending on their programs, whether or not politicians or citizens wanted it (*CQ Almanac*, 1969, pp. 101A–103A). In its description of vertically integrated functional specialists, this diagnosis was not unlike Deil Wright's discussion of "picket fence federalism" (Wright, 1982). And in its assertion of a relationship between functional policy control and increased federal spending, the diagnosis was not unlike Beer's "overload" (Beer, 1976). As president, however, Nixon was able to move beyond analysis.

The president's remedy was simple: return power and resources to elected state and local officials. The components of this prescription were two straightforward changes in the design of federal programs. First, separate federal programs dealing with similar problems were to be linked together into a much smaller number of "block grants," reducing program fragmentation and complexity. Second, authority to determine the uses of block grant funds was to be placed in the hands of local and state governments. Mayors and governors rather than national agency directors were to decide how funds were to be used. Following these principles, the Nixon administration laid before Congress a series of New Federalism proposals calling for revenue sharing, consolidation, and devolution in several functional areas, including education, transportation, employment training, and urban assistance ("Transcript of Nixon's Address to Nation Outlining Proposals for Welfare Reform," 1969).

Although these proposals attracted broad support from the state and local officials who expected to benefit from them (Beer, 1976), congressional reaction was mixed. Liberals distrusted the president's ideology, conservatives were troubled by the loss of control over programs for which they had to vote funding, and beneficiaries of the programs designated for consolidation were concerned over the possible loss of substantial benefits (Dommel, 1974; Dommel and Associates, 1982). These concerns were compounded by an early administration focus on foreign policy and, after Nixon's reelection in 1972, by the rapid escalation of the Watergate crisis.

Despite these obstacles, three of Nixon's initiatives were successful. General Revenue Sharing was signed into law on October 20, 1972—just in time for the November election. CETA, the Comprehensive Employment and Training Act, was signed into law in December 1973 (Franklin and Ripley, 1984). CDBG, the Community Development Block Grant program, was signed into law by President Ford in 1974, after Nixon had been forced to resign (Dommel and Associates, 1982). The programs Congress passed were substantially different from the programs Nixon had proposed, and they included less than half of the proposal he originally had offered. What began in 1969 as a full-blown effort at structural reform was transformed into three new federal programs that represented some significant change, but hardly major reform.

That a strong presidential initiative was required to achieve even this limited success is revealing. Both the changes made in the Nixon proposals and the length of time required to achieve congressional approval—only General Revenue Sharing was passed during Nixon's first term—suggest that this effort to lead from the top generated no more than a fragile base. The fragility of the support became apparent during the next decade, when CETA lost the support of many national politicians. By 1985 both programs had been terminated, leaving only a substantially reduced CDBG program as a reminder of one president's effort to reshape American federal governance.

Reagan's "New" New Federalism

Between 1970 and 1978, federal assistance programs grew to unprecedented levels, becoming the largest single source of revenue for state and local governments (Chapter 6). Nixon's limited success at returning power to states and cities was more than matched by other developments that expanded national authority: Food Stamps expanded from an experimental to a fully national program; the national government assumed responsibility for Old Age Assistance, Aid to the Blind, and Aid to the Disabled in the new SSI (Supplemental Security Income) program; and other new programs with additional regulations proliferated.

As the decade wore on, complaints about system complexity became even more widespread and intense, in part because they were now joined by a more ominous theme—namely, that the system appeared beyond control. It was, as an ACIR study suggested, a ". . . monster of excessively pervasive and inordinately complex proportions . . . a largely uncontrolled and unaccountable system—a kind of 'big brother run amok'" (ACIR, 1981, p. 9). President Carter was able to bring a halt to increases in federal aid in 1978, but even so, federal aid in 1980 was three times what it had been in 1970.

Ronald Reagan's victory over Jimmy Carter in the November 1980 presidential election brought to the White House a former California governor who was not only sensitive to these developments, but determined to do something about them. Reagan's diagnosis of the problem was similar to Nixon's in many ways, but it was more political and less analytic in expression:

> The Constitution provides clear distinctions between the roles of the Federal Government and of the States and localities. . . . During the past 20 years, what had been a classic division of functions between the Federal Government and the States and localities has become a confused mess. Traditional understandings about the roles of each level of government have been violated. . . . By 1980, total Federal grants to States and localities exceeded $90 billion, meaning that 18% of Federal tax receipts were being passed through to States and localities for one reason or another. However, these funds were not passed through entirely benignly. Attached to them were Federal rules, mandates, and requirements. This massive Federal grantmaking system had distorted State and local decisions and usurped State and local functions. I propose that over the coming years we clean up this mess. I am proposing a major effort to restore American federalism. (OMB, 1983a, p. M22)

The "mess" theory presented an interesting contrast to Nixon's views. Nixon's New Federalism proposals were forward-looking, designed to develop a system better able to deal with the problems of the next decade ("Transcript of Nixon's Address to Nation Outlining Proposals for Welfare Reform," 1969). They included innovations such as direct federal assistance to local governments that would lead to a more sophisticated system without doing away with existing structures. By contrast, Reagan's perspective looked backward toward a point in time when an ideal system existed. A strong sense of loss characterized Reagan's vision, and a desire to restore what had been lost. In this sense, Reagan can be thought of as a traditionalist, compared to the more pragmatic Nixon.

This traditionalist view emerged very quickly in the new administration. As part of the massive Omnibus Budget Reconciliation Act of 1981, which cut taxes, reduced social service expenditures, and increased defense spending in one all-embracing piece of legislation, some 57 separate federal programs were combined into just 9 new block grants. Authorized expenditures for these new block grants were reduced by 25 percent, in keeping with the president's determination to reduce federal social services spending, and federal influence over the distribution of block grant funds was reduced. But unlike Nixon's programs, which gave local governments some of the influence taken away from national bureaucrats, Reagan's block grants favored the states: The discretionary authority removed from Washington agencies was in each case reallocated to state governments. Less than a year after assuming office, President Reagan had achieved a reordering of federal grant programs beyond anything contemplated by Presidents Eisenhower and Nixon and, in the process, reasserted the traditional significance of the states.

Given his first opportunity to develop a national budget, for fiscal 1983, Reagan transformed his sense of traditional federal and state responsibilities into the most comprehensive reform of federal governance proposed in this century. Beginning in fiscal 1984, he proposed that the federal and state governments "swap" responsibilities: The states would assume full responsibility for the AFDC and Food Stamp programs; in return, the national government would assume full responsibility for Medicaid, the program of medical assistance for the poor. In addition, the president proposed that some 44 federal programs be "turned back" to the states beginning in 1984, along with federal revenues sufficient to fund those programs, albeit at substantially reduced levels (OMB, 1983b, pp. 17–34).

Had the swap and turnback proposals been accepted, national responsibilities would have been substantially reduced in virtually all social services except health, leaving defense, foreign affairs, and income security as the major national concerns. Nearly everything else, including large federal programs in education, welfare, transportation, and community and economic development, would have become state responsibilities. This was clearly reform on a grand scale, presumably reflecting Reagan's sense of what was once the "proper" division of national and state authority.

Mr. Reagan's 1981 successes were not to be repeated, however. Offered to the Congress and the public in January 1982, the swap and turnback proposals were abandoned in April, after it had become clear that they would not be seriously considered (Pear, 1982). Hindsight suggests that the proposals may have been too radical for either politicians or the public to accept. It is also clear in retrospect that reduction of an additional $45 billion in federal spending called for in these proposals could not have been supported by state and local officials, already facing a deep economic recession that was forcing them to raise their own taxes. Important as these considerations may have been, there were two others that were even more serious flaws in the swap and turnback proposals.

The first was that state and local officials were never seriously consulted in developing the plan. Although congressional hearings and numerous other meetings were held during the summer and fall of 1981 to discuss federalism reform, the president refused to engage either governors or local officials in detailed discussion. By December, rumors of impending administration proposals had created so much anxiety that the chairman of the National Governors Association, Governor Richard Snelling of Vermont, wrote to President Reagan to suggest that a domestic "summit meeting" be held to develop some agreement on further action. Discussing this proposal on the *MacNeil-Lehrer Report* on PBS, the president's advisor on intergovernmental affairs argued that the president already had met with hundreds of state and local officials and questioned the value of a summit without a specific agenda. Snelling responded:

> . . . the governors wanted more than just meetings; they wanted true consulta-
> tions and would be happy to work with the President in coming up with an
> acceptable agenda. Snelling also argued that it was essential for such a meeting
> to occur before the President announced his fiscal year 1983 budget. He
> pointed out that the potential for further cuts was of great concern to state and
> local governments already beginning to suffer from the cuts initiated by the
> President and Congress in 1981. The President ignored Snelling's plea.
> (Matheson, 1986, p. 29)

One important consequence of ignoring state and local officials in developing the swap and turnback plan was that the details of implementation were left unexamined. Details, however, were critical to any serious proposal. Consider the funding mechanism for the swap of 44 federal programs from federal to state administration. Beginning in 1984, these programs were to be funded by a special $28 billion trust fund made up of revenues from excise taxes on cigarettes, alcohol, telephone service, and gasoline ($12 billion), as well as the windfall profits tax on oil production ($16 billion). From 1984 to 1987, the 44 programs turned back to the states would be supported by this trust fund, with each state's allocation based on a three-year (1979–1981) average of its receipts from each program.

Beginning in 1988, the 44 federal programs would be terminated, leaving states free to continue them or not as they saw fit. The trust fund, however, would also be reduced by 25 percent in 1988 and in the three succeeding years, terminating entirely in 1991. During that phase-out period, states would be free to levy the same excise taxes to provide continued support for the programs, or they could discontinue the programs, or they could use other revenues to fund them. By 1991 the trust fund would have expired, but the states, in theory, would have gained new tax sources to continue the programs.

Had President Reagan's advisors consulted the governors or taken the time themselves to consider the working out of this plan, they might have discovered its flaws. Because states receive very different mixes of federal program dollars and operate very different tax systems (Anton et al., 1980), the turnback and trust fund operations would have created severe inequities during the 1984–1987 period. North Carolina, which paid more than 12 percent of the taxes included in trust fund revenues, would have received only 2.97 percent of trust fund spending in 1984; California, which paid 10.48 percent of the revenues, would have received 7.8 percent of expenditures; Virginia, which paid 6.92 percent, would have received 2.2 percent, and so on (Anton, 1982). Even worse, the "gift" of federal tax resources after 1988 would have worked in only a few states:

> Four states pay 53 percent of the federal excise tax on gas, six states pay 51 percent of the alcohol tax, seven states pay 55 percent of the telephone excise, and adding Virginia and Kentucky to North Carolina incorporates nearly 95 percent of the tobacco tax. For each of the tax sources to be returned, therefore, only a few states would gain very much; most would lose far more in federal funds than they would gain in new tax revenue. . . . [Moreover], the windfall profits have been nationalized. It is thus unlikely that even these few [oil-producing] states can look forward to this new source of state tax revenue after 1988. For them, as for the other states, the turnback programs that remain will have to be funded from existing state revenues, or eliminated. (Anton, 1982, p. 32)

Little wonder, then, that states adopted what former Utah Governor Scott Matheson has described as a "computer printout mentality" (Matheson, 1986, p. 32), carefully scrutinizing proposals to determine winners and losers. Nor is it surprising that the governors, having finally been given an opportunity to consider the proposals after they were made, found them unacceptable.

The second major flaw in the swap and turnback plan was that it was unprincipled, in the sense that the criteria used to select programs for swapping or turning back were never articulated. When the first round of block grant reforms was debated in 1981, most state governors reacted cautiously at first. Then they gradually expressed a growing concern that reform was little more than an excuse to justify further reductions in national government spending. "The battle cry of federalism," said one governor in a June 1981 speech, "has served as a bludgeon to balance the federal budget, not to balance the federal system" (Matheson, 1986, p. 26). Later, when the president first refused to consult the governors in developing his swap and turnback plan, and then refused to provide any details on, for example, implementing the proposed Medicaid swap, the governors concluded that their concern was fully justified. Governor Matheson of Utah, chairman-elect and then chairman of the National Governors Association during the 1982 discussions of swap and turnback proposals, has provided firsthand evidence of why the governors were so concerned in his recent book, *Out of Balance* (1986). Of his discussions with Budget Director David Stockman over the federalism issue, Matheson writes:

> I had several meetings with Stockman. My judgment, as I had feared, was that he looked at the federalism initiatives strictly as a means of reaching budget objectives. His comments were always confined to numbers. He never discussed the concepts of federalism or the merits of public programs. (pp. 32–33)

Of the negotiations that took place between the governors and the administration after the swap and turnback plan had been announced, he says:

> What most troubled me about the character of these negotiations was that they were driven solely by dollar tradeoffs without any kind of underlying philosophical basis for sorting out the program elements (p. 38). . . . Despite the administration's lip service to the establishment of a "safety net" for the poor, its effort to shift AFDC to the states was totally inconsistent and suggested to me that they had no clear concept, nor any genuine philosophy, concerning the nature of the federal system. (p. 39)

And he reports the administration's complete unwillingness to deal with the disparities inherent in its federalism reforms:

> Budget Director David Stockman, while arguing in the short run that there would be no winners or losers in the President's proposal, admitted that under the Reagan plan, the trust fund would disappear by 1991, and the states would be on their own. He candidly stated that the Reagan plan is simply not designed as a "solution to the fiscal disparities problem." He questioned whether the federal government should even address the disparities issue, saying that such proposals were "a dangerous thing to get into." (p. 32)

In the face of these attitudes, the governors were forced to conclude that the serious component of Reagan's federalism initiative was not structural reform, but budget reduction. The governors did propose alternatives, based on their theory that economic and income security was a national rather than a state problem, but the administration was unwilling to consider them. In the end, the early promise of the most comprehensive reform proposal in a half century was reduced to a far less significant achievement: enactment of several additional block grants that reduced national financial participation in federal social service programs.

TOWARD A THEORY AND PRACTICE OF SYSTEM BETTERMENT

The limited accomplishments of three Republican presidents in their efforts to reform American federalism make clear that reform is extraordinarily difficult to achieve. Presidents Eisenhower, Nixon, and Reagan all were persuaded that the system itself had become too unwieldy; all were committed to substantial reform; all had achieved a strong electoral mandate; and all exerted considerable leadership on the issue. Eisenhower's efforts failed completely; Nixon achieved no more than a watered-down and tiny portion of what he had proposed to Congress; and Reagan's major initiative—the swap and turnback plan—never became a serious legislative proposal. Why is reform so difficult?

The Barriers to Reform

One important clue emerging from these three major efforts is that all of them were presidential initiatives, following a pattern referred to earlier (Chapter 5) as a "top-down" process. In no case was there a large existing coalition, pressing for reform; in no case was there a broad public consensus on the nature of the problem; in no case was there a clear and widely accepted solution to the problem. Instead, it was the president who tried to stimulate a coalition in each case, and it was the president who tried to sell his version of both the problem and the solution to potential partners.

Although presidential leadership was successful in recruiting some supporters, particularly among elected national politicians and a few policy professionals, in no case was the president able to recruit and sustain a coalition large enough to enact his program. Indeed, even a president as popular and as committed as Ronald Reagan was unable to prevent the issue of reform from being submerged as other matters appeared more pressing. Top-down coalitions are inherently fragile, and coalitions for federalism reform may be among the most fragile of all.

A major problem, of course, is that the benefits of reform are difficult to identify, because they seem so abstract. Even when they can be identified, their appeal is bound to be limited. How many people, after all, are likely to be interested in simplifying complexity, or achieving better coordination, or improving accountability, or efficiency. For government officials and members of professional policy communities, these are very important concepts, used repeatedly in efforts to improve performance. For the public at large and most elected politicians, however, such terms lack the symbolic power necessary to attract broad support, particularly in a highly volatile political environment. Federal governance is an extremely important issue, but it has not been and is unlikely to be an issue of great salience to the American public; it is an issue for government elites and their policy advisors.

But managing the issue is no easy task because the costs of reform are far easier to identify than the benefits. To achieve reform, abstractions such as "accountability" or "coordination" must be translated into specific proposals. Specific proposals, however, immediately reveal which individuals or governments will pay the costs of achieving some set of benefits. Opposition from those for whom projected costs exceed anticipated benefits is bound to arise and, in a system as diverse as American federalism, bound to be widespread. President Reagan's swap and turn-back plan, for example, was announced as a plan that would create no winners and losers because the revenues turned back to the states would equal the expenditures made in the states. As soon as the specific programs and tax resources for the trust fund were identified, however, it became clear that a national revenue-expenditure balance would in fact have very different effects among the states, and cause many of them to become losers. The president's refusal to consider the issue of disparities was a guarantee that his plan would itself become a loser.

Conditions That Favor Reform

The record of three presidential initiatives suggests nothing more than some of the conditions that inhibit reform. To discover some of the conditions that may promote reform, we can turn to the field of govern-mental regulation, which was extensively reformed between 1975 and 1985. In their fine study of these events, *The Politics of Deregulation*, Martha Derthick and Paul Quirck offer a number of provocative insights regarding the sources and processes of successful reform (Derthick and Quirck, 1985).

Although regulation raises different issues, it is similar to federalism in its lack of clear symbolic appeal to mass publics—a quality that sup-pressed the development of a large and broad-based coalition. Derthick and Quirck point out that a smaller but nonetheless influential coalition, dominated by professional economists, had been developing for two decades prior to the initiation of regulatory reform. First in journal articles and books, later in public testimony before Congress and elsewhere, and finally from high-level appointive positions in Washington, these policy professionals repeatedly expressed a consensus they had reached on regulation: It was inefficient and unnecessary. Having agreed on the nature of the problem (economic inefficiency), this policy community also came to agreement on a solution derived from economic analysis— namely, eliminate as many regulations as possible and allow the market to regulate economic behavior.

By the mid-1970s, economists had become both numerous and influen-tial in Washington. Many of them, in fact, had been appointed as senior officials in such regulatory agencies as the Federal Aviation Agency, chaired by Cornell University economist Alfred A. Kahn. Because the FAA and other regulatory bodies were authorized to act independently, Kahn and others like him were able to develop and implement comprehensive deregulatory plans. Observing the popularity of these plans, Congress followed with actions that in some cases legitimized, and in other cases extended, action already taken. Not all industries experienced deregula-tion, but major industries such as the airlines, transportation, and telecom-munications emerged in the 1980s in substantially deregulated form. A relatively small coalition, dominated by a professional elite, united in its diagnosis of and solution to a problem, successfully persuaded Congress and successive presidents to enact policies that were strongly opposed by industrial giants such as AT&T. As much as anything else, deregulation reflected a politics of ideas that demonstrated the power of ideas to change institutions (Derthick and Quirck, 1985).

The Late 1980s: Context for Reform

Federalism remains high on the national political agenda in the late 1980s. Scholars continue to analyze federal governance, politicians continue to debate it, and proposals for reform continue to be made. Viewed against a background of past failure in federalism reform and success in regulatory reform, the continuing interest in federalism seems significant. The way the issue is being framed, the nature of the coalition being developed, and the processes pursued by this developing coalition all differ considerably from past experience. Public interest and involvement remain minimal, as has been true in the past, but the fairly small elite of government officials and policy professionals who continue to debate the issue appears to have become different in several important respects. Prediction would be rash, but it seems apparent that today conditions favoring reform are more powerful than they have been in some time.

One major development that reflected several important changes was the convening of the Committee on Federalism and National Purpose in the summer of 1984. Initiated by the National Conference on Social Welfare, with funding support from the Alfred P. Sloan Foundation, this committee met six times between July 1984 and July 1985 before issuing its final report in December 1985. Chaired by Republican Senator and former Governor Daniel J. Evans of Washington and Charles S. Robb, former Democratic Governor of Virginia, the committee included distinguished academics such as Samuel H. Beer of Harvard University and Richard P. Nathan of Princeton University, distinguished Republican politicians such as Senator Dave Durenberger of Minnesota and former Representative Barber B. Conable of New York, distinguished Democratic politicians such as Representative Richard A. Gephardt of Missouri and former presidential counselor Stuart E. Eizenstat, and a variety of foundation presidents and corporate executives, as well as journalist Neal R. Pierce. It was clearly a very capable and influential group.

Quite apart from the contents of the committe report, its composition was a reflection of two important political developments. The first was that this was a "bottom-up" initiative, arising from the interests of citizens, governors, mayors, and other elected politicians, rather than the interests of a president. While hardly a grassroots movement, creation of a major nongovernmental committee to examine the federal system, with representation from a broad array of public and private sector organizations, was a clear sign that interest in federalism reform had become widespread and would no longer depend on a presidential commitment. The second important development reflected in the committees's composition was that federalism had become much more of a nonpartisan issue. After nearly two decades of criticism and debate, Democrats as well as Republicans had begun to accept the significance of structural problems in American federal governance. It was thus no accident that the committee had Democratic and Republican co-chairs as well as membership balanced to reflect both major political parties. By the mid-1980s, a coalition in support of reform had become less partisan and more inclusive. This, in turn, opened up the possibility of developing a broad national consensus on a reform strategy.

The committee's report, *To Form a More Perfect Union* (National Conference on Social Welfare, 1985), was obviously written to provide a foundation for just such a consensus. It began by rejecting the idea (and the conflict that would accompany the idea) that system reform can be based on some set of hard and fast rules:

> This Committee agrees on the necessity for a greater separation of responsibilities. However, we do not agree on what the philosophical basis for such a change should be. In this respect our views mirror those of the nation as a whole. The United States has never developed a commonly held philosophical rationale for division of labor within the federal system (p. 6). . . . We do not believe there are any hard and fast rules about which levels of government can perform which functions best. (p. 7)

Instead of rules, the committee offered "guidelines" based on "experience and common sense" (p. 7) that supported a new division of labor. The committee recommended that the national government assume greater financial responsibility for the two major welfare programs by providing 90 percent of funds to support new minimum benefits. The states would continue to administer these programs, but they would also assume "full financial, policy and administrative responsibility for many community development, local infrastructure and social service programs" (p. 17) such as CDBG, wastewater treatment, or Title XX social services.

To deal with the problem of fiscal disparities among states, the committee proposed that a system of fiscal capacity grants be established, providing unrestricted funds to states with the least ability to fund services up to new minimum standards. To deal with the problem of fiscal disparity within states, the committee proposed a transitional assistance program for localities, providing federal grants ". . . to states for targeting and distribution to those localities most in need of general purpose assistance" (p. 22). Other recommendations were offered as well, but these were the major components of a carefully researched and thoughtful report.

Whatever the intellectual merits of these ideas, their political significance seems quite substantial. By proposing greater national responsibility for welfare assistance programs, the committee reflected ideas that already had gained wide support among governors and local officials (Matheson, 1986). And by proposing to provide funds to compensate state and local governments that would become losers under a national system of minimum welfare standards, the committee dealt with a major obstacle to the development of a coalition capable of achieving comprehensive reform. To be sure, offering such proposals does not guarantee their acceptance. The 5,000 city officials who gathered in San Antonio for the annual convention of the National League of Cities in November 1986 expressed concern that city interests might be injured, despite the transitional assistance plan (Herbers, 1986, p. B-7). What is politically important, however, is that the proposals recognize the legitimate fiscal interests of the cities and provide an opportunity, through further negotiations, to accommodate those interests in a larger coalition.

Similar ideas were also gaining impressive support among other members of the policy community. An important study published by the Brookings Institution in 1986, for example, concluded that the federal system could be noticeably improved if the national government assumed greater responsibility for "redistributive" programs and gave less attention to "developmental" programs that state and local governments were far better equipped to pursue (Peterson, Rabe, and Wong, 1986, pp. 230–236). Although the conclusions offered in this study were an indication of a growing policy consensus among intellectuals as well as officials, it is also important to note that the authors did not derive their recommendations from an exaggerated sense of system failure. On the contrary, their careful analyses of a number of education, health, and housing programs over an extended period of time led them to conclude that federal governance worked reasonably well. In contrast to many earlier characterizations of the federal "mess," Peterson, Rabe, and Wong offer a more discriminating view that reports considerable success as well as a number of difficulties that require corrective action. By moving beyond exaggerations to more balanced and analytic statements, these authors suggest that the time for analytic consensus may have arrived.

All this suggests that many conditions which favor reform of federal governance have fallen into place. After thirty years of tinkering and ten years of sustained criticism, a broadly based coalition appears to have emerged that is significantly less fragile and less partisan than earlier presidential coalitions. Even more important, perhaps, is the emergence of a more analytic, less rhetorical, diagnosis of the "problem," as well as a growing consensus among officials and intellectuals regarding what to do about it. Senator Evans and Representative Downey have introduced legislation in the Congress designed to implement the recommendations of the Committee on Federalism and National Purpose and provide a focus for further coalition development. If these and other politicians are skillful enough, and if the coalition is strong enough to prevent the issue from again being submerged, there is real prospect for significant federalism reform in the late 1980s.

Two major political obstacles stand in the way of this major reform. The first is that the developing coalition lacks a very important actor: the president of the United States. The second is the enormous political uncertainty created by enactment of the Gramm-Rudman-Hollings legislation to eliminate the federal budget deficit over the next five years (Pl 99–177, the Balanced Budget and Emergency Deficit Control Act of 1985). Depending on choices not yet made by both President Reagan and Congress, these obstacles could well prevent any major reform.

Although President Reagan's ambitious reform plan was not successful during his first term, his interest in the issue remained strong. After his landslide reelection, the president established a Working Group on Federalism of the Domestic Policy Council. Chaired by Assistant Attorney General Charles J. Cooper and made up of representatives from nine federal agencies as well as the White House itself, the group was charged with developing ". . . 'a basic, administration-wide strategy' for ensuring that federal law and regulations are rooted in 'basic constitutional federalism principles'" (U.S. Domestic Policy Council, 1986). Its report, issued in November, 1986, made clear that the Reagan administration had again chosen to position itself well apart from the consensus view of the federalism policy community expressed by the Committee on Federalism and National Purpose.

Faithfully reflecting the president's own views, the Working Group concludes:

> The Framers' vision of a limited national government of enumerated powers has gradually given way to a national government with virtually unlimited power to direct the public policy choices of the states in almost any area. States, once the hub of political activity and the very source of our political tradition, have been reduced—in significant part—to administrative units of the national government, their independent sovereign powers usurped by almost two centuries of centralization. (p. 2)

Attacking and rejecting nearly two centuries of judicial interpretation of the "necessary and proper" clause, the commerce power, the Tenth Amendment, the spending power, and other constitutional provisions, the Working Group asserts the preeminence of perceived constitutional principles and offers a series of proposals designed to ". . . return to the Framers' vision of a nation of states—a system of government in which the national government exercises sovereign authority in accord with the letter, and the limits, of its constitutionally enumerated powers, and the States exercise sovereign authority in all other areas" (p. 59).

Although the Working Group denies that its proposals are ". . . a call to disassemble the government in Washington and return all power to the States" (p. 59), it also makes clear that its view of federalism can be reestablished ". . . only if limits are placed on the national government's ability to invade the sovereign authority of the States" (p. 70). The group's proposals are designed to impede national government action, and include the suggestion that the Constitution be amended to limit national authority (p. 69).

In its vision of a federalist Paradise Lost, its retrospective rather than prospective orientation, its belief in a "dual" federalism that clearly separates national from state powers, and its generous use of politically charged symbolism ("sovereign authority," powers "usurped"), the Working Group report is vintage Reagan. It is also very different, in tone and in result, from the more pragmatic and analytic consensus developing among governors, mayors, intellectuals, and other members of the policy community. To be sure, many of the specific recommendations offered by the Working Group—including, ironically, proposals for greater consultation with the states—seem more practical than ideological. Nonetheless, the Working Group's report underlines again the considerable policy distance between the Reagan administration's view of federalism and the views of others. Should the president decide to maintain his position rather than join in negotiations for more pragmatic action, reform could become even more difficult to achieve.

The potential consequences of Gramm-Rudman-Hollings are equally difficult to predict. This deficit-reduction legislation requires annual reductions in the national budget deficit leading to a zero deficit by 1991. If annual targeted reductions are not agreed to by the president and Congress, the law authorizes automatic spending reductions to reach the specified targets, with half of the reductions taken from defense and the remaining reductions taken from other programs. Social security, veterans pensions, and large welfare programs such as Medicaid, AFDC, Food Stamps, and Supplemental Security Income are exempt, but all other domestic programs are subject to automatic annual cuts if the president and Congress fail to agree ("Dole Says Plan on Deficit Is No Panacea," 1985). Although one portion of the legislation has been declared unconstitutional (Rauch, 1986), the remainder remains in effect, including the annual deficit reduction targets.

Although Gramm-Rudman-Hollings was designed to deal with a national fiscal problem, it will clearly have a powerful impact on state and local governments if the process it mandates is carried out. As former Utah Governor Scott Matheson pointed out recently: ". . . total funding in fiscal year 1985 of every program which Congress did not exempt or subject to limited cuts under Gramm-Rudman was only $46.5 billion (including $13.5 billion in the Highway Trust Fund), or twenty-three percent of the budget reductions needed to balance the federal budget by 1991" (Matheson, 1986, p. 12). If the process mandated by this legislation were to be taken seriously, therefore, it would be reasonable to expect that all nonexempt domestic programs would have to be terminated, including major programs in highways, environmental protection, education, housing, and community development.

Such action would immediately upset state and local budgets and lead to increased pressure on states to replace lost federal revenues. Matheson himself predicts ". . . a three-way struggle for scarce state resources among educators, local officials, and advocates for the poor, all attempting to replace declining federal revenues" (Matheson, 1986, p. 13). Unless Congress acts to alter the Gramm-Rudman-Hollings process, state and local governments are bound to experience increased tension in the short run, leading to significant change in, if not reform of, current activities.

But whatever the short-run outcome of the current interest in reform, change is certain to occur. American politicians appreciate the difficulty of changing the structure of federal governance, which helps to explain why comprehensive reform is attempted so rarely. But American politicians are also interested in solving social problems and, in reaching for solutions, they often cause major structural changes. In this respect, Gramm-Rudman-Hollings may be taken as a 1980s analog of the interstate highway program of the 1950s or the social programs of the 1960s. Those earlier programs were designed to achieve substantive policy objectives, but, in pursuing those objectives, federal relations were changed. If Gramm-Rudman-Hollings remains in effect, it is certain to cause similarly widespread changes.

Such changes, in turn, will cause other modifications of the intergovernmental system that will have to be addressed by another generation of federal politicians. American federal politicians are more numerous, better-trained, and more resourceful than ever before, which means that cycles of response to problems may become more rapid than before. If so, the constant changes built into an experimental system may lead to a system in which reform is as common as change. In either event, dynamism will remain the most obvious and most important quality of American federal governance.

PATTERNS OF FEDERAL POLITICS

American federalism, with its thousands of governments and other thousands of private and nonprofit agencies interacting constantly to generate various public benefits, is a supremely political institution. To achieve anything, officials within the system must overcome built-in barriers to accomplishment by exercising the political skills of communication, persuasion, and cooperation. Existing conceptual frameworks derived from economic or administrative theory have largely failed to capture these complex realities of federal politics and policy, leaving us with no clear sense of the political patterns that define American federalism.

In the face of enormous complexity, some analysts have suggested that the variety and dynamism of the system are so great that few general patterns can be identified. While I appreciate this argument, I have tried to show that observing federalism through the lens of an explicitly political conceptual framework can reveal patterns of behavior that tell us a great deal about how the system works. In this supremely political environment, it is supremely important to understand not only what government does, but who benefits from government action, and how.

Americans generally view their governments as instruments to produce goods and services they value, from clean water to cash payments. To gain these benefits, citizens join together in coalitions that advocate and monitor programs which distribute the benefits. Federalism guides the processes of coalition formation in three major ways. First, the federal structure provides many routes of access for those seeking public benefits. Local, state, and national governments are all potential coalition targets, and, within each level, various executive, legislative, or judicial agencies are available. By banding together, weak local or state coalitions often gain the strength to generate some benefit from higher levels of government, and higher-level agencies frequently gain strength by participating in lower-level coalitions. Federalism thus provides opportunities for both vertical (multilevel) and horizontal (single-level) coalitions.

Second, the many governments of American federalism produce large numbers of officials who have incentives to participate in benefit coalitions. Authority in most policy fields is shared among national, state, and local governments. To gain or change a benefit, therefore, officials are often required to create or join coalitions that lobby other governments. This lobbying function of both elected and appointed officials is neither accidental nor rare; it is built into the fabric of American federal politics and is one of the most important qualities of the federal system. Citizens continue to press their governments by mobilizing coalitions, but it is a rare coalition that lacks participation by public officials.

Third, shared authority combined with political autonomy leads to a system in which relationships among governments are permanently unstable. Because authority is shared for a wide range of functions, governments constantly intrude into one another's policy space. And because each autonomous government can levy its own taxes, set its own budget calendar, organize its own personnel system, and otherwise act with considerable independence, opportunities for intrusion are generated constantly. With each intrusion, existing relationships between governments can be called into question and new coalitions formed to maintain or change those relationships. American federal governance is thus constantly in flux as officials respond to the demands of existing and newly created coalitions in pursuit of some desired benefit.

Viewed across time, these dynamic activities appear to fall into identifiable patterns of surge, spread, and reform that structure cycles of change. Once a benefit coalition has achieved sufficient political strength, a "surge" of policy occurs, often in the form of an economic benefit, but also in the form of a symbolic affirmation of some purpose or some juridical right. To maintain and expand political support, particularly for economic benefits, they are then "spread" around to more and more beneficiaries, to form larger and more powerful coalitions. The process of spreading, however, often leads to adjustments in program design that weaken the support of some participants. If coalition support becomes sufficiently weak, a period of "reform" sets in, during which the original terms of the benefit program are renegotiated. These reforms often produce a very different program benefit, reflecting the interests of a changed coalition. After reform, the new program begins the process of surge, spread, and reform all over again. These cycles differ in length from one benefit program to another, and there is some evidence that they generally have become shorter in recent years. The cyclical pattern itself, however, has been observed in a great many federal programs.

Successful coalitions are not necessarily large coalitions. As we have seen, tax coalitions typically are tiny because of the interdependent complexity of federal taxation. Many public-private coalitions are small for similar reasons, and coalitions that form to influence federal regulations are also small and largely hidden from public view. In some cases, successful coalitions include no more than a handful of people. Many recent federal programs, for example, have distributed legal rights to citizens and given citizens legal standing to go to court to enforce those rights. Thus individual citizens, their lawyers, and judges have frequently formed tiny coalitions that have successfully enforced or extended civil rights, environmental rights, or affirmative action rights.

Larger coalitions remain essential, however, particularly in areas that lack broad symbolic appeal. In such areas, of which structural reform of federalism is a leading example, even determined presidential leadership has been unable to mobilize coalitions large enough to produce action. Such areas are often very important to effective governmental performance, but without broad consensus among members of relevant policy communities, change is very difficult to achieve.

By attending to the central political issue of who gets what from American federalism, and by linking that issue to the processes through which individuals mobilize support for government programs, the benefits coalition framework allows us to see important patterns of federal politics that are otherwise hidden from view. Viewing federal policy this way leads to no all-encompassing theory, nor does it offer any easy solutions to difficult problems. It does, however, force us to come to grips with the inherently political quality of federal programs by recognizing that beneficiaries are as important as purposes. For the reformers who seek improvement in the quality of federal governance, as well as the curious who seek nothing more than a better appreciation of our system, no lesson could be more important.

REFERENCES

ACIR, 1981. Advisory Commission on Intergovernmental Relations. *The Federal Role in the Federal System: The Dynamic of Growth.* Washington, D.C.: Government Printing Office. Report A-86.

Anton, 1982. Thomas J. Anton. "Turning Back the Clock: The New Federalism in Illinois, Part II." *Illinois Issues* 8 (June): 26–33.

Anton, 1984. Thomas J. Anton. "Intergovernmental Change in the United States: An Assessment of the Literature." In *Public Sector Performance: A Conceptual Turning Point,* ed. Trudi C. Miller. Baltimore: The Johns Hopkins University Press.

Anton, et al., 1980. Thomas J. Anton, Jerry P. Crawley, and Kevin L. Kramer. *Moving Money.* Cambridge, Mass.: Oelgeschlager, Gunn and Hain.

Beer, 1976. Samuel H. Beer. "Political Overload and Federalism." Paper prepared for the Annual Meeting of the Northeastern Political Science Association, November 12, 1976.

Commission on Intergovernmental Relations, 1955. *Final Report.* H. Doc. 198. 84th Congress, 1st Session.

CQ Almanac, 1969. *Congressional Quarterly Almanac.* 91st Congress, 1st Session. Vol. 25.

Derthick, 1975. Martha Derthick. *Uncontrollable Spending for Services Grants.* Washington: The Brookings Institution.

Derthick, 1986. Martha Derthick. "Our Changing Federalism: Madison's 'Middle Ground' in the 1980's." Charlottesville, Va.: University of Virginia. Unpublished manuscript.

Derthick and Quirck, 1985. Martha Derthick and Paul Quirck. *The Politics of Deregulation.* Washington: The Brookings Institution.

"Dole Says Plan On Deficit Is No Panacea," 1985. *New York Times,* December 9.

Dommel, 1974. Paul R. Dommel. *The Politics of Revenue Sharing.* Bloomington: Indiana University Press.

Dommel and Associates, 1982. Paul R. Dommel and Associates. *Decentralizing Urban Policy Case Studies in Community Development.* Washington, D.C.: The Brookings Institution.

Eisenhower, 1953. Dwight D. Eisenhower. "Special Message to the Congress Recommending the Establishment of a Commission to Study Federal, State and Local Relations." *Public Papers of the Presidents.* Washington, D.C.: U.S. Government Printing Office.

Eisenhower, 1957. Dwight D. Eisenhower. "Address to the 1957 Governors' Conference," in *Public Papers of the Presidents.* Washington, D.C.: U.S. Government Printing Office.

Foote, 1987. Susan Bartlett Foote. "New Federalism or Old Federalization: Deregulation and the States." *Perspectives on Federalism: Papers from the First Berkeley Seminar on Federalism.* Berkeley, Calif.: Institute of Governmental Studies.

Franklin and Ripley, 1984. Grace A. Franklin and Randall B. Ripley. *CETA Politics and Policy, 1973–1982.* Knoxville: The University of Tennessee Press.

Hansen, 1983. Susan B. Hansen. *The Politics of Taxation.* New York: Praeger.

Herbers, 1986. John Herbers. "Mayors Fear Loss of Aid to Cities." *New York Times,* December 1.

Kirlin, 1982. John J. Kirlin. *The Political Economy of Fiscal Limits.* Lexington, Mass.: D. C. Heath.

Matheson, 1986. Scott M. Matheson, with James Edwin Dee. *Out of Balance.* Salt Lake City: Gibbs M. Smith.

Monypenny, 1960. Phillip Monypenny. "Federal Grants-in-Aid to State Governments: A Political Analysis. *National Tax Journal* 13 (March): 1–16.

National Conference on Social Welfare, 1985. *To Form A More Perfect Union: The Report of the Committee on Federalism and National Purpose.* Washington, D.C.: National Conference on Social Welfare.

OMB, 1983a. Executive Office of the President. Office of Management and Budget.

Budget of the United States Government. Washington, D.C.: Government Printing Office.

OMB, 1983b. Executive Office of the President. Office of Management and Budget. *Major Themes and Additional Budget Details*. Washington, D.C.: Government Printing Office.

Pear, 1982. Robert Pear. "White House Halts Attempts to Shift Welfare to States." *New York Times*, April 7, p. 1.

Peterson, 1986. Iver Peterson. "Rebellion Gains in West and the Plains Over U.S. Speed Limit." *New York Times*, June 13.

Peterson, Rabe, and Wong, 1986. Paul E. Peterson, Barry G. Rabe, and Kenneth K. Wong. *When Federalism Works*. Washington, D.C.: The Brookings Institution.

Rauch, 1986. Jonathan Rauch. "The Thickening Fog." *National Journal*, July 12.

Stanfield, 1986. Rochelle L. Stanfield. "Environmental Focus: Just Saying No." *National Journal*, November 15.

Sundquist, 1986. James L. Sundquist. "American Federalism: Evolution, Status, and Prospects." Paper prepared for delivery at conference in observance of the Bicentennial of the Constitution, University of Nebraska-Lincoln, May 23–25.

"Transcript of Nixon's Address to Nation Outlining Proposals For Welfare Reform," 1969. *New York Times*, August 9, p. 10.

U.S. Domestic Policy Council, 1986. *The Status of Federalism in America: A Report of the Working Group on Federalism of the Domestic Policy Council*. November.

U.S. Treasury, 1985. U.S. Department of the Treasury. Office of State and Local Finance. *Federal-State-Local Fiscal Relations: Report to the President and the Congress*. Washington, D.C.: Government Printing Office.

Weisman, 1984. Steven Weisman. "Reagan Signs Bill Tying Aid to Drinking Age." *New York Times*, July 18.

Wright, 1982. Deil S. Wright. *Understanding Intergovernmental Relations*. Monterey, Calif.: Brooks/Cole.

Yin et al., 1979. Robert K. Yin et al. *Federal Aid and Urban Economic Development: A Local Perspective*. Santa Monica, Calif.: RAND Corporation.

INDEX

ABOUT THE AUTHOR

THOMAS J. ANTON earned his A.B. in history from Clark University and his M.A. and Ph.D. in politics from Princeton University. He taught at the Universities of Pennsylvania, Illinois, and Michigan in the United States and was visiting professor at the University of Stockholm, Sweden, before joining the faculty of Brown University as director of the A. Alfred Taubman Center for Public Policy and American Institutions. He has held Guggenheim, Fulbright, and American Philosophical Society fellowships, served as consultant to a variety of government agencies and foundations, and is a former editor of the journal, *Policy Sciences*. His published works include *Federal Aid to Detroit, The Politics of State Expenditures in Illinois, Moving Money: An Empirical Analysis of Federal Expenditure Patterns*, and *Governing Greater Stockholm*, among others. In addition to his academic work, he currently serves as a member of a quintessential federal agency, the Providence Public Housing Authority.